NET EFFECTS

NET EFFECTS

How Librarians Can Manage the Unintended Consequences of the Internet

Edited by
Marylaine Block

Information Today, Inc.

Medford, New Jersey

Net Effects: How Librarians Can Manage the Unintended Consequences of the Internet

Library of Congress Cataloging-in-Publication Data

Net effects : how librarians can manage the unintended consequences of the Internet / edited by Marylaine Block
    p. cm.
Includes bibliographical references and index.
ISBN 1-57387-171-0
1. Libraries and the Internet. I. Block, Marylaine, 1943–
Z674.75.I58N47 2003
025.04--dc21

2003008872

Printed and bound in the United States of America

Publisher: Thomas H. Hogan, Sr.
Editor-in-Chief: John B. Bryans
Managing Editor: Deborah R. Poulson
Editorial Services Manager: Lauree Padgett
Copy Editor: Pat Hadley-Miller
Graphics Department Director: M. Heide Dengler
Book Designer: Kara Mia Jalkowski
Cover Designer: Laura Hegyi
Indexer: Sharon Hughes

Contents

Chapter 3—Making Them Adapt to Us: Training Our Users 73

Chapter 4—The Shifted Librarian: Adapting to the Changing Expectations of Our Wired (and Wireless) Users 111

Chapter 7—Running to Stay in Place: Continuous Retraining 227

Chapter 8—Up to Our Ears in Lawyers: Legal Issues Posed by the Net 255

Acknowledgments

I'd like to thank all of the writers and publishers who allowed me to make use of their work here. Even when copyrights for these articles belonged to the publishers, whose permission I obtained, I obtained the consent of all the authors as well.

I'm also immensely grateful to those who digitized these articles, making the preparation of this manuscript far easier than it otherwise would have been. That includes the publishers—especially those of *Chronicle of Higher Education*, *Library Journal*, and *Computers in Libraries*—who have posted so many articles on their Web sites. It also includes the folks at OCLC who make FirstSearch available; the access it gave to Periodicals Abstracts and WilsonSelect was invaluable.

I'd like to thank John Bryans and Deborah Poulson at Information Today, Inc. for moving this project forward and editing it, and Lauree Padgett who worked with me on obtaining reprint permissions. Eve Cotton at the American Library Association and Anne Kim at *Library Journal* were also very helpful with permissions.

As always, I am grateful to my friend, Mark Coburn, who has listened to me throughout the writing process and who has taught me a great deal about the business and craft of writing.

About the *Net Effects* Web Page

http://marylaine.com/book/index.html

I've posted annotated links here for all the Web sites I personally selected for the book (though not for links mentioned by authors of the individual essays), and I will update them and add to them on a regular basis. They'll be organized by chapter, for easy topical access.

I'll use the Web site to amplify the book's content as well. As I find interesting new articles online detailing other solutions to the problems I've identified, I will link in those articles under the appropriate chapter heading.

Introduction

Do you ever feel as though the Internet has caused you to lose control of your library? That the machines and the Net are now driving decisions as much as you are? That the Net has complicated your life at least as much as it has benefited your library services? Then you're just the person for this book.

The idea for the book was born in the following essay, which I wrote for my e-zine, ExLibris:

Planning for Side Effects:
The Case for Semi-Luddite Management

When I tell people what I do for a living, they always say, "Oh, you must really love computers!" Well, no, not exactly. I NEED computers, but I approach them, and their consequences, in the same spirit an apprentice lion-tamer approaches her charges: with wariness, respect, a preference that experts handle the tricky bits, and an awareness that even the best lion-tamers can't always predict or control what the beasts will do.

The thing is, the Luddites were right. They knew that mechanized looms would produce a new set of winners and losers, and that they would be those losers. Any technology upsets applecarts, both by intention and through unintended side effects; the more powerful the technology, the more profound those side effects are.

When it comes to machines, Americans are classic early adopters; we've always rushed to embrace new technologies and worried about side effects later. We sincerely believe machines can solve social problems: School violence? Metal detectors. Education? Educational television, videos, the Internet. Even when we realize the machines themselves cause problems, like when the Internet makes porn available to children surfing the Net, we look for mechanical solutions like filters (and don't seem to notice or care that filters don't work very well).

That's why I think it's important to have a few Luddites on the library staff; when administrators are charging ahead full steam, they're the ones who are going to say, wait a minute, what are we going to do about the unintended side effects?

They're the ones who, when we abandoned our card catalogs and Readers' Guides in favor of OPACs and databases, said "What are we going to do for users who are intimidated by machines?" They're the ones who understood that long-time library users would really hate the new-model library.

Our Luddites told us that if we HAD to replace the catalogs, we would have to make the interface as easy to understand as an ATM machine. They insisted we offer lots of classes to teach people how to use our OPACs and our databases, from the library or from home. Our Luddites told us that because all the garbage on the Net would frustrate our users, we would have to teach them how to find good stuff on the Internet, and show them the wonderful stuff we'd linked on our home pages.

Our Luddites were the first ones who realized that Internet content would be a problem for us. Though all audiovisual technologies—movies, radio, television, the Net—were first promoted as great educational tools, people have always preferred to use them for entertainment and communication and advertising, with violence and sex as ploys to grab our attention. Knowing this, our Luddites warned us that pornography would be an issue, and that we'd need to devote a lot of time to public meetings, hammering out Internet use policies we and our users could agree on.

Our staff Luddites are the ones who keep telling gung-ho administrators that machines don't do much good if you don't spend time and money training librarians how to use them, and if you don't hire somebody to maintain them. (Since that money could have been spent on more and better-paid librarians, they may not have warm fuzzy feelings about the machines and the systems technicians.)

Our Luddites pointed out that, by substituting educational CD-ROMs and videos for teachers, and giving kids direct Internet access to information, teachers and librarians were cut out of the loop. By failing to train teachers and librarians to know more about the machines than the kids did, school administrators devalued both. (Which kids would have understood in any case—when school boards cut library budgets and lay off librarians, pay low salaries to teachers and librarians, and then spend lavishly to put computers on every desk, kids get the message about what matters in this world.)

Our staff Luddites foresaw how the book and the printed journal would be devalued; they correctly warned us that books and pre-1995 articles would vanish from the bibliographies of student research papers. They recognized that the new problem would not be the availability of information, but students' ability to evaluate and make sense of it. They're the ones who talked with teachers about how to counteract the effects on students' reasoning and writing and critical thinking skills when they moved from a linear-reasoning book culture to a collage-assembly, hyperlinked culture.

Luddites look at events like the "one city one book programs" and say, "we should do that in our school or campus or library." Luddite librarians work with teachers to make sure there will be good, thought-provoking books available to support whatever topic has been assigned. They work together with teachers creating writing assignments, and teaching students to evaluate Web sites and other information.

I'm not saying all Luddites are right, mind you. Sometimes they guess wrong. And we all know some librarians whose resistance is based not on principle but on the devout hope that they can make it to retirement before they're forced to learn new ways of doing things.

I'm just saying that we need to pay attention to Luddites because even when they're wrong, they're canaries in coal mines, giving early warning about misgivings our users will also have. They have a stronger sense than charge-ahead futurists do of what's going to be lost when we adopt new technologies. Only when we understand the risks of new technologies can we plan ways to compensate for those losses.

So, cherish your Luddites. In fact, take a Luddite to lunch today, why don't you? And while you're at it, listen to them.

That essay stuck with me. The more articles and news stories I read about current problems in libraries, the more I realized that I was on to something: most of these problems are side effects of the Internet and our other technologies. Think about it:

- Locus of control: Suddenly, all kinds of nonlibrarians are selecting what comes into our library—the filter vendors, the database vendors, the wild and woolly Internet itself.

- The survival of the book is threatened.

- Our point-and-click users think—incorrectly—that they can find everything they need to know on the Net.

- Our point-and-click users want information delivered to them, where they are, whenever they want it.

- Large segments of society are being left behind, unable to access digital data.

- More and more of our budgets are diverted from books, magazines, and librarians to machines, software, databases, and technical support people.

- As soon as we learn a technology, it changes; we spend all our lives running to stay in the same place.

- We're up to our ears in lawyers—we get sued if we don't use filters and sued if we do, we're asked to hand over our Internet use records to the FBI, etc.

- Disappearing data—Web sites come and go, digital data degrades over time or can't be retrieved as formats change, and government documents that used to be published in print and preserved by librarians are now posted on Web sites from which they may disappear without warning.

But problems are simply opportunities in disguise, and we librarians have plunged enthusiastically, even joyfully, into solving them. This book is an anthology of some of our solutions. Think of this as an idea book. You can read it straight through, or dip into it to see how librarians are dealing with the specific issue that's bothering you.

I asked only two things of the articles I chose: that they offered interesting solutions, and that they were readable. I avoided academic articles that smacked of publish-or-perish, articles that were full of acronyms and jargon, articles that elucidated the entire history of librarianship before getting to the point, and articles that were excessively technical, though the recommended readings point to such articles for those who want to pursue the topics. I figured that articles that made my eyes glaze over would make yours glaze over too.

I did choose several of my own articles. I realize there's some conflict of interest between my role as editor and my role as writer, but I have tried to use my own work only when I couldn't find anybody other than me proposing a solution.

The format for each chapter is statement of the problem, followed by possible solutions, each of which is illustrated with at least one article. My commentary is enclosed in gray-shaded boxes. I hope that by showcasing the ideas of these talented librarians in the context of other solutions to similar problems, I may give some additional value to their work.

Chapter 1

Regaining Control over Selection

Having the Internet in our libraries means that now all kinds of other people are doing our selecting for us. We cannot, of course, control the content of the Net itself, unless we use filters, in which case we are transferring our right to select to commercial companies that will not disclose what they block.

And while licensing electronic databases allows us to deliver significant journal, newspaper, and reference content to our users 24/7, it also transfers our power to select and maintain periodical collections to aggregators, who may add and drop journal titles with little advance notice, and to publishers, who may demand that we take all of their titles in order to get those titles we wish to offer our users. Julia Martin and David Coleman point out that "When publishers hold the right to withdraw materials from the public domain, charge access fees, and, more disturbingly, easily alter materials at any time, their suitability to act as archivists must be questioned" (Martin and Coleman, par. 7).

Following are some ways librarians are reasserting their right to select.

Solution
Create Our Own Web Indexes, with Selection Policies for Inclusion

To Link or Not to Link

Joyce M. Latham

The World Wide Web may be a morass of information, but a library is making a value judgment when it identifies and selects sites it considers important and links to those sites from its own web page.

In the same way selecting a book, video, CD, or magazine for inclusion in a library collection represents the recognition of some value to the users of that item, the act of selecting a web site also ascribes another level of value to that site. Traditional collection development is often shaped by an active documented policy reflecting the institution's values, however, the selection of web sites tends to be left to the staff members as a subjective judgment call.

In many cases that judgment call is perfectly valid. There are, after all, guidelines professionals use in evaluating web sites. But how do professionals explain the process of collecting web sites, of creating relationships among various sites relative to particular subjects? Why do they create the juxtapositions that they do? Which lists are regularly updated, and what collections languish once posted? How do professionals justify the costs of their collections, when we investigate the staff time, server time, and cataloging time involved in the process?

A Legal Defense

The Bettendorf Public Library, IA, created a link selection policy for its web site on the advice of the city attorney. Bettendorf was concerned that white supremacist groups active in the area would request a link from the library web site to its own. Without a policy, the library had no grounds by which to refuse a request for a link, and so the board passed a "Policy for Links" to the library web site in May 2001.

This is a common stimulus for any selection policy, in large part a defensive maneuver to thwart the strategies of special interest groups to, in effect, manipulate a practice to further their own ends. If the group is mainstream and innocuous, there is seldom a problem. If its views are marginal, the stage is set for fireworks.

The case of *Putnam Pit* v. City of Cookeville has highlighted the need to document the decision-making process by which links are added to governmental web sites. Geoffrey Davidian was the publisher of the *Putnam Pit*, a watchdog newspaper that monitored the government of the City of Cookeville, TN. Davidian had requested that the city provide a link from its web site to the web site of his tabloid. When Cookeville refused, Davidian filed suit, claiming a violation of his First Amendment rights.

The Cookeville site had been maintained by the city computer operations manager, who usually simply added any requested link to the city site. In this case, however, given the nature of the requestor, the computer services staffer referred the decision to the city manager. The city manager denied the request and then instituted a policy requiring that links be limited to nonprofit agencies. He apparently also made the statement that he would not allow a link to the *Putnam Pit* under any circumstances, as the newspaper was often critical of city government. The city then determined that links would be required to promote the economic welfare and appreciation of the city. Several links were removed from its site that did not fit this policy.

The lower court found for the city, but Davidian appealed. It was in the appeal that the lack of a selection policy became prominent. The court found that the city web site qualified as a nonpublic forum, but, as a result, the regulation of that forum must be viewpoint neutral. The policy requiring that sites promote the economic welfare, tourism, and industry of the city allowed too much discretion to the city; it allowed for the possibility of discriminatory practice. The Sixth Circuit Court basically found the city of Cookeville vulnerable to a charge of First Amendment violations. Cookeville is not the only city to have faced a challenge of discrimination regarding a decision not to link to another web site. As a result some lawyers are recommending link selection policies for city web sites.

Get Specific

The Bettendorf policy states that its links are added and evaluated based on its collection development policy, that sites are not added upon request, and that it does not intend to "open up the Library or city's web site as a full or partial public forum."

As public forums are not often intentionally created, but tend to grow through a process of public appropriation, such a statement does not provide much protection. The League of Wisconsin Municipalities, in its interpretation of the decision, listed several strategies for dealing with the situation:

- Ideally, include no other links besides those of other government agencies. This strategy would obviously not work for libraries and basically turns the web site into an electronic brochure;

- Have a policy governing web site selection that is viewpoint neutral;

- Adopt a policy based on information type, such as government, schools, and cultural institutions and eliminate resources also by type, such as commercial sites, illegal sites, or sites violating city policies;

- Avoid broad categories to avoid vulnerability to viewpoint discrimination charges.

The need for a policy that governs selection should be obvious for any public web site, especially library sites. Materials selection is a large part of what libraries do; many libraries already have materials selection policies, and those that do not have them certainly should. If we extend the role of selection to library web site link collections, the need for a link selection policy is obvious.

G. Edward Evans and Margaret R. Zarnosky devote a chapter of *Developing Library and Information Center Collections* (Libraries Unlimited, 1999. 4th ed.) to the development of collection policies, characterizing selection as a subprocess of collection development.

The point of the policy is to outline the plan, which maintains the strengths of a library collection while addressing the weaknesses.

Evans outlines a number of elements to fashion within a collection development policy, including the intended service community, specific subject areas for collecting, the programming requirements of the community (educational, recreational, etc.), details about the collection, who does the selecting, how they select (i.e., which resources do they use), what criteria they employ, how the library handles miscellaneous items, the evaluative process, and, finally, the process for handling collection challenges.

While Evans does address electronic resources, the selection of web links is not considered a part of the collection development process. Electronic resources are purchased materials, either directly or through participation in a consortium, and they are often related to a text resource, which may or may not already be part of the collection. As libraries develop a stronger and more robust web presence, as they attract greater numbers of users, and as they expend professional time and energy in expanding access, the need for a link collection policy becomes apparent, even without legal challenges looming.

Some Examples

The Bettendorf Public Library "Policy for Links for the Library's Web Site" is a simple two-paragraph statement that clarifies the purpose of the link selection, and it is useful to staff in answering patron questions. It states twice that the selection must be consistent with the library collection development policy and lists a simple set of criteria that includes "currency, authority, organization, and accessibility." With the addition of the statement indicating that neither the library nor, by extension, the city library web site was to be considered a public forum, the counselor for the city was satisfied with the policy.

Web site selection policies do not need to be extensive documents. However, other libraries have taken a more detailed approach to policy development. Monroe County Public Library, Bloomington, IN, states that its selections are oriented to users, with the intention of providing access to good information. According to Paula Gray-Overtoom, information systems librarian, a committee drafted the policy to parallel the materials collection policy. "We have a web committee composed of staff who create web pages, department managers, administration, and any other staff interested in the development of our web site. Since we have a large number of people who create web pages, the committee decided that we should have standard guidelines that everyone could follow."

The recognition that the policy should guide the selectors is significant. The assumption that web links are free is a misperception. While one web site may occupy a limited amount of a staff member's time in identifying, annotating, and marking up, the accumulation of sites can begin to develop real costs. Pennies do, after all, add up. Also, a mass of links can be as useless as no links at all, if the end-user is overwhelmed. Monroe County was interested in publishing the policy so that patrons could be aware of it. Admittedly it also serves as a "right of refusal" document when external agencies request links.

The Wyoming-based GoWYLD! site constitutes an online "special collection." As it immediately states in its policy, "The GoWYLD! Wyoming Collection contains Wyoming-related Internet resources of interest to librarians, teachers, students, and citizens of the state of Wyoming." The developers of GoWYLD have included five different criteria: access, design, content, scope, and authority. The policy emphasizes ease of use, quality and persistence of content, ADA accessibility, and accountability. The policy is detailed without being wordy, making the policy itself as readable and accessible as the web sites it evaluates. It is also available online, and the last update is noted on the page.

It's Academic

Academic libraries are not exempt from the need for link collection policies. The Newman Library of Baruch College, CUNY, includes link selection in its electronic collections policy, which is another strategy to pursue in the development of a policy. It states, energetically, that the goal of collecting must be "to insure the incorporation of the best in educational technology into the Baruch academic environment.

All resources accessed through the Newman Library home page, whether to internal resources, to CUNY, or to other web sites, must reflect the mission of the library, the curricular and research interests of the faculty and students, and undergo a rigorous process of selection for comprehensiveness, for relevance to the collection, for quality, and for educational value." The library goes on to explain that the selection of web links is not quite as demanding as selection of other resources, since the expenditure of library funds is not involved. However, the expectation of a quality product remains. There is little detail outside the broad scope of quality, but it does go on to tie the selections to the curriculum and the existing collections, not only within Newman but through all shared resources.

The Internet Collegiate Reference Collection (ICRC) of Bloomsburg University's Harvey A. Andruss Library, PA, includes selection resources in its document. It includes the Best Free Reference Web Sites from the American Library Association's Reference and User Services Association (RUSA), Internet Scout Report, and Librarians Index to the Internet. It also lists various resources from which links have, euphemistically, been "borrowed," such as Digital Librarian: Reference Sites, Louisiana State: Ready Reference Sources, and Martindale's—the Reference Desk.

The most extensive policy, however, belongs to healthfinder(R), the online information and referral resource for health questions. Within the introduction to its Content Selection Policies and Procedures is the following: "The goal of the Web site is to improve consumer access to selected health information from government agencies, their many partner organizations, and other reliable sources that serve the public interest."

Its 12-page document is divided into six sections that wed policy and procedure. In addition to identifying the goal, the introduction identifies the target groups and what it calls "credible organizations" and selected individual resources, i.e., web pages that are part of a larger site but may be lost in a more general organizational link. It identifies its relationship to the Federal Health Information Clearinghouse network and outlines the characteristics of organizations that are included in an evaluation. It indicates that the development of the Internet has allowed it to expand the number of inclusions.

With its high visibility and accountability, healthfinder(r) has provided a very thorough analysis of its process, has used its professional credibility to ground its policies, and has made the product readily available. It also recognizes that, as a web-based service, link selection is neither a casual nor an add-on service. As libraries begin to expand their concept of the web site as an online branch, they must also come to grips with the particulars of the web-based collection.

Documenting E-Sources

In considering a link collection policy, we are actually engaging in an analysis of the role of such a collection within the library service model. Link collections began as ad hoc assortments of Internet resources usually grouped by topic. The web has grown to include a great deal of chaff, but the wheat is also much more robust. There are real, persistent resources available to be documented and maintained. As Baruch's Newman Library's collection policy states in its opening paragraph, "The Internet, with its rapid growth, decentralized architecture, vast resources, and lack of standards, demands the information access skills the library faculty have traditionally provided on this campus. With so many faculty members at Baruch and elsewhere skeptical of electronic information sources and dubious about the educational value of the World Wide Web, it is important that the Newman homepage reflect the best in electronic collection management."

Davidian won a retrial of his case for *Putnam Pit*'s link to the city of Cookeville's web site, but the jury did not find that his paper's content fit the requirements outlined in Cookeville's selection policy. It may be a loss in terms of free speech, but it certainly demonstrates the significance of the policy.

Crafting Your Own Link Selection Policy

Where to begin? The first question is, does the library have a materials collection policy and, if it does, is it up-to-date? Is it more than a defensive document? Is it intended to direct the development of collections? Does it include electronic resources the library is currently purchasing? Does it include web link collections? If not, is there really any reason for all of them to be separate?

Secondly, who is doing the selecting now? How has that been determined? What guidelines for selection are in use? Are they based on professional literature? Do the various collectors meet regularly to discuss strategies and procedures?

Third, what does the library want to achieve with a link collection? A link collection policy? How extensive a policy serves the purpose of the collection? Is the practice supported by the administration?

Fourth, are the resources available to maintain a collection once it is developed? Who will be responsible for link checking? How often will collections be updated?

Finally, will the links be annotated? If not, why not? Will they be cataloged? If not, why not? Are they included in library pathfinders? Are pathfinders included on the web? What is their relationship?

One of the first selective indexes of Web sites was the Librarians' Index to the Internet. Originally the brainchild of one librarian, Carole Leita, it is now an index funded by the state of California and contributed to by a team of California librarians, currently under the guidance of Karen G. Schneider. Following is the recently updated selection policy its librarians use.

Selection Criteria: lii.org
Scope of the Collection

The lii.org Mission Statement: The mission of Librarians' Index to the Internet is to provide a well-organized point of access for reliable, trustworthy, librarian-selected Internet resources, serving California, the nation, and the world.

1. In general, lii.org seeks for and enters sites that reflect:

   a. Unique, important content across the full scope of information

   b. Contrasting viewpoints on major issues

   c. An awareness of current affairs and issues in the public's mind

   d. The information needs of library users and librarians

   e. The information needs of underserved groups

   f. Local and regional content pertinent to California and to our Regional Partners

2. The lii.org selection scheme is not age-specific. However, we do not collect intensively in resources targeted for children. Some of our records may point to resources intended for mature audiences.

Key Selection Criteria: The Big Five Factors

These five factors are the "show-stoppers" for lii.org content. In most cases, Web sites that do not meet all five key criteria will not be included in the lii.org database. These factors also provide critical guidance for our weeding program; sites that no longer meet these criteria will in most instances be removed.

1. lii.org does not include sites that are fee-based or sell a product unless the site also offers important informational content for free.

2. The site should contribute current, accurate information about the topic.

3. Content should be competently written, with few if any grammatical or spelling errors.

4. For all sites, links should lead to appropriate content. For directories—sites that primarily provide links to other sites—a strong majority of the links should work.

5. The author should be legally entitled to present the content within copyright and fair use guidelines.

Beyond the Big Five Factors: Evaluative Criteria

The following criteria are more fluid and conditional than the "Big Five Factors." lii.org emphasizes collecting sites that reflect its motto, "Information You Can Trust." However, as our selection criteria below suggest, we will consider including sites that may have "quality" issues, yet present unique and important information. Context is everything.

These criteria should be used to evaluate the site not only on its own merits, but also with respect to peer resources in lii.org. In most cases, the lii.org record description should note strong deviances from these areas; exceptionally high quality in any of these areas may also be noted.

Authority

a. Can an author be identified, and is there contact information?

b. What is the author's reputation and qualifications in the subject?

c. Does the author provide sources for information?

Scope and Audience

a. Why does the site exist? What is its purpose—to instruct, inform, amuse, or persuade? Is its purpose clearly stated or easily inferred?

b. Who are the audiences for this site? Is the site appropriate for the intended audiences?

c. How does the site compare with other sites on the same subject?

Content

a. How thoroughly does the site cover its content areas? For example, a site describing dachsund breeds should list all known breeds. Take a rough count: for example, a site providing recipes may have "dozens," "hundreds," or "thousands" of recipes (or it may have just one, but it's really special!).

b. If the site provides opinion, rather than facts, are these opinions clearly identifiable as such?

c. Does the point of view help balance the lii.org collection?

d. Does the site provide illustrations you would expect to find? (For example, a resource describing knot-tying would be expected to have illustrations of knots in various stages of execution.)

Design

a. Is the site well-organized and easy to navigate?

b. Does the site display well in popular browsers? Do all features work in current versions of Netscape and Internet Explorer?

c. Is the site complex or simple in design? Is the level of complexity appropriate for its audience?

d. Is it searchable or browsable? Is the search box or browsing hierarchy easy to find? Does the user have to read instructions to search or browse successfully?

e. Is the site consistently available? If you visit it over several days, can you always retrieve it? If not, does it offer an explanation?

f. Is the site visually appealing, particularly for its target audience? (Examples include a brightly colored children's site, or a site for teens with dramatic yellow lettering on a black background.)

Function

a. Do key features work? Do search engines function?

b. How fast does the site load? If it is "bandwidth-hungry," is this justified by special features, such as high "teen appeal" or elaborately detailed scientific images?

c. Does the site display error messages?

d. If the site includes video and audio files, is it clear what plug-ins are required to make them work? Can you play the files?

e. Are there pop-up ads? How frequently do they appear? What kind of content do these ads provide (and is this content appropriate for lii.org)?

f. Does the site require registration in order to access information or use features? Why does the site require registration? How much information is available anonymously? How much personal information is required to register?

Shelf Life

a. Is the site established for a temporary event or activity?

b. Is the site a "personal" page (often indicated with a tilde before the directory name, as in www. myfunpage.com/~bobsmith)?

c. Is it a student or class project?

Solution
Create Our Own Databases

JSTOR and Electronic Archiving

Ron Chepesiuk

In 1995, David M. Pilachowski, then a librarian at Denison University in Granville, Ohio, got involved with a new project called JSTOR (Journal Storage), which offered to help his library reduce the costly space necessary to house large back runs of journals. Like many libraries across the United States, the Denison University library had been under pressure to provide increased services and to do more with less. And with huge numbers of old scholarly journals cramming its shelves, the library simply didn't have the money or space to buy and house new acquisitions.

To address formidable library challenges like this, the New York City-based Andrew W. Mellon Foundation, under its president, William G. Bowen, launched JSTOR as a pilot project in August 1995 by providing a grant to the University of Michigan to create a modest electronic database that would include 10 journals in economics and history. Denison University was selected as one of the project's first test sites.

"At that time, there was little, if any, indexing for the early issues of academic journals and certainly none that could match the ease of access JSTOR promised to provide," explained Pilachowski, who is now college librarian at Williams College in Williamstown, Massachusetts, also one of the original test sites. "Even those libraries owning the full back run understood that the material was underutilized, since bibliographic and intellectual access to it was inadequate. JSTOR has radically changed that situation."

Juliana Mulroy, associate professor of biology at Denison, also recalled her early experience with JSTOR. She realized that the new electronic archiving project could help her find all references to a particular plant she was studying by searching the JSTOR database for its scientific name. This would give her a quick way to get a sense of its ecological significance, its habitat, and its range in North America. Mulroy could have done a Biological Abstracts (BIOSIS) database search, but that would have meant the time-sapping process of going to another building or remote-storage location to retrieve the articles and lift volume after volume off the shelves.

"Not only was JSTOR a quick and easy way to do something I otherwise wouldn't have done, but I actually picked up one hit in the literature-citation section of an article that I would not have found in more traditional searches," Mulroy recalled.

A Success JSTORy

But that was then and this is now. In a little more than five years, JSTOR has shed those modest beginnings to become a central player in the efforts of libraries, publishers, and scholars to gain access to the back files of important scholarly journals. As an independent and self-supporting nonprofit corporation, JSTOR has grown from 10 journals in two disciplines with 10 participating universities in 1995, to 124 academic journals in 16 disciplines and a subscriber list of 857 institutions in 41 countries in 2000.

> As of 4 June 2003, JSTOR reports 322 journals online, and 1,674 participants in 73 countries.

The number of new users, moreover, is constantly increasing. In October 1999, the Smithsonian Institution and its 19 branch libraries worked out an agreement with JSTOR that offers desktop access to the JSTOR database from any office or lab at the Smithsonian to any affiliated researcher. Members of the general public will also be able to use JSTOR for research by appointment at any of the branch libraries, including the Cooper-Hewitt National Design Museum in New York City and the Smithsonian Tropical Research Institute in the Republic of Panama.

The stats are impressive, given that JSTOR began to make its database of complete runs of important scholarly material available to libraries only on January 1, 1997. "JSTOR has succeeded beyond my wildest expectations," said Bowen, who serves as chairman of the JSTOR board of trustees. "In retrospect, I clearly underestimated how valuable it would be to scholars seeking to unlock earlier literature and for scholars simply trying to find articles that they already knew were there. But the response of the user community has been extremely gratifying."

Scholarly Preservation and Access

Even administrators of libraries that are not JSTOR subscribers say the project is making a vital contribution to scholarship and enhancing the profession's role in making scholarly resources available.

"JSTOR's electronic archive represents one of the most important contributions to the preservation of scholarly literature to date in the cyber age," said Mark Y. Herring, dean of the library at Winthrop

University in Rock Hill, South Carolina. "While major databases capriciously drop titles of retrospective years from their offerings, only JSTOR provides libraries with a product of consistent high quality."

JSTOR's potential extends beyond preservation and space savings, according to Fred R. Shapiro, associate librarian for public services at Yale University Law School in New Haven, Connecticut, and compiler of the *Oxford Dictionary of American Legal Quotations* (Oxford University Press, 1993). Under a grant from the Mellon Foundation, Shapiro has been investigating the capabilities JSTOR has for linguistic research, especially for uncovering uses of words and phrases earlier than the first uses of the terms recorded by the *Oxford English Dictionary* (OED).

In hundreds of instances, Shapiro has been able to find occurrences of important terms antedating the earliest evidence in the OED. These terms include such common ones as "racism," "software," and the "United Nations."

"JSTOR's coverage encompasses crucial journals in multiple fields, and they have substantial chronological depth," Shapiro explained. "Since JSTOR has the ability to search the full text of these journals, it has enormous potential for rewriting the history of significant segments of the English language."

An Overview of the Process

In pursuit of its mission, JSTOR has developed a well-organized production process that involves coordinating efforts with journal publishers. Physical copies are first collected at JSTOR's two production facilities at the University of Michigan and Princeton University. JSTOR staff then inventories the shipments, takes necessary observation measures, and creates guidelines for indexing. The journals are then sent to an outside agency for scanning.

Once scanned, the files are converted into digital text through the use of optical character recognition software, metadata is formulated by production librarians and keyed manually to maximize searchability, and a graphic image is captured for the full journal run. Next, the three files—the metadata, page image, and text—are downloaded to a CD-ROM and shipped to JSTOR, where they are uploaded to servers at UM and Princeton and to a mirror site at the University of Manchester in England. After the JSTOR staff performs a variety of quality checks on the vendor's work, the files are finally prepared for release to JSTOR participants.

Although JSTOR still maintains user-services and production staff at the University of Michigan, the operation has been independent of the university library since shortly after the beginning of the pilot project. "We still provide guidance and service when needed—for example, cataloging support and use of collections—but JSTOR's staff has grown sufficiently to support its own operations," explained Wendy P. Lougee, associate director for digital initiatives at the University of Michigan library, who was instrumental in the design and launch of JSTOR in 1995.

JSTOR has not geared down in the months since December 1999, when it reached the end of its first three years by making available a total of 117 titles in its Arts and Sciences Collection to participating libraries. On February 16, JSTOR launched its General Science Collection of serials, which will ultimately provide 1.4 million pages of such titles as *Science*, the *Philosophical Transactions of the Royal Society of London*, and the *Proceedings of the National Academy of Sciences*. An additional 29 titles in an Ecology and Botany Collection are being released in December [2000].

While happy with the progress they have made and confident about the future, JSTOR officials revealed that in its short history the project has had to deal with many important challenges, both technical and economic. It may be difficult to imagine today, but when the project first began, much discussion actually took place within JSTOR about whether it should be a CD-ROM or an Internet-based project. At that time, cyberspace had not captured the public's imagination yet and the Web was just beginning to be spun.

JSTOR decided that delivering its database on CD-ROM would simply exacerbate the space problem, since a physical object would still have to be preserved for future researchers. Better to pool the resources, store one of the copies at a mirror site, and distribute the journals online.

Still, the decision was not as straightforward as it might seem in retrospect; relying on the Internet has involved tradeoffs, said JSTOR officials. For example, the high-resolution color and grayscale images in the database are large files that load and print more slowly than text.

Another important challenge involved deciding whether to store and deliver the JSTOR material as image or text. One of JSTOR's prime objectives has been to replicate the journals accurately, so the organization decided it was important to deliver the content in image format. Writing in the July–August 1997 *D-Lib Magazine*, JSTOR President Kevin Guthrie explained, "Given the technology available to Web browsers, the most accurate way to replicate completely the originally published material, which is full of special characters, foreign languages, mathematical symbols, charts and pictures, is with scanned images. In addition, our commitment to make the material more accessible to scholars led us to use optical character recognition software to build a corresponding text file that would allow the user to search the full text of the journals in the database."

Some of the challenges have been ongoing. One of the most difficult has been the so-called "research access question." How can JSTOR be sure that people accessing its services are indeed registered users from a college or university? Addressing the issue, said Guthrie, has involved both technology and policy. "We actually don't know what faculty member has retired or what student has graduated, so there has to be a trusting relationship between a resource provider like JSTOR and a licensing institution," he explained.

Verifying users is difficult these days, but some libraries have been hard at work looking for ways to help JSTOR do that. "A lot of libraries have tried to solve the problem locally by setting up proxy servers of one type or another, and we've developed some software to make it a little easier for institutions to authenticate users," revealed Amy Kirchhoff, a software developer on JSTOR's technical staff.

A License for Back Issues

JSTOR offers site licenses to academic institutions that permit their registered students, faculty, and staff to have access to the Arts and Sciences archive. What an institution pays depends on its size and nature. A one-time database development fee for permanent-access rights to information in the archive can range from $45,000 for a large institution to $10,000 for a small one, while an annual access fee, to help cover the recurring costs of maintaining and upgrading the archive, ranges in price from $5,000 to $2,000. [As of March 2003, the annual fee ranged from $2,000 to $8,500. Initial fees continue to range from $10,000 to $45,000.]

Some library administrators say that JSTOR's price tag is the biggest drawback to an otherwise excellent product. Herring pointed out that the entrance fee is close to $30,000 for his library (Winthrop University has about 5,000 students), and this "borders on exorbitant," especially since libraries have faced stagnant or declining budgets in the last decade.

"Robbing the Peter of book purchasing to pay for the Paul of serial access will eventually result in two impoverished budgets," he predicted.

"We endeavor to set fees that are fair not only to institutions considering participation, but also are fair to those that are already supporting JSTOR," said Bruce Heterick, JSTOR director for library relations. "The intent is to set fees that enable us to recover the costs of providing access, while adjusting those costs to reflect the actual value derived by different types of institutions." Besides, JSTOR's annual charge is quite reasonable compared to other databases, both bibliographic and full-text. "Given the cost of preparation, production, maintenance, and user support, the cost does not seem out of line," the University of Michigan's Lougee said. "We feel it has been a very cost-effective investment."

JSTOR hopes that the cost will go down as it continues to add more institutions to its subscriber base. "As more institutions are added," Guthrie said, "it will be possible to spread the costs of maintaining the database over more institutions. In addition to increasing the number of participating colleges and universities, we are also reaching out to other types of institutions, like public libraries, schools, and research institutions such as the Smithsonian. Our goal is to keep the costs of continued participation as low as possible while insuring that we meet the archiving promises we have made."

Reprinted from *American Libraries,* Dec. 2000. Copyright 2000, Ron Chepesiuk. Used by permission.

Solution
Choose Your Journal Titles and Let Vendors Bid for Your Package

California State U. Adopts New Model to Pay for Journals

Lawrence Biemiller

Seven months ago [1999], California State University officials said they wanted to create a new model for subscribing to scholarly journals, one that took advantage of the 23-campus system's buying power to get scholars easy electronic access to a wide range of titles. Now, the officials say, they have succeeded.

Instead of negotiating with multiple publishers over packages of titles dictated by the publishers, the university system asked for bids on a single contract to provide access over the World Wide Web to 1,279 journals on a list created by university librarians. The contract spelled out how the articles could be used, and guaranteed that scholars would always have access to issues of journals the university had paid for, even if the university later canceled the subscription.

Cal State is signing a contract for journal access with EBSCO Information Services, says Evan A. Reader, the university system's director of software and electronic information resources. And although the contract includes access to only about 500 of the journals on the librarians' list, he says, it nevertheless represents a shift in the balance of power between journal users and publishers.

"We feel it's the wave of the future," says Mr. Reader, who handled the negotiations for the university system. "We intend to make this very public. We want others to follow our lead. That's the only way we can convince the large bulk of publishers to start considering our requirements as buyers."

David S. Kerin, who represented EBSCO in the negotiations, says that the Cal State deal is "an exciting project" and that it "puts in place a foundation on which we want to build." Mr. Kerin, who is vice-president and general manager of the company, adds that other institutions are "in the wings watching" what the university system has been doing.

Mr. Kerin notes that EBSCO Information Services is both a subscription agency and a supplier of aggregated databases—electronic products that contain information merged from many sources. The company, a subsidiary of EBSCO Industries of Birmingham, Ala., handled all the negotiations with the publishers whose journals were on the Cal State list.

Mr. Reader says that the contract "is being written not to exceed $500,000," and that it will provide journal access immediately for approximately 350,000 students and 45,000 faculty members. The materials will be available at off-campus Cal State facilities, as well as to university users who are traveling and to students in Cal State distance-education courses.

Avoiding Preset Packages

From academe's point of view, the deal is especially notable because it offers an escape from the tyranny of publishers' preset packages, which bundle popular journals together with titles that comparatively few scholars have any interest in. In Cal State's case, Mr. Reader says, the packages meant paying for journals that were never used, as well as paying for multiple copies of titles that appeared in more than one package.

Some publishers, however, were unwilling to go along with all of the university's stipulations, and their titles are not included in the deal. Of the journals on the initial list, about 980 are available in electronic form, Mr. Reader says. Of those, some were dropped to keep the cost of the deal within the university's price range, but some were excluded because their publishers refused to agree to Cal State's terms.

Mr. Reader says he's disappointed that the university was not able to include more than 500 journals in the current contract, but he says additional titles will be added in the months ahead.

"As publishers agree to meet our terms," he says, "we will continue to acquire more of these titles." The university's original request for proposals noted that it might award contracts to more than one vendor.

Perpetual Access

The publishers' most common objection, he says, was to the demand that scholars have "perpetual access" to electronic articles that the university had paid for, even if its subscription was subsequently dropped. Some publishers offer access to their on-line journals only to current subscribers—a practice that puts electronic access at a significant disadvantage, because libraries can store printed copies of journals almost indefinitely.

As finally negotiated, the deal provides that EBSCO will maintain an electronic archive of lapsed subscriptions at one-third the cost of what the university would have paid in subscription fees. Mr. Reader says the price was reasonable, given what it would cost the university to maintain such an archive itself.

Another deterrent for some publishers, Mr. Reader says, was that the contract gives the university the right to use on-line versions of journals the same way it uses printed editions. Publishers, he says, had previously tried "to write out in their contracts our fair-use rights in respect to sharing information that we had subscribed to."

Major fair-use sticking points have included interlibrary loans of journal information and electronic transmission of article files. "We wanted to share information with non-subscribers in ways permitted by the fair-use provisions of copyright law," Mr. Reader says.

He says humanities journals were, "in general, more willing to agree" to Cal State's terms. Among publishers of science journals, he says, there was "a lot of consternation." EBSCO's Mr. Kerin notes that the deal does not involve any journals published by Elsevier Science, one of the most prominent scholarly publishers.

Ferment in the Industry

While the university will continue to receive printed copies of most journals, Mr. Reader says, "ultimately the reality is that we're going to be canceling the print."

The deal comes at a time of considerable ferment in scholarly publishing. For three months, scientists have been debating a proposal by Harold E. Varmus, director of the National Institutes of Health, to create a new Web site that would give researchers a quicker way of publicizing their findings than journals currently offer. The site would be called "E-biomed" (*The Chronicle*, July 9 [1999]).

More recently, the editors of a British medical journal, *BMJ*, said they would open a similar site in September or October, in hopes of breaking journals' hammerlock on the dissemination of scholarly information.

Solution
Create Our Own Web Search Engine

If you can't beat 'em, join 'em. If our users' preferred strategy for finding information is using a search engine, maybe we should create a search engine that out-Googles Google.

Creating a Yahoo! with Values

Karen G. Schneider

Fiat Lux is a collective of librarians from web portals around the world, dedicated to planning a major, high-quality web presence. We intend it to be as well known as Google, as authoritative as the best library collections, as painless to use as a soda machine, and as high-tech as the Human Genome Project. Our timetable? Now or never.

The first Internet directories came from librarians, not from Yahoo!. These portals were designed to be easy to use, objective, and high quality. Yet you can walk down any busy street in America and not find a soul familiar with them. In the hectic dot-com mania of the 1990s, our sparsely funded portals, with their homespun interfaces and high-quality records, largely puttered along anonymously, while the world went gaga over Google.

I love Google. But Google and its compatriots fail at "identifying related topics and collecting the best sources on those topics," says Rebecca Cawley of the Michigan Electronic Library (MEL). "That requires experience and thought ... and that is why we use librarians as selectors." Cawley is one of the librarians behind Fiat Lux. The other reason Fiat Lux is so important is that librarians aren't for sale. Many commercial search engines practice a variation of paid placement, meaning you can purchase prominence in search results.

What We Bring

Google and its competitors are wonderful information trash barges. But the tasks of selection and organization are very human, and the values that reject paid placement and encourage free access are the values of our profession.

The members of Fiat Lux are combining existing efforts with groups in California, Canada, and Europe. In California, the Librarians' Index to the Internet (lii.org) and INFOMINE are the "Click and Clack" of library-based web portals. For 12 years, lii.org has provided a friendly, authoritative first stop for high-quality web resources for public librarians and the people they serve, while INFOMINE has provided a similar service for academic audiences. Few people outside of librarianship know we exist, but we collectively get close to 30 million hits every year.

Michigan's two web portals have different missions and target audiences. MEL—now ten years old and very possibly the model Yahoo! cribbed from—is a rather plain-looking suite of links. Yet it has over 20,000 resources, lovingly groomed by paid librarian selectors, and is an arm of the Library of Michigan, meaning it is firmly ensconced at the top levels of the state. The Internet Public Library, at the University of Michigan School of Information and Library Sciences, has had an experimental, research-directed flavor since its earliest days and contains a valuable reference section and a large collection of public-domain texts.

Our international colleagues include the Toronto Virtual Reference Library, of the Toronto Public Library, and BUBL, at the University of Strathclyde, UK. The Virtual Reference Library is a front end not only for freely available Internet resources but for library catalogs, fee-based databases, and similar value-added services. BUBL is unique among its peers in assigning Dewey numbers to its records, which has given it a way to direct collection development by requiring minimum records for every Dewey number (a method that is easy to measure and evaluate).

What We Can Become

The six participants of Fiat Lux have over 100,000 records, 44 years of experience, 280 librarians, 30 million annual searches, and the fire-power of six combined budgets. Our pooled resources can help us find additional funding, develop the tools we need, scale for the Internet of tomorrow, and move us past the endless cycle of year-to-year funding.

One of the important roles for Fiat Lux is to put the librarian back in the driver's seat, not merely by asserting our preeminence but by harnessing and mastering technology. Most of these tasks directly address the problem of scale—designing Internet finding aids that are capable of serving the information needs of an ever-burgeoning, ever-ubiquitous Internet.

On the most mundane level, all of us agree that a pooled record database will have significant economies for Fiat Lux members by preventing duplication of effort. In the days following September 11, all of us rapidly indexed the same three-dozen sites. Why wouldn't we? Our users needed this information.

Our other ideas are far from mundane. We all find Internet sites and create records for them manually, a process that easily takes two hours per record. We plan to use machine-assisted harvesting to pre-identify potential records. Computers aren't superb at classification or writing, but they aren't too bad at it, either—the computer-generated records I've examined lack flair or human insight. But then, that might describe *USA Today*. It would be the role of our superior human index-ers to buff and polish computer-generated records.

Retrieval is also a big issue. Search logs indicate that people are using very specific, highly granular terms to locate records in our data-bases. This makes sense; users come to our smaller portals with expec-tations learned from larger portals. For example, someone might type the term "chili" or "Denzel Washington" when our records say only "recipes" or "movie stars." We need to add keywords to our records, but that requires manually consulting thesauruses, racking our cerebral cortexes, or similarly inefficient methods to improve retrieval.

Yet INFOMINE, whose programming team has spent the last three years developing open-source portal software, has created an automatic keyword generator. Key in a record, then select the generator; it prowls through the files associated with the URL you are indexing and retrieves related terms. A record for the September 11 collection maintained by librarian Gary Price will be retrieved by anyone looking for "United Nations Security Council Resolution 1368," "Pentagon," "suicide terrorism," or "emergency response."

This kind of technology is both sexy and important; it can turn six homespun web portals into the amazing search tool of the future.

Time Is Running Out

All of us in Fiat Lux can see the sand funneling to the bottom of the hourglass. After 12 years of hard work, the Librarians' Index to the Internet barely has 10,000 records; meanwhile, in January 2002, there were nearly 150 million domains on the web. The single most important reason searches fail in Librarians' Index to the Internet is that the content isn't in the database. The most common reason people don't use us is that we're too small. Like other Fiat Lux participants we are not scaling well to the growth of the web.

"Size isn't everything," observes Dennis Nicholson of BUBL. "But we need to provide what people are looking for, or, quite reasonably, they will go elsewhere. The bottom line is service to our users. In that context, survival is insufficient."

To keep up, we all need to move past the "proof of concept" stage and become a real, funded library service. It is notable that MEL, with its 12 paid (part-time) selectors, has 20,000 resources. If every state had that many people dedicated to contributing to Fiat Lux, we would have a joint database of one million records. A million records may not seem much compared with the Googles of this world, but searches that produce live links, deep in content, and that actually satisfy a user's query will certainly set us apart.

However, the migration from unstable funding to a sustainable cost model has been elusive for most of us. No matter how valued our resources, our independent futures have been consistently precarious, and this budget year promises to be a killer. Some library-based services have quietly died, and others are on life support. Most of us feel the Grim Budget Reaper breathing down our necks, and a lot of our energy is consumed with looking for the funds to keep us going.

This spring we generated key proposals for the Institute of Museum and Library Services, the National Science Foundation, and private grants. We have also explored funding through the Library Services and Technology Act (LSTA). While it may not be too difficult to secure start-up money, the really crucial problem is how to build a sustainable funding model. Would we expect to be integrated into a funding plan for national library services? Would we set up a tithing model for state library agencies and assign regional content in the Fiat Lux portal according to the level of funding each state provided?

Turf Wars

The members have been in this business for a long while, and we all believe our resources are vitally important. We've battled for the same pots of money. Our funding agencies—as well they should—feel proprietary toward us. Finally, we're attempting to pull off a major collaborative venture when we barely have enough funding to maintain our services.

Nevertheless, Fiat Lux will work because we're knit together with an old-fashioned, pre-automation concept: values. Any one of us individually could have jumped ship to go commercial. We all have our stories of cash offers from some overeager dot-com. But we're still here, driven by stubbornness, vision, and the thrill of the chase.

Also, an interesting thing happens when librarians with a common cause unite: it becomes easier, not harder, to work together. The walls around us are "torn down by cooperative efforts," says Sue Davidsen of the Internet Public Library. This ability—even need—to collaborate is "a trait of the profession," notes Sabrina Pacifici, librarian and editor-publisher of LLRX.com, a respected legal portal.

State and Main

Librarians just aren't wired to think globally, let alone nationally, despite the creation of such national resources as MARC, OCLC, and the Library of Congress. Our local focus—the inevitable outcome of our dedication to our user communities—makes creating a global resource intimidating.

LSTA funds still provide the most significant source of seed money for library technology projects. These funds are distributed through state library agencies and are nearly always used for local or statewide projects. Interstate LSTA grants are rare, even though the legislation doesn't forbid this. Yet many library services—such as literacy and service to disabled users—which started as LSTA projects—are now well integrated into our national library budget. What we need to do is become—if you will—dual-boot librarians: thinking locally, acting globally.

A Critical Juncture

Our librarian colleagues must recognize that we are at a critical juncture. In one direction we move toward becoming a significant resource—as powerful as the role of Carnegie in the 20th century—while in the other we become a fondly remembered anachronism. Can we generate a sense of urgency strong enough to overcome the boundaries of parochialism, territory, and inadequate funding? Can we develop a global resource that can move librarianship to the web?

The Fiat Lux initiative requires our profession to take ownership of a big idea and to act. "Too often we wait like cargo cults for others to come up with these large metasolutions and parachute them down to us," says Steve Mitchell of INFOMINE, whose team spearheaded several grant proposals for Fiat Lux. "This has been the profession's approach to the Internet."

We need to build a Yahoo! with values and a brain, and we need to do it now. We aren't going to blow the commercial portals out of the water. But we can be to the Internet what public radio and television are for these other media: a single place for local and global content that our public can trust.

Reprinted from *Library Journal NetConnect*, 15 July 2002. Copyright 2002, used with permission of *Library Journal*, a publication of Reed Business Information, a division of Reed Elsevier

Recommended Reading

Branin, Joseph, Frances Groen, and Suzanne Thorin. "The Changing Nature of Collection Management in Research Libraries." Association of Research Libraries, Washington, DC. 10 June 2002. 10 Aug. 2002. http://www.arl.org/collect/changing.html

Foster, Andrea L. "Second Thoughts on Bundled E-Journals." *Chronicle of Higher Education* 20 Sept. 2002. http://chronicle.com/free/v49/i04/04a03101.htm

Frazier, Kenneth. "The Librarians' Dilemma: Contemplating the Costs of the 'Big Deal.'" *D-Lib Magazine* Mar. 2001. 20 June 2002. http://www.dlib.org/dlib/march01/frazier/03frazier.html

Pearlmutter, Jane. "Which online resources are right for your collection?" *School Library Journal* June 1999: 27–29.

Price, Gary D. "The librarian's librarian, Carole Leita." *Searcher* Nov.–Dec. 2000: 69–73.

Chapter 2

Rescuing the Book

Libraries have always been about books and reading. We've added videos and CDs and Internet access and databases, but we have always assumed that we are serving readers.

But in our technology-soaked world, the future of the book is in doubt. A recent report by the Book Industry Study Group indicates that "total sales of trade units declined 6.4 percent in 2001," that "the estimated number of books sold in 2006 is predicted to be lower than the total sold last year," that sales of mass market paperbacks and university press books will remain flat, that book club and mail-order sales will decline, and that the sales of juvenile books will also decline (Weeks, par. 3).

A nationwide survey of the reading habits of 509 American adolescents, conducted for the National Education Association in 2001, revealed some potential problems for the future of the book, especially with boys:

- Asked how important reading is to them on a 10-point scale, 40 percent of girls said 8 or higher, but only 31 percent of boys said the same thing.

- Asked why they read, 48 percent of girls said "for fun and pleasure," while 44 percent of boys said "for facts and information."

- Asked if they read every day things that weren't assigned, 30 percent of girls said yes, but only 19 percent of boys. (NEA)

Our technologies bear a large part of the blame, in part because they compete with books for our time and attention. More important, though, is the click effect. We click to zap alien invaders, click to different channels or web sites the moment our interest lags. We type a word or question in a search engine and click to get something resembling an answer. Within an electronic page or article or book, we click on "find" and zap down to the one little word or name that interests us, without having to read the surrounding paragraphs.

The click means users now are in control. Users atomize content, selecting and combining bits from all the different pages they visit. They ignore the authors' context and create their own, freely roaming back and forth between multiple open screens.

This is an environment that breeds restlessness, impatience, an urge to see what else is out there. It is not an environment that breeds readers of books, which require sustained attention. Concentrating, following a narrative or an argument, understanding the logic of the presentation— these are not inborn abilities but skills developed by practice.

In books, the authors, not the readers, are in control of the narrative voice, the point of view, the plot or argument, the characters or evidence, the pace, the style and vocabulary. The only times readers exercise control are when they decide to pick the book up in the first place, and when they decide to stop reading.

Libraries are not insulated from the world around them. When our users change, we have three choices: try to change our users, change ourselves to adapt to them, or some combination of the two. In this chapter, I will present some innovative things librarians are doing to respond to the challenge to the book and to the traditional library.

Solution
Easier Access by User-Friendly Cataloging

The Convenience Catastrophe

Roy Tennant

Anyone who has worked a reference desk has seen users pleased with a quick and mediocre answer when, with a bit more time and effort, they could get a better one. It's called 'satisficing.'

It's human nature to seek that which is 'good enough' rather than the best. For many, it's a simple equation of effort vs. payback. At a 'good enough' point that can only be determined by a specific individual, it becomes too much trouble to reach the optimum for the perceived gain.

Nobel prize–winning economist Herbert A. Simon came up with the concept of 'satisficing' in 1957. Although he was attempting to explain the behavior of firms, the concept appears to apply to individuals as well, and perhaps even more aptly.

Such behavior by and of itself is neither surprising nor necessarily detrimental. But when this aspect of human nature intersects with digital libraries, we have all the makings of what I call the 'convenience catastrophe.'

This catastrophe is nothing more or less than the disappearance of our print collections in the face of more easily obtained digital content. Collections that are easy to access by using a computer and an Internet connection will very frequently win out over print collections—no matter how much better and more inclusive our print collections may be. Once our clients begin to see the Internet as the answer to all or most of their questions, our sources of support will be in jeopardy.

So how do we fight this tendency? We must provide more information online about what our print collections hold, so that potential users of our holdings can more easily discover the treasures they contain. Converting our card catalogs into digital form was merely the beginning. A title, an author, and a few subject headings are often inadequate to determine if a particular book will be useful or not. We need to work cooperatively to provide much more information about our books, particularly nonfiction works.

Tables of Contents

For nonfiction works, the best first step is to provide the table of contents. Can you imagine a student's face lighting up when a book with an entire chapter on his/her paper topic is discovered? How could a student find this from the comfort of a dorm room unless we have made such information available online?

Luckily, we don't even have to do it ourselves. Blackwell's Book Services has sold digital tables of contents of books since the early 1990s. The company web site has a great deal of information on the topic, including an argument for the added expense and an explanation of how such information can be integrated into a MARC record.

MARC record enhancement is already happening. OCLC recently announced it would bolster WorldCat records with tables of contents provided by Ingram Library Services.

At Cornell, a 1997 report made the case for adding tables of contents to the catalog and summarized the state of such enhancement services at the time. Although that report focused on books, Cornell is now developing a MyContents component for its MyLibrary system that will enable users to select journals they wish to track and have the tables of contents of those issues e-mailed to them. The tables of contents are provided by vendors. The system is being constructed using open-source components, and the university plans to make the code available as open source.

Online Indexes

Providing indexes online is less important, overall, than providing tables of contents, but it can be a useful service if done appropriately. To be most effective, the indexes must be searchable. This can be done very simply by using optical character recognition software to turn scanned images into text and not bothering to correct any mistakes (which is costly in time and money). Instead, when a user discovers that a particular index has the terms searched, the page images will be displayed rather than the converted text file.

This technique is used by JSTOR and others to cut down on the expense of fully correcting the scanned text, while still providing a search function. A few years ago I proposed such a project at the

UC-Berkeley Library, and the proposal and demonstration site are still available. (The project wasn't funded.)

Making Reviews Available

Librarians write a lot of reviews. By and large, these reviews appear in professional journals such as *Library Journal* and *Choice* and are never seen by most library users. Admittedly, they are written for other librarians to make purchasing decisions, but such reviews could also be desirable for library users. Some libraries are already offering library reviews to their users.

Many books never get reviewed by the standard review media, however. By reviewing these books cooperatively, as we do for cataloging, we could begin providing hundreds (and soon thousands) of additional reviews that would help users select books.

Seeing Covers

Part of making books desirable is creating interest and intrigue. Book covers have been designed to do this for many years, since trying to get a customer to buy a book in a bookstore isn't all that different from getting them to come down to the library to get it. So why not use the marketing savvy of the publisher? Amazon.com certainly uses book covers (and not just the cover image, but also front and back flaps) as well as book excerpts, customer reviews, and even pointers to books that others bought at the same time. Institutions like Ferguson Library, Stamford, CT, and some 300 others provide similar information via companies like Syndetic Solutions, which supplies reviews, book jackets, and summaries, as well as excerpts, tables of contents, and more.

Integrated Searching

If a business sees a fall-off in customers, it would be wise for that business to consider what it is no longer doing right. We should be no different. Our customers are increasingly leaving us for the Internet.

We need to create powerful, effective, and easy-to-use search systems that integrate access to not just Internet resources but also our rich set of online databases and print content. If libraries began providing the kind of integrated portal services that I profiled in "Cross-Database Search: One-Stop Shopping" (*Library Journal* 10/15/01), users would beat a path to our doors. And in so doing, they would discover that print collections have something to offer as well. But to enable them to discover this, we will need to have much more information in our online catalogs.

The Convenience Opportunity

Everyone has heard the saying that if life gives you lemons, make lemonade. Trite but true: we now have our opportunity to take this 'catastrophe' and fashion an opportunity from it. If we can meet the challenge of moving our users from satisficing to satisfying, from minimizing to maximizing, we will have done not only our users a favor but ourselves as well.

Link List

Blackwell's Tables of Contents Bibliography
[no longer extant]

Blackwell's Tables of Contents Enrichment Service
<http://www.blackwell.com/level2/TOC.asp>

Ferguson Library Catalog <http://www.futuris.net/ferg>

Ingram Library Services <http://www.ingramlibrary.com>

OCLC Announces Enhancements to WorldCat
<http://www.oclc.org/oclc/press/20010918.shtm>

Table-of-Contents Enhancement of the Catalog
<http://www.library.cornell.edu/cts/martyrep.htm>

UC-Berkeley Library Proposal
<http://sunsite.berkeley.edu/PEP>

Reprinted from *Library Journal*, Dec. 2001. Copyright 2001, used with permission of *Library Journal*, a publication of Reed Business Information, a division of Reed Elsevier.

Solution
Easier Physical Access to All Nearby Library Collections

The Best Little Library System in the World

Marylaine Block

For 22 years I worked in an Iowa library that by the blessings of God and geography was part of an Illinois library system, the River Bend Library System, whose directors have always worried less about boundaries than about how to provide maximum service to their library users. They didn't worry about boundaries of type, either; the system embraces the libraries of three colleges, four community colleges, schools, hospitals, corporations and cities in three counties in Iowa and four in Illinois, not separated but joined by the Mississippi river.

Over the years, River Bend matured from a system that navigated all those libraries' separate catalogs to figure out who had the books we needed and get them to us, to a system that built a joint online catalog and circulation system (Quad-LinC—for Quad-City Libraries in Cooperation) that allows patrons of any library in the system to check books out from any other library, or even check them out online and have them delivered to their chosen library for pickup. Everyday, a River Bend van shuttles between libraries, delivering materials.

Next River Bend produced a union list of serials held by all participating libraries, and initiated a joint collection development program;
knowing that St. Ambrose University's library, for instance, would
keep key Catholic publications like *Commonweal* forever, other
libraries were free to keep more limited runs of these, and save their
space for long runs of other titles more basic to their own users' needs.

Everything this library system does is decided by librarians from all
over the Quad Cities, working in committees that do everything from
setting policies to choosing databases. Those committees are a splen-
did opportunity for librarians across all types of libraries to get to
know each other and find out about the special resources of each
individual library that are available to all of us.

The benefits for Iowa libraries that participate are obvious; we pay
our own fair share, but get the benefits of major capital investments
made up front by a well-funded Illinois system. Illinois citizens,
though, also benefit from this ignoring of arbitrary geographical
lines. They draw heavily on the holdings and knowledge of Iowa
libraries and librarians.

People in the Quad Cities tend to think of their cities—Davenport,
Bettendorf, Moline and Rock Island—as a seamless whole. We travel
freely back and forth across our bridges and boundaries. QuadLINC
and the River Bend shuttle system allow citizens to see the libraries of
the Quad Cities as a seamless whole as well, open to all comers.

What's more, we take seamlessness for granted. We tend to think all
systems operate like that, and are puzzled by the "mine, mine, mine!"
attitude of other libraries, the needless barriers thrown up against
people who don't fit inside a narrowly defined service community.

Praise goes to the unusually collaborative, forward-looking, service-oriented people who run the River Bend Library System. But
ideas and enthusiasm can only go so far without adequate funding.
Which is why full credit must be given to the state of Illinois, which
thinks it's important to make information widely available to its citizens, and thinks libraries are the key to doing so. Illinois' government

is a generous funder not only for day-to-day activities, but for special projects that require up-front capital, such as the building of our joint online catalog. As the world becomes ever more dependent on swift access to information, River Bend and the Illinois State Library are models for what other states and communities can and should do for their citizens.

Addendum from Robert McKay, System Director, River Bend Library System

The balance of library resources in our area provides a powerful pre-condition for cooperation. The population of the Quad City area, about 350,000, is pretty evenly divided between Illinois and Iowa. Quad City library resources are also pretty evenly split between the two sides of the Mississippi River. There are many excellent local collections and staff, but no collection is so large and powerful that its managers and staff can provide all of their customer's needs. The area has several fine private colleges and community colleges, but no major state or private university with a huge collection and staff. Davenport Public Library is a Major Urban Resource Library, but it is not the Chicago Public Library. No one library is so strong that it can meet all its customer's needs by itself. Every area library can see how cooperation within our area can improve service to its primary clientele.

The Quad Cities has created a powerful resource-sharing ethic that sustains and builds on itself. All the area's major academic, public, and special libraries participate in the River Bend Library System automated circulation project, known as Quad-LinC. Quad-LinC is managed by the libraries that participate and is operated by River Bend. Quad-LinC has more than 2.5 million items and one million titles. This means we have a relatively large bibliographic pool that is also relatively shallow.

Reciprocal borrowing has become a very popular program with library customers and managers—one out of every six items borrowed through Quad-LinC is borrowed by a customer from another library. Visiting another library and getting what you want makes navigating the broad, shallow lake of our area's bibliographic resources a pleasurable, rewarding experience for area customers. After more than three decades of successful library cooperation, area library customers' expectations foster even more cooperation and program integration.

Solution
One City, One Book

In 1977 the Library of Congress established the Center for the Book (http://www.loc.gov/loc/cfbook/ctr-bro.html) to promote books, reading, and libraries. Its projects have included "Read More About It," a Promoting Literacy project, and Letters about Literature, in which students write to their favorite authors to tell them how their lives have been affected by the author's books.

The 47 affiliated state centers for the book have produced projects such as the Vermont Center for the Book's Mother Goose Asks Why (http://www.vermontbook.org), which uses picture books to teach preschool children the process skills of science; Alaska Center for the Book's annual Writing Rendezvous (http://www.alaskacenterforthebook.org), where aspiring writers meet authors and learn about the craft and business of writing; and the Colorado Center for the Book's Authors in the Classrooms program (http://www.aclin.org/~ccftb).

But without a doubt the program that has caught the imagination of the American public and spread to city after city is the one that began at the Washington Center for the Book at the Seattle Public Library when Nancy Pearl, its director, asked the question, "What would happen if all Seattle read the same book?" (http://www.spl.org/wacentbook/centbook.html).

"If All Seattle Read the Same Book"

Nancy Pearl

The idea for this project was an outgrowth of two of my most strongly held beliefs as a librarian (and as a human being): good discussion of a book broadens and deepens a readers' understanding of and appreciation for that book; and people coming together for a discussion of a work of literature can help build community through the interchange of ideas and opinions, as well as help participants to develop a common vocabulary.

We had received a grant from the Wallace-Reader's Digest Fund to develop a three-year program to promote audiences for literature—this gave us the funds to get the project going and to continue it for all three years.

We worked closely with the independent booksellers in the Seattle area and with all the branch libraries in Seattle. We have an advisory group for the Center for the Book and we use them as a sounding board for our ideas. But basically, since there was minimal media interest (and no interest from the local government), we did it all ourselves.

The Center for the Book is part of the Seattle Public Library—there were discussions with the authors each year at two branch libraries and the main library downtown. In addition, the majority of the book groups that meet at libraries took part in the project by reading and discussing the book in their own groups.

We work closely with reading groups all over Seattle—we have a book club collection of recommended titles for discussion (the purchase of these books is funded by the library's Foundation). These books are not in the catalog and are sent out from our office. We have over 200 book groups who make use of the collection, some regularly, some infrequently. We are contacted each month by approximately 10 new groups wanting to borrow books from us. Typically we order 400 copies of the paperback to circulate to book groups.

Public participation went up each of the first three years; the fourth year there was a smaller turnout at the large public program, but more participation from book groups borrowing the book from the book club collection. The author was much less well known (Molly Gloss, *Wild Life*) than any of the other three. We have numbers of attendees at programs for each of the four years—what can't be measured quantitatively is the "broadening and deepening" part, which to me is the most important aspect of the project.

My one tip (or word of advice) to a group wanting to do this is to not be afraid to pick a book just because the fear is that someone or some group won't like it. We choose the books on the basis that each one makes for a good discussion—we know going in that some people will love the book and some will hate it, but that there's a lot to say about the book as a work of literature. This was never intended to be a social studies lesson, nor was it intended to bridge the racial divide or cure AIDS—it's a reading and discussion program that introduces people to books they might or might not be familiar with, gives them an opportunity to come together to talk about the book with other people in the community, and then offers them the opportunity to meet with the author.

Solution
Creating Readers Through Outreach and ESL

The New Americans Program: Twenty-One Years of Successful Partnerships Serving Diverse and Changing Communities (Part One)

Fred J. Gitner

"Bonjour. Je suis un nouvel immigré qui vient d'arriver aux Etats-Unis. Je ne parle pas l'anglais. Je ne lis pas l'anglais. Je suis un peu perdu, un peu dépaysé. Mes enfants sont à l'ecole où ils apprennent l'anglais. Mais je travaille et j'ai si peu de temps libre. Je commence à faire la déprime. Ce pays est si grand et si compliqué. J'ai des amis qui me parle de "la bibliothèque," mais c'est pour des chercheurs, n'est-ce pas?..."

That brief statement gives you an idea of the situation faced by new arrivals to the United States every day. For more than twenty years, the New Americans Program of the Queens Borough Public Library in New York has been helping to make life a little easier for Queens residents whose primary language is not English.

Queens Borough Public Library (QBPL), chartered in 1896, always has been a community-oriented institution. It now comprises a central library and sixty-two neighborhood branches, including the recently opened Flushing Branch that houses an International Resource Center. The library mission statement affirms its commitment to "provide quality services, resources, and lifelong learning opportunities in books and a variety of other formats to meet the informational, educational, cultural, and recreational needs and interests of its diverse and changing population." According to the 1990 census, Queens' population of almost two million residents includes 36 percent who are immigrants and 44 percent who speak a language other than English at home. In fact, Queens, one of New York City's five boroughs, is recognized as the most diverse county in the United States, with more than one hundred languages spoken.

The New Americans Program, an agency within the Programs and Services Department, is a unique mix of interrelated programs, services, and collections designed to reach these diverse and constantly changing potential user groups, many from countries without a public library tradition. It introduces a wide array of library programs and services so that the library becomes for them, as well as for more traditional customers, a community center and a place of lifelong learning.

Over the past twenty years, the New Americans Program successfully has forged partnerships in a variety of areas described below, to
provide quality service to all of the diverse groups in Queens. A proactive approach—including personal contacts by phone and in-person
to local community agencies, attendance at community fairs, and
press releases to the ethnic media—has served to let immigrants know
that the library welcomes them and has many programs and services
to offer them and their families.

Background

The project began in 1977 with funding from a federal LSCA grant.
The goals of the preliminary project included: to expand library services to immigrants whose primary language is not English, and to
attract newcomers to the library and assist them in adjusting to their
new surroundings through acquisition of appropriate materials and
creation of special training programs, workshops, and services, while
fostering an appreciation for their unique cultural makeup. In order
to determine which groups to target and what programs and services
should be offered, community studies were conducted, branch managers were surveyed regarding their neighborhoods, and contacts
were made with police precinct community relations officers and the
borough president's office. The local ethnic press was examined, as
were the local telephone directory and community organizations in a
variety of categories, including social service, ethnic, schools, and
churches. Bilingual flyers and brochures promoted the program, and
it quickly became apparent that staff with language capabilities
would be essential to success. Initial groups targeted were the
Hispanic, Greek, and Chinese communities. The project began with a
staff of two; today the New Americans Program has a staff of nine,
including seven professional librarians with knowledge of Spanish,
Italian, Portuguese, French, Chinese, Tagalog, Russian, and Yiddish
(and all have come in handy!).

English for Speakers of Other Languages (ESOL)

With seventy-five classes in twenty-four branches, the New Americans Program runs the largest library-based ESOL program in the country. Our ESOL coordinator, who is a librarian, and her assistant—a specialist with a degree in teaching ESOL—supervise a staff of twenty-five part-time teachers who are experienced in teaching English to adults. Each year almost three thousand students who are from eighty-eight different countries and speak fifty different languages take classes. Special features of the curriculum, which is based on everyday library situations, include a library lesson tailored to the Queens Library, a library orientation, and ensuring that all students register for library cards, which makes students feel a part of the library user community.

Another special aspect of our approach includes ESOL literacy classes for those immigrants who are not literate in their native language. These smaller classes allow for individualized attention and begin right at the beginning with how to hold a pen, and how to write on paper. About half of the students completing this class are ready to move into a regular beginning ESOL class the following year—which is a very good success rate.

Most recently we have added an exciting feature to our Advanced level ESOL class. All students attend a session that introduces them to the computer and its use in the library. For those who are unfamiliar with the mouse, a preliminary training session is given, followed by an introduction to the library's Web-based OPAC, InfoLinQ. The students are then ready to join the next session where they learn more about the features of InfoLinQ and receive an introduction to the Web, with a selection of sites tailored to their interests, including how to get daily news from their home country!

Coping Skills

The library offers practical workshops in the major Queens immigrant languages: Spanish, Chinese, Korean, and Russian, with other languages added from time to time, including Haitian Creole, Hindi/Urdu, Bengali, and most recently, Turkish. Teachers, lawyers, social workers, and psychologists fluent in the target language present workshops. Topics covered affect the lives of new immigrants, such as changes in the immigration laws, job training, the American educational system, parenting skills, family reading, health issues, tenants' rights, and domestic violence. Speakers are located by contacting community agencies and topics are not imposed, but arrived at by the New Americans Program's Coping Skills Librarian in conjunction with practitioners familiar with community needs. In many cases speakers are provided free of charge and agencies assist with publicity and provide relevant handouts to attendees in their language. At each program a brief introduction to the library's services is presented in the language of the program and a book display is prepared. One particularly successful program has been a workshop in Spanish on "Starting a Home Day Care Business." This fall we plan a series of workshops in Spanish, Chinese, and Korean in collaboration with Fannie Mae on "Buying Your First Home."

Cultural Arts

Assisting immigrants in the acculturation process is a primary goal, but at the same time we feel it is important to assist in maintaining native languages and cultures that enrich New York for all who live here. To that end, regularly scheduled programs of music, dance, storytelling, and crafts celebrating the diverse ethnic groups in Queens are presented using primarily local artists and performers. Bilingual flyers mailed to community organizations and the ethnic media, press releases, and visits to local merchants promote the program. A bilingual introduction about the New Americans Program and library services is presented along with an appropriate book display. Recent cultures that have been featured include Bengali, Filipino, Korean, Russian, Haitian, Chinese, Hispanic, Turkish, Polish, Greek, and Afghan. Our aim is to attract a mixed audience of 60 percent from the ethnic group featured, and 40 percent from the public at large, fostering cross-cultural interaction. These programs are among our most popular, with up to seven hundred people attending our all-day festivals, and are an excellent way to attract new immigrants to the library. Program planning takes into account community make-up in selecting the location to present a particular ethnic group. A successful partnership with the Queens Council on the Arts Folk Arts Program has involved sharing costs, assisting with publicity and promotion, and increasing the pool of performers from which to choose.

Collection Development

The collections we develop in languages other than English have goals similar to the programs described earlier. We provide practical popular materials to assist new immigrants in adapting to life in America, e.g. citizenship and ESOL materials. We also provide general popular materials from their home countries on the same topics that we provide our English-speaking customers, i.e. fiction, parenting, cookbooks, biographies, romances, children's books, videos, and music CDs. This demonstrates that the library respects their native culture, language, and customs. We currently support five major programs (Spanish, Chinese, Korean, six South Asian languages, and Russian) and five other programs (French/Haitian Creole, Greek, Hebrew, Polish, and Portuguese) for a total of sixteen languages. All materials purchased by the New Americans Program become part of the local branch collection, so that it is only after community analysis—discussed in [part two of this article]—that branches are added to a program. The literature and language division of the Central Library provides rotating collections to branches in those two subject areas in almost fifty languages, which allows branches to "test-market" a language. Bilingual promotional brochures have been created for the four largest collection programs.

One additional aspect of collection development is our Mail-a-Book program in seven languages. These are annotated lists of about one hundred titles each that act as a public-relations tool and allow customers to become acquainted with the library without having to come in or get a card. These lists, in the various languages, are made available at our programs and through community organizations. Once readers have gone through the entire list and request additional titles, they are sent information about the library and invited to borrow in person from the full range of available materials.

Solution
Creating Readers Through Outreach to Boys and Men

You Go, Guys!

Shannon Maughan

Jon Scieszka, an author (and former second-grade teacher) whose goal has always been to "reach the guys in the back of the room," goes to the head of the class, as it were, speaking out on how to encourage boys to read. On April 30, appropriately enough during the International Reading Association convention, Scieszka outlined the philosophy and strategies of his new literacy initiative for boys called Guys Read, a project enthusiastically supported by his publisher, Penguin Putnam, as well as the Association of Booksellers for Children. Scieszka recently spoke with PW about the campaign.

"I think the whole thing crystallized when I was talking with my editor, Regina Hayes president and publisher of Viking Children's Books," Scieszka explained. "We were discussing some projects and talking about how I've always tried to write books that will reach those guys we seem to miss. Regina said, 'You should tell people about that.'"

Hayes had a similar recollection. "It really grew out of our work on the *Time Warp Trio* books [an early reader series]," she said. "Jon really understands those boys he's trying to reach. He's one of six brothers, he's a father, a former teacher and an avid reader himself. He's always had the philosophy that if you find the right stories to hook them, boys will read. The Time Warp Trio books have humor, short chapters and cliffhanger endings, and some of those funny or slightly gross things that make boys feel that what they're reading is a bit subversive. It's similar to the way many kids feel about Roald Dahl's books." In Hayes's estimation, "It seemed to me that Jon was the perfect spokesman for Guys Read. He feels so strongly about this issue, he knows the educational rationales, he has practical experience and he's a natural speaker."

Scieszka's and Hayes's focus dovetailed with recent efforts of the ABC. "We've been realizing in the past couple of years that we needed to create some sort of campaign for kids ages 8 to 12," said ABC executive director Caron Chapman. The organization's longstanding and successful "Most Important 20 Minutes of Your Day" campaign, which encourages adults to make a daily habit of reading to a child, is primarily aimed at preschoolers.

As ABC officers and members formulated the beginnings of a Hey Girls! campaign for girls, according to Chapman, "we thought, now what about the boys?" The group discussed commissioning artwork for the boys' reading initiative and illustrator Lane Smith's name came up (Smith is Scieszka's long-time collaborator, having illustrated nearly all of his books). After the ABC spoke with Scieszka and learned of their common purpose, ABC, Penguin Putnam and Scieszka pooled their efforts to create the formal concept of Guys Read.

Getting the Word Out

Scieszka has written a Guys Read brochure that highlights the reasons a literacy program for boys is long overdue, and offers concrete suggestions on how parents, teachers, booksellers, librarians and others can participate in and promote the cause. Much of the advice centers on providing boys with role models. "We need more men standing up as reading role models for guys," Scieszka said. "When I was a teacher, I was pretty much the only guy teaching in the lower elementary grades. Most teachers, librarians and even booksellers in kids' lives are women; this gives boys the idea that reading is not a masculine activity." He cites one of his neighbors as a shining example of connecting boys with books. "My neighbor started a father-son reading group," he explained. "They call it Books and Balls. The sons choose the books. Then, once a month or so, the dads and sons meet at a local indoor soccer place where they have pizza, discuss the books and then play ball. It's terrific—the kids, mostly third and fourth graders, and the dads all love it."

The Guys Read brochure goes on to list Scieszka's personal book list, called "A Few of My Favorite Books for Guys," which he hopes will inspire adults who work with children and books to be more conscious of the titles they assign and recommend. "I saw my son struggle through *Little House on the Prairie* in fourth grade," said Scieszka. "He and his friends just hated it. But it wasn't because it's a bad book, it's because girls are much quicker to develop an emotional connection to fiction. We have to remember that guys are different and they need special attention when it comes to reading. They want to read books that will titillate or electrify them first. Then we can move them into something more sophisticated, with an emotional palette that helps them become more well-rounded people."

Not recommending specific titles is where Scieszka believes some other literacy initiatives fail. "The 'Get Caught Reading' campaign is a great idea, but they don't take the next step and recommend specific titles. And in a recent ad, they show baseball star Sammy Sosa reading *Green Eggs and Ham*. What kind of message does that send to guys?" he remarked.

In addition to the brochure, Lane Smith has designed (along with his wife, Molly Leech) and illustrated a poster and button featuring what Scieszka calls a "cool, every-guy logo" to promote the campaign. Penguin Putnam will underwrite the cost of these materials, as well as Scieszka's conference appearances, for the first year/tier of Guys Read (2001-2002), and the ABC will distribute promotional items to member stores (free, save for shipping costs). Nonmember booksellers may also request materials from the ABC office (800-421-1665), but will be required to pay a fee, which has not yet been determined.

Scieszka will also spread the word as he presents the Guys Read initiative to booksellers at BEA during the ABC breakfast on May 31, promotes it at the ALA annual convention in San Francisco this June [2001], and on the June bookstore tour for his new picture book, *Baloney (Henry P.)*, illustrated by Smith (Viking).

Going forward, Scieszka hopes that the campaign will serve as a starting point for many more people to get involved. On May 1 [2001] GuysRead.com officially launched, designed as a true electronic community where "people can connect and share ideas" about the program. He mentioned as future goals posting celebrity reading lists, obtaining corporate partners/sponsors, and giving guys themselves a stronger voice.

He also hopes that the forthcoming *Time Warp Trio* animated television series (launching next year on PBS) will provide other opportunities to promote Guys Read. "I never really saw myself in this role, talking to crowds of people as a spokesguy," Scieszka said. "I'd rather just make the guys laugh."

"We're not trying to be something for everyone," he added. "But the response to this idea has been phenomenal. People have a visceral reaction to it. I hope we can channel all that interest and really help get guys through the struggle they have with reading."

Reading Is 'In'

Janet L. Balas

While libraries have been busy promoting technology, other businesses have been promoting reading. The irony is stunning.

Several months ago I attended a brainstorming session where the question under consideration was, "What services will the library need to deliver in the future in order to remain a viable institution?" One participant declared that in order to draw patrons into the library and keep them coming back, we needed to always have technology that was newer, faster, and better than the technology patrons had in their homes. I know of many libraries that are following this model of development, offering the latest computers, printers, scanners, and CD-RW drives for patron use in their computer labs or technology centers. They have trumpeted their Internet access and other available technologies in their publicity materials. And many libraries offer a wide range of computer classes, believing that the primary reason patrons come to the library is to use computers.

In the months since the brainstorming session, while I have been pondering the question of whether the library should concentrate its planning and development efforts primarily on acquiring the latest cutting-edge technologies, I have noticed some interesting developments in the world outside the library.

Bookstores Are 'In'

We have a Borders bookstore in our community, and every time I visit, it is always full of people. It's true that some are in the cafe area while others are listening to the entertainment, but the vast majority of the people in the store are in the aisles of books, browsing through the various titles or unabashedly reading a particular book or magazine. What is most interesting is that I could find no more than two computers in the store for customer use, and even they were only to check on the availability of items. There was no e-mail, no chat, and no Web browsing—which is what many people insist that libraries need—yet the store had plenty of customers looking at the CDs, videos, magazines, and of course, the books.

Techies Know Books

Part of my job is to keep abreast of the latest developments in information technology, so I read a number of technology related publications. One print publication that comes across my desk regularly is *Information Week*. Several months ago, the magazine debuted a new section entitled Breaking Away, which acknowledges the need for technology staff to have a life outside the technology-laden workplace.

One weekly feature that appears to be very popular with readers is the Open Book literary quiz. Each issue, several excerpts from a particular book are presented, and readers are asked to identify the book and the author. Entries may be submitted by mail or online. Recent titles selected for the quiz include: *Blue Highways* by William Heat Moon, *The Killer Angels* by Michael Shaara, *The Cardinal of the Kremlin* by Tom Clancy, *The Tale of Jeremy Fisher* by Beatrix Potter, and *The Odyssey* by Homer. Contest answers are printed in the next week's issue, along with reader comments of special interest. There's even an online forum where readers can discuss the quiz. I find it quite interesting that a technology magazine would use a literary quiz to increase readership. What is even more surprising is the enthusiastic response to the quiz from supposedly hard-driving, ambitious high-tech professionals.

I've noticed the same renewed enthusiasm for books in my library. After years of unsuccessful attempts to organize book discussion groups, we now have not one, but two book clubs that meet here regularly. Our summer reading program this year set a new daily circulation record on the first day, and a teen reading program that is only in its second year has grown both in participants and in enthusiasm. It would seem that while librarians have been busy promoting our technology to attract patrons, businesses outside the library have been promoting reading in order to attract customers and, through their marketing efforts, have rekindled the public's interest in reading.

While I certainly wouldn't suggest that we turn our backs on technology in the library, I would suggest that we also not turn our backs on books and reading. It should be possible to support both, and I have discovered that many libraries have implemented some innovative uses of technology to promote books and reading.

Taking Discussions Online

I mentioned the resurgence of interest in book discussion groups here in Monroeville. Often when a group is involved in an interesting discussion, the available meeting time doesn't seem long enough. Perhaps with that thought in mind, the Fairfax County (Virginia) Public Library has instituted an online book discussion service that it calls The Front Porch. Readers are invited to visit The Front Porch to post messages about books they've read and enjoyed, whether old or new. The discussion is organized into separate conferences on fiction, mystery, nonfiction, science fiction, and one devoted to a specific book discussion group. Guests may browse the conferences and read messages, but posting messages and participating in chat is restricted to registered users.

Readers, including librarians, who enjoy reading and writing book reviews should also enjoy visiting BookCrossing.com, a site with an unusual premise. Visitors are invited to register a book they have read and enter comments about it as a journal entry. They are then invited to share the book with others by either lending it, donating it to a charity, or simply leaving it somewhere to be found by another reader. Every time someone else reads the book and records new journal entries for it, the original reader is notified by e-mail and can track the book's journey. Of course, we can't exactly give away our libraries' books, but we, or anyone else who can't part with their books but still wants to share them with others, can record journal entries on the ones they've read. While browsing through the journal entries, I noticed that one reviewer mentioned that the book she read was from a library.

Strategies to Get People Hooked on Books Again

Libraries can take advantage of an online book club service from Chapter-a-Day that is designed to encourage busy people to take time to read. Each weekday, Chapter-a-Day members receive an excerpt from a popular book in their email. The excerpts are short enough to be read (or in the case of the audio club, to be listened to) in 5 minutes. After the first two or three chapters have been sent, the club will move on to a new title. The service has several sections: its original book club that selects from a wide variety of popular titles, an audio book club, a business book club, a teen book club, a good news book club, and a fiction book club.

Libraries can offer this free service to patrons from their own Web sites using the graphics and other promotional materials supplied by Chapter-a-Day. Participating libraries will be notified about upcoming selections 8 weeks in advance to give acquisitions departments plenty of time to place their orders. Librarians can learn more about implementing this service by visiting the Chapter-a-Day site, where a sample e-mail excerpt is available. You can also read about the inspiration behind the concept as described by the site's founder, Suzanne Beecher. A list of publishers participating in the service is available as well. Librarians can try out the book clubs by signing up for free on the Chapter-a-Day site. I've already used the test audio sample to make sure my Mac has the appropriate version of RealPlayer installed for the audio club, and I'll be receiving my first text excerpts and a link to the audio excerpt in my e-mail tomorrow.

I was especially interested to see a teen book club offered by Chapter-a-Day because my library has been making a sincere effort in the last few years to interest teens in reading and the library. It had seemed to us that young children loved the library, but that they fell away during their teen years, only using the library when absolutely necessary to complete a school assignment. Jon Scieszka, author of *The Stinky Cheese Man* and *Time Warp Trio*, has been particularly concerned that boys don't seem to enjoy reading and don't read as well as girls. He has developed a Web site, Guys Read, to address this issue. [Ed note: See "You Go, Guys!" on p. 56.]

Some of the goals of this initiative are: 1) to call attention to the issue of boys' literacy, 2) to motivate adults who select books for children to examine the role that gender plays in their selections for boys, and 3) to tell boys about books recommended by other boys. The site offers a list of recommended titles that should appeal to guys, as well as ideas for promoting the enjoyment of reading to them. The site does not provide an extensive list of titles nor does it discuss the issue in depth, but it does raise an issue that those of us who work with children and teens should consider. The Guys Speak section provides boys with the opportunity to submit their favorite titles for inclusion on the site, so its resources may develop over time.

Even though young children seem to love the library, we shouldn't take their interest for granted. We still need to promote reading through programs and services designed especially for them. An online reading promotion that does exactly that is StoryPlace-The Children's Digital Library from the Public Library of Charlotte & Mecklenburg County.

Available in English and Spanish versions, the site offers both a Pre-School Library and an Elementary Library. The Pre-School Library offers online stories and activities, take-home activities, and reading lists organized around themes which, at the time of my visit, included shapes, colors, animals, monkeys, crocodiles, teddy bears, babies, and bath time. The Elementary Library used a similar format offering topsy-turvy tales, printout activities, and reading lists around themes that included critters, mammals, and the upcoming magical places. StoryPlace is colorful and easy to navigate using the freely available Flash plug-in to provide the interactive features. Themes change monthly, so frequent visitors might want to sign up for the free e-mail newsletter to stay informed on the latest updates.

Vacationing with Books

I began this column by pointing out several examples of a resurgence of interest in reading. I'd like to end it with one last example that I found particularly interesting. Information professionals who visit bookstores or libraries while on vacation are often accused of taking a busman's holiday. For the librarian, or any avid reader, who truly wants to be immersed in books while on vacation, there is now The Library Hotel in New York City. The hotel, which describes itself as "fully booked," is organized according to the Dewey Decimal System with each floor corresponding to a major division and each of its 60 rooms devoted to a different subject. Common areas are also stocked with literature. Even if you're limited to only dreaming about such a vacation, visit this Web site to watch the video and see pictures of the rooms. Nearly all the librarians I know chose this profession because they loved books and reading. Despite the advantages offered by technology, many of my colleagues have caught themselves longing for the good old days when they talked about books, rather than computers, with patrons. Those days aren't gone, however, as I've discovered. Our patrons may use our computers, but they are also interested in our books. Reading, and using technology to promote it, is most definitely "in."

Resources Discussed

Information Week: Breakaway
<http://www.informationweek.com/breakaway>

The Front Porch: An Online Book Discussion-FCPL
[no longer extant]

BookCrossing.com <http://bookcrossing.com>

Chapter-a-Day <http//www.chapteraday.com>

Guys Read: A Literary Initiative for Boys <http://www.guys read.com>

StoryPlace-The Children's Digital Library <http://www.story place.org>

The Library Hotel <http://www.libraryhotel.com>

Solution
Partnerships

Making Bookstores Your Partners

Marylaine Block

In a previous article <http://marylaine.com/exlibris/xlib121. html> I suggested that the net has led libraries, publishers, writers, bookstores, schools, scholars, and readers, all former partners in the knowledge and reading enterprise, to regard each other as dangerous competitors. I pointed out how self-destructive this was, since we all continue to provide different but equally valuable contributions to the success of the others.

Libraries and bookstores in particular should be natural allies, since we both want to serve readers and increase their number. In fact, our readers and theirs are essentially the same people—virtually every reader survey shows that people who use libraries also buy books. Libraries are to bookstores what tasting parties are to wine shops—places where people can sample and find out what they like.

Readers who discover a favorite author in a library and read their way through all the author's previous work, often go out and buy not only the newest work by their chosen author, but their favorite older books as well, both for their personal collections and for gifts. Parents who take their kids to story hours often take them to the bookstore and buy them the latest Harry Potter or Lemony Snicket books. Libraries, in short, create bookbuyers.

Bookstores, on the other hand, may create library users. A devoted Gordon Korman fan who has bought all the Korman books still in print may go to the library to find the ones misguided publishers have allowed to die, like the wonderfully funny *No Coins, Please*, or *Don't Care High*.

How might we collaborate? Let me count the ways:

- Libraries create lots of reading lists: If you like cat mysteries, try these titles; if you like John Grisham's legal thrillers, try these. We provide topical reading lists—on terrorism, coping with grief, women's history, the Olympics, etc. We even do complete author bibliographies, both their in-print and out-of-print titles. Wouldn't the bookstores like to have copies to post in their stores in the relevant areas, or stick in the bag along with a book purchase?

- We sponsor lots of book-related events, and so do bookstores. Shouldn't we share? Can't we jointly sponsor author appearances and book talks?

- Couldn't our book discussion groups get special discounts at local bookstores? For that matter, shouldn't librarians? Shouldn't the top ten readers in our summer reading programs get gift certificates from the local bookstores?

- Couldn't we give bookstores advance notice of the books, authors and topics we're going to feature in exhibits, story hours, and special events so they could stock up?

- Couldn't they publicize our story hours—and beef up their own sales—with an alcove of "story hour books"?

- Shouldn't bookstores route copies of their own readers' magazines to us so we can stock up on multiple copies of the stores' featured items?

- If we choose a particular kind of e-book technology, shouldn't we notify local bookstores so they can stock some titles in compatible format?

- We have deeper collections than the bookstores on virtually every topic; when people want to know more on any topic, shouldn't bookstores refer people to us?

- We have a backfile of magazines, and they only have current issues; they have lots of titles that we don't subscribe to [quick, how many of you get *Guns and Ammo*?]. When someone wants what isn't on our shelves, shouldn't we refer people to the bookstores, and shouldn't they refer people to us? Do your local bookstores even know what magazines you subscribe to? Have you given them a copy of your serials list?

- Bookstores get reference questions and questions about out of print books all the time that they can't provide answers to. Shouldn't they say, "Hold on, let me call the library and see if they can answer that question/have that book?" Couldn't they tell people seeking an out of print book that the library may either have it or get it for them on loan?

- For that matter, shouldn't we be their reference source of choice for author and book information beyond the purview of *Books in Print*—for author biographies, book reviews, the value of that first edition of *Gone with the Wind*, identifying a book when the patron knows only the plot line, and such? Do the bookstore folks even realize that we could search WorldCat, or NoveList or *Fiction Catalog* for them?

- Shouldn't bookstore owners be working members of our Friends of the Library groups, and board members? Shouldn't they be defending library budgets in city council and Chamber of Commerce meetings, and helping us on bond issue campaigns?

I'm sure there are other ways of collaborating that haven't occurred to me. The point is, libraries and bookstores are as complementary as salt and pepper, serving the same purpose for the same people, but in slightly different ways. We should be working together.

Reprinted from *ExLibris*, 25 Jan. 2002. Copyright 2002, Marylaine Block.

Solution
Blogs and Personalized Services by E-Mail

A good patron-oriented blog for readers is a wonderful service. For example, the one offered by Waterboro (ME) Public Library (http://www.waterborolibrary.org/blog.htm) provides links to news stories about books and authors, book reviews, reading group guides, author interviews, and more. The webmaster maintains reading lists as well, of Maine Writers, Fiction with a Maine setting, Golf Mysteries, and some other interesting mystery reading lists. The blog is not only updated several times each day, but is also available by e-mail subscription and as an RSS feed.

Morton Grove Public Library (IL) offers an outstanding Readers Services program, making the reading lists from the FICTION-L discussion group available on its Web site and using them as the basis for its MatchBook program, which allows users to create a profile of their individual reading interests, and automatically notifies readers when the library has a new book fitting their profiles.

The MatchBook Program

Readers Services, Morton Grove Public Library

Have you ever wondered if anyone cares what YOU like to read?

The Morton Grove Public Library does! We've created a new service to tell you about the new books in the Library that will interest you.

MatchBook is a special service that allows you to pick the subjects that interest you: antiques, hobbies and crafts, or sports, to name just a few. You can also select your favorite authors or fiction categories: mysteries, romances, historical fiction, and many more. Any patron twelve years or older and registered with the Morton Grove Public Library may use the MatchBook service. Fill out a Patron Profile and we'll create a list every month of new books in the Library that match your profile exactly!

Recommended Reading

Abramson, Marla. "Lunch Special: Over Books and a Meal Senior Citizens and Sixth-Graders Have a Meeting of the Minds." *Book*, Sept.–Oct. 2002: 34–35.

Bailey, Ian. "Reading Group Closes the Book on Allowing Women." *National Post*, 20 July 2002.

DeGroot, Joanne. "You Want Me To Do What?" http://www.yrl.ab.ca/You%20 Want%20Me%20to%20Do%20What%20Presentation.ppt *An excellent presentation on drawing kids to books and to the library.*

Dubois, Deborah L. "Taking It to the Streets: The Life and Times of a Children's Outreach Librarian." *Wilson Library Bulletin* Feb. 1995: 18–19.

Fine, Jana R. "From the Field: Reaping the Benefits of Partnerships." *Journal of Youth Services in Libraries* 15.1 (2001): 16–22.

Gitner, Fred. "New Americans program: Part 2."*Reference & User Services Quarterly* 38.3 (1999): 243–4.

Olsen, Florence. "Virginia Commonwealth U. Creates Virtual New-Book Shelves for Every User." *Chronicle of Higher Education* 17 Apr. 2001. http://chronicle.com/free/2001/04/2001041701t.htm

Raiteri, S. "Recommended Graphic Novels for Public Libraries, Selected and Annotated by Steve Raiteri." 26 May 2002. 20 Aug. 2002. http://my.voyager.net/~sraiteri/graphicnovels.htm

Ramirez, Mark. "On the Same Page? The Plot's Thickened as Other Cities Copy Seattle's Novel Reading Idea." *Seattle Times* 24 Mar. 2002. http://seattle times.nwsource.com/html/education/134425244_seattlereads24.html

Weiner, Robert G. "Graphic Novels in Libraries." *Texas Library Journal* 77.4 (2001): 130–5.

Chapter 3

Making Them Adapt to Us: Training Our Users

The Internet generation is something outside our experience. How are these people different?

Attention span: Ted Selker, an expert in online behavior from MIT says, "If we spend our time flitting from one thing to another on the web, we can get into a habit of not concentrating" ("Turning into Digital Goldfish" par. 4). That's certainly the assumption my editor worked under when I was a columnist for Fox News Online—she told me to never write more than 700 words or my readers would click away.

Patience: Readers want information to be available the instant they want it, on demand, 24/7/365. They "favor least cost efforts in order to save time and avoid embarrassment" (Young and Von Seggern, par. 11). Like the scientists who asked the computer the meaning of life, the universe, and everything, they head to Google or Yahoo! before they've even figured out exactly what they need to know about their topic. The answers, like the computer's answer, "42," may leave them scratching their heads. In the focus groups Young and Von Seggern looked at, "knowing where to start" was the biggest problem. One person said, "I wouldn't have known a second word to type in because I didn't know what I was looking for" (Young and Von Seggern, par. 33).

Willingness to expend effort: They don't want no stinkin' citations, even to journals sitting right there on our shelves. They want it full text, so all they have to do is push the button and print. Undergraduate citation behavior has changed; between 1996 and 1999, book citations decreased from 30 percent to 19 percent, and Web citations increased from 9 percent to 21 percent (Davis and Cohen, par. 2).

Preferred communication systems: Instant messaging, e-mail, cell phone, PDA.

Ability to analyze information: We know that they confuse information with knowledge, and the delivery system—

computers—with what is delivered. Jeffrey Hastings, a school librarian, explains why the Internet has made it impossible for him to teach students good research method:

> I wonder if she didn't approach the computer that day possessing an outspoken assumption. Something like this: You push buttons on computers and you get them to do things. Once you make them do the right things you are done. On this day, maybe for the first time in her experience, the computer was presenting her with something that she would have to process. I don't think she had bargained on that. And, I know it sounds far-fetched, but I think her conceptual model of the human-computer relationship still exists today among the students I serve and gets in the way of their "getting down to business." The inescapable fact seems to be that students delay the brainwork involved in research when they're using electronic tools. (Hastings, par. 25)

In the focus groups Nancy Young reported on, "undergraduates revealed that they perceived no difference between the computer labs that are housed in the University of Idaho Library and the library itself. . . students think that the lab monitors are library employees who can assist with research techniques, and conversely, the library staff is assumed to know how to help in the labs with questions about software problems" (Young and Von Seggern, par. 44).

In a Canadian study of student Internet use, while the majority of respondents said that 50 percent to 70 percent of the information on the Internet was true, 369 students (21.8 percent) thought 80 percent to 100 percent of what they saw on the Net was true (Gibson and Tranter, par. 12). Fifteen percent of these students said outright that they did not know how to distinguish true from false information on the Net (Gibson and Tranter, par. 16). The aura of inerrancy surrounding computers tends to attach itself to material delivered by way of computers. We know that users are satisfied with results we would consider totally inadequate.

Of course librarians could help them find better resources and more reliable answers, but a recent OCLC White Paper on student research behavior revealed that when students need help finding information on the Web, more than 60 percent of them will first go to a friend, but only a fifth of them will go to a librarian.

Still, there is some ground for hope. When Young asked focus group members to describe the "dream information machine," it bore an astonishing resemblance to a librarian:

> The qualities that were listed . . . as important characteristics of a "good" information source (accuracy, reliability, authoritativeness, timeliness, cost, currency, accessibility, completeness, organization, etc.) were apparently taken for granted by most participants when it came time to talk about a "dream information machine" or an ideal information source. Descriptions were remarkably consistent across all groups, especially in the use of terms such as "mind reader" and "intuitive." Voice recognition and natural language were also mentioned by all groups, as was the idea of a single source, expressed as "one source," "complete," "comprehensive," or "everything." In addition, portability and 24/7 access were expressed as attributes of the ideal source (Young and Von Seggern, par. 38).

So all we have to do is convince them that we are the information machines of their dreams. One way is to train them.

It is true that our efforts to do so don't seem to have worked all that well so far. On the other hand, we often do the training in terms of classroom assignments that do not engage student interest in the first place. We could change that.

Solution
Teach Them While They're Asking for Information

Reference as a Teachable Moment

Marylaine Block

Doing reference can be kind of like doing magic tricks. The patron wants an answer—quick, what's the national enrollment in private schools?—and we deliver it, along with the source we got it from ("according to *Statistical Abstract*, in 1998—the last year they have final figures for—enrollment was 9,142,000"). We pull the rabbit out of the hat and leave it at that.

But knowing that there's a lot more to statistics than that, we could carry on a running commentary about what we're finding— "It gives projected numbers for 2000 and 2004, too, if you want those, and it breaks the figures down by grade level. Did you want to compare that with previous years? It gives comparative enrollment data back to 1980, and comparisons with public school enrollment, too, if you're interested."

You see, that's another approach to reference: showing our patrons the art behind the trick while we're looking for their answers, so that they can learn to find their own rabbits. We do it by thinking out loud, letting them hear our thought processes.

Why? Because when people have a need to know is when they are most open to learning not just the answers but how to find answers. Suppose someone asked you to track down a quote about how progress depends on the unreasonable man. We could take them to Google, and say something like, "Let's type in PROGRESS + "UNREA-SONABLE MAN," since those are the words you're pretty sure about. Of course we always put quotes around things we want to search as exact phrases."

As we sort through the results, we could say something like, "Hmm, there seem to be at least six different versions of that quote. I can't tell which one is correct, either, because the only source given on each of those pages is George Bernard Shaw, and we can't really go through everything Shaw wrote to check it. Let's go to X-Refer <http://w1.xrefer.com/> or Bartleby <http://bartleby.com/>, where we can look it up in online quote books.

"OK, according to the *Oxford Dictionary of Quotations* on X-Refer, the quote goes this way: "The reasonable man adapts himself to the world: the unreasonable one persists in trying to adapt the world to himself. Therefore all progress depends on the unreasonable man." It says the quote came from George Bernard Shaw's *Man and Superman, Maxims.* You know, I always trust it more when they tell us exactly where the quote came from—it gives us a way of double-checking."

Of course we could also say, "You know, I don't trust the web because so many of the quotes online are just wrong; I'd rather use a quote book," and take them directly to our reference section or to the quotation sources on XRefer or Bartleby, but in my experience, showing is more effective than telling. By bumbling through Google search results with them, we show them how unreliable the open web can be; actually seeing the problem should make them welcome the discovery of reliable online databases that are part of the invisible web.

I once helped some business students who were doing a project on community development along the Mississippi River and wanted to know where they'd find information on inland ports and barge traffic. I started musing out loud about who would logically be conducting research on it—the Department of Transportation, the U.S. Department of Agriculture (which inspects grain barges), the Army Corps of Engineers, the Coast Guard, state and regional boards and such, all government agencies. So I suggested we use SearchGov <http://searchgov.com/>, which indexes federal, state and local government web pages, where indeed, we found lots of good statistics and research reports. On the other hand, I said, there would also be articles about it in business and trade magazines and journals, so I also helped them search it in our full-text business databases.

I wasn't just giving the students answers. I was also teaching them my first rule of information: Go where it is. Find it by figuring out first where it's most likely to be.

When a faculty member once asked me what science databases were available on the web, I talked him through a mental process like this: "Hmm, interesting terminology problem, since a chemistry database, for instance, would be called a chemistry database, not a science database. How do we get around that? I know, let's use a search engine like SciSeek <http://sciseek.com/>, which searches nothing but science sites [SciSeek is no longer extant]. Now, let's just type in DATABASE and see what we get. OK, SciSeek found 495 science databases—for hazardous materials, software for chemists, aquatic plants and such." He learned a little that day about the complexity of terminology problems, about searching within restricted universes, and about a search engine he'd never heard of before that he's been using ever since.

If a student asks for information on schizophrenia, you could explain your reasoning as you escort him to the computer and help him begin his search: "OK, you say your instructor expects you to use psychology literature for this, so we should search *Psychological Abstracts*, which indexes the behavioral science journals. But if all we type in is schizophrenia, we're going to pull up thousands of references, so how can we narrow it down? If you found the perfect article on your topic, what would it be called? OK, let's take this word and this other word and add those to schizophrenia in your search."

Of course if the student really doesn't know enough in the first place to be able to narrow down the search, you could say, "Well, would you like to see what current psychological research is being done on schizophrenia? We could probably find a review of the research in *Annual Review of Psychology*. Or we could start with an expert site for the field, say the American Psychological Association, and see if it guides you to the best research in that area. Or, if you like, before we go to the psychology literature, we could start with MedlinePlus <http://medlineplus.gov/> where the National Library of Medicine has linked in some good background information on it. OK, let's do that. I see it's got some overviews, and information on symptoms and diagnosis. Hmm, they also link in a couple of news items about psychedelic drugs and schizophrenia. Oh, look, here's a report on the evidence for a biological basis, and one on a possible genetic cause, and something on schizophrenia and suicide. Do any of those ideas grab you? Why don't you explore a little and I'll get back to you in a few minutes." Once the student arrives at a narrower topic THEN you can show him how Psych Abstracts works and help him explore the psychology literature.

You can teach quite complicated strategies by thinking out loud while you're finding things for your patrons. You can show them how to pick up new terms as they sort through results, and suggest different ways of narrowing the search—were you interested in genetic aspects, or maybe therapeutic drugs?

Of course reference is not a monologue but a dialogue, and how much you say will be determined by how your patron responds. But if your patrons find the perfect article or web site and want more like it, it's an opportunity to show them hyper-linked subject headings or bibliographic references they could click on, or suggest using the authors' names or terms from that article in new searches. You can suggest other databases to search and explain why they'd be good sources. For that matter, you can show them why, in some cases, the best thing they could do is start with a good book on the topic.

Why should we demystify ourselves like this, give away some of our best tricks? Why not just take credit for being the sees-all-knows-all wizards that we are? Because bad information far exceeds good information, and most of our patrons have no good way to tell the difference. Their best defense is skepticism, not blind trust in anyone's authority, even ours. When they come to us for answers, let's also give them some of the tools they need for self-defense.

Solution
Raise the Stakes. Make Them Care Whether the Information Is Right

It's Not Just for Term Papers: Solving Real-Life Problems in an Information Literacy Course

Sarah Kaip

After living in Montana for one year, I decided it was time to assimilate into the state's culture by buying a gas-guzzling, air-polluting 4(times)4-sport utility vehicle. Impulsively, I stopped at a dealer one day on my lunch hour to look at two used Ford Explorers.

I knew no car dealer would ever take advantage of an innocent-looking, little library lady like myself, so how could I doubt him when he said these Ford Explorers were a couple of the best on the market? However, when I returned to work, a quick glance at newspaper articles retrieved from "Lexis/Nexis" revealed that 1992–94 Ford Explorers were under investigation due to 135 reports of fires or thick smoke in the ventilation systems (FN1). I realized how foolish I would have been to make such a big decision without doing an investigation of my own.

Designing a Credit Course

About the same time I was in the hunt for an SUV, I was also pursuing the design of a creative project for my two-credit Information Literacy course taught at the Montana State University College of Technology in Great Falls.

The previous year, I had students write a research paper but found that not only were students uninspired by yet another term paper, but they finished the class with a view of research as something needed simply to complete an assignment. This time I wanted students to see how information empowers us to make responsible and informed decisions in our personal lives, such as buying a new vehicle.

Therefore, the new final project required each student to "solve" a personal problem by the end of the semester using information he or she gathered throughout the course. Students were expected to enact their solution sometime during the semester using what they learned from their research and then report the outcome.

The students' problems varied dramatically. One student chose to research how to sell her house. She had never sold a house before and was very anxious to get the best price possible. Another student, a substitute teacher for a school district that integrates deaf children into regular classrooms, wanted to know how to teach deaf children effectively. Another student was asked to coach a teenage hockey team, but she knew nothing about the sport. One student's grandfather was recently diagnosed with prostate cancer, and he wanted to know how to help his family cope with the psychological effects of having a family member with cancer.

I was more concerned with the process than the result. If students failed to solve their problems, they could explain why they were unable to solve it. If that was the case, I wanted to know whether their information was inadequate, irrelevant, or even an obstacle for coming up with a solution. For example, the information I found about fires in the ventilation systems of Ford Explorers was an obstacle for buying the SUV model and year I wanted.

Furthermore, this wasn't simply a process of gathering information and then solving a problem. As they made decisions throughout the semester, students confronted new and unanticipated problems, which made it necessary to go back and do more research.

The student coaching a hockey team, for instance, realized that she struggled to assimilate into the hockey culture because she was unfamiliar with the players' language and jargon. This led her to read popular hockey magazines, which helped her communicate with her players on their level.

For many students, the search for solutions involved juggling their actions and knowledge with their need for additional information and vice versa.

Articulating a Problem and Choosing Sources

The first task was to articulate the problem, tell why it was a problem for them, and figure out what they thought they needed to know to solve the problem. This is harder for students than might be expected. Students tend to zero in on one specific aspect of a problem and have a hard time looking at the big picture and its different components.

For example, when the semester began, Cara, the student selling her house, was mostly concerned with getting a fair price. As she progressed, she was able to articulate more specific things she needed to know. These included how to choose a realtor; what to expect from a realtor; what her responsibilities were as a seller; what to expect from a buyer; what paperwork she should become familiar with; how to prepare the house for viewing; how to negotiate a price; and how to close a deal.

Students were then asked to think of characteristics of information that would be appropriate for their situation. Cara thought information that was geared to a general audience, current, and written from the perspective of buyers and sellers rather than real estate agents would be best. She knew most of her information would be opinionated, but some things would have to be factual, such as the worth of her house.

After students thought of general characteristics, I asked them to think more specifically about sources. Since Cara knew nothing about how to sell a house, she started with Dummies and Idiots books to give her an overview. She also looked for personal Web pages authored by sellers and buyers for tips and advice. Personal interviews from friends who had sold homes proved to be valuable resources, as well. I encouraged students to be creative and think of sources outside of the library.

Part of the assignment was graded on how well students were able to justify using the types of information they chose. Obviously the student coaching hockey did not need to have peer-reviewed journals. However, the student learning how to teach deaf children was expected to use professional education journals. Students learned that knowing when it is appropriate to use different types of sources is part of being information literate.

Solutions

Students then needed to make an outline and write a paper. The paper was a forum to tell me what happened. I wanted to know what types of information were found and how it was used, what decisions were made and why, what unexpected problems arose and how they were dealt with, what changes and adjustments were made, and what was the level of satisfaction with what took place.

I was particularly impressed by Cara's experience. The change in her level of knowledge and her attitude throughout the semester was significant. She began the semester frightened by her own ignorance. She experienced a great deal of anxiety because selling her house seemed overwhelming. There was so much to do and she didn't know where to start.

Furthermore, realtors who did not want to provide her with written information about the process of selling a house frustrated Cara. In fact, one realtor told her that it was the realtor's job to inform her of what she needed to know. Cara felt like realtors wanted to keep her ignorant. She explained to me, "I am a person who wants to do some searching on my own so I know how to sell a house myself."

Once she started researching, she began to understand how the house-selling process worked. Organization and confidence replaced her feelings of anxiety, confusion, and frustration. It occurred to her that instead of being talked at by the realtor, she could communicate on an equal level, which earned her respect from the realtor. Given Cara's new knowledge, she became a partner rather than simply a client.

Changes for Next Time

There are two things I will change if I decide to do this again. I will have students keep a log or journal instead of writing a paper. I would like to see how information helped them solve a big problem by making several little decisions over a period of time. I got the sense that some students waited until the end of the semester to research and write. Hard to imagine.

I also would not allow students to choose a problem that is actually a topic for which they must write a paper for another class. This defeated the purpose, which was to show students that information is more than something needed to finish a term paper.

At the end of the project, students had to write a personal statement explaining what they learned about research and information. From these statements, it was clear most students realized libraries and research serve a higher purpose than simply getting them to the graduation podium.

Endnotes

1. Associated Press, "Utility vehicle fires are probed," *The Boston Globe*, 23 February 1999, sec. A7. Accessed online: "LEXIS-NEXIS Academic Universe," 7 November 2000.

Teaching Kids Indirectly (Effective Online Searching)

Marylaine Block

We librarians know much more about the net, and for that matter about information, than students do. And they don't believe that for a minute.

While students might in fact wish to improve their searching skills, they very much doubt that we're going to be any help. After all, they've spent their lives showing grownups how to do every technical thing from programming the VCR to installing software and navigating the web. They have no reason to believe we know more than they do about the net, especially since we're only librarians. Too often, they don't distinguish between information and the computers that deliver it—techies will get their automatic respect, but librarians have to earn it.

In short, we start with zero credibility. Students will resist learning from us because they don't believe we have anything useful to teach them. If we try to teach them in a classroom setting, if we lecture at them, they will tune us out. Before we can teach them, we have to prove ourselves.

Tools They Can Use

One of the ways we can do that is to build pathfinder web pages that make it easier for them to find quality material, both for term papers they're required to write and for subjects that genuinely interest them.

In an ideal world, teachers would notify librarians of their assignments in advance, and we could build pages for those assignments. But even if they don't, we can build web pages for each department and build pages around absolutely predictable assignments like Martin Luther King, Jr., Women's History Month, science fairs, and such. We can also create web pages on topics that regularly arouse students' interests. (I've often suspected that students meet secretly every September to decide which six topics they will all write term papers on simultaneously.) Topics might include abortion, gun control, censorship of student newspapers, child labor, Internet filters, rock music, Napster, etc.

By preparing such web pages, not only can we demonstrate that we are certified Internet gurus, we can also indirectly teach some of the skills students need to know.

First, Give Them Answers

A great frustration for most searchers is getting a bunch of web pages when all they really want are answers to specific questions. Students will already be impressed if you can link directly into repositories of reliable factual information on each page. Xrefer, for instance, searches through over 60 online reference books. A search here on Martin Luther King yields biography, history, and quotations from and about him. Documents in the News lets students find out for themselves what relevant laws and court cases, like Roe v. Wade, actually say. Statistical Resources on the Web answers students "How much?" "How many?" questions on a wide variety of topics (abortions, hate crimes, drunk driving, etc.). Polling Report gathers in one place public opinion not just on politics but on a variety of issues such as school safety, genetically modified food, privacy, etc.

Teaching Skepticism

Students lack a necessary skepticism about biased and inaccurate web resources. They have a kind of mystical faith that what they find on the net is true. For that reason, we might consider how the very structure of a pathfinder can teach students good research methods.

By indicating the sponsoring/authoring organization right in the annotation, we demonstrate the importance of such factors. By classifying the sites, we show that some pages may be great for one type of information, or one side of the story, but sketchy in other areas.

Consider Multnomah County Library's Social Issues page. Librarians have divided each hot topic into logical categories like topical "Megasites," "Support," "Oppose," and "Legislation." They've written brief annotations describing the purpose and content of each site. By indirection, the librarians at Multnomah are teaching students the value of using specialized directories, like UNICEF's guide to child labor issues; the importance of law and other documentary evidence; and the need to recognize bias in sources.

Use the Entire Web

Students usually use only publicly searchable web sites. But, properly understood, the web is three things: web sites, a medium of communication, and a delivery system for proprietary information like books, articles, and other kinds of documents. We should include good bulletin boards or discussion forums for our pathfinder topics whenever possible.

There are also hidden treasures inside the "invisible web" that we can point them to by linking both for-pay and public databases that general search engines cannot search through—data sets, concordances, indexes, or bibliographies, for example.

This is also a good place to stress the unique value of web-delivered full-text journal databases—unlike many a web site, any magazine or journal article has gone through at least one level of editorial scrutiny. It's not enough just to link in our databases, though; we need to tell them what search terms are productive. We can also insidiously teach them how to ask good questions, a skill they need on the Internet as well as in the databases. With broad topics we can show them ways of thinking about their topic, of narrowing their focus to smaller aspects of the issue. On the abortion pathfinder, ask them to try choosing a subcategory like abortion and ethics; abortion and religion; abortion and economics; late-term abortion; abortion and choice; or right to life.

In addition to showing students our own licensed databases, we can point them to open search tools like the Online Books Page and both FindArticles.com and MagPortal, which index magazine and journal articles.

Narrowing the Universe

Another way we can help students get fewer, but better, results is to show them how to search not the entire web but a narrower universe that is specific to their subject through specialized portals and search engines. Any time we construct web pages for courses like biology, for instance, we should include directories of major biology resources, like Academic Info's Biology and Biological Sciences Gateway and topical search engines like SciSeek.

And we can show them selective general directories they can start with: Librarians Index to the Internet, Scout Report Archive, About.com, and Internet Public Library (which, incidentally, has outstanding pathfinders on literary criticism, military history, punk and indie rock, multiethnic/multiracial Americans, and lots more). These general directories make a point of finding the excellent gateways, databases, and search engines for a broad array of subjects. We can also point them to SearchIQ, which is not only a guide to topical directories and search engines but also a source of tutorials and reviews of search engines [SearchIQ is no longer extant].

The Search Tips Page

Once we've succeeded in convincing them that we know how to find really good resources on the web, students are going to start wondering how they can find such good resources themselves. Now we can start directly teaching them search strategies they can use in unrelated assignments.

Point out that in a general search engine they can add powerful words to their search topics that tell search engines the exact types of resources they want, like search engine or gateway or guide, or the exact aspect of a problem they want to address, like ethics. I call these powerful words "wedge words." *FAQ* (frequently asked questions) is one of the most powerful words we can show students, because experts on virtually every topic have created FAQ files on the Internet. They're great starting places on topics we don't know anything about. In any search engine, they can type *mytopic FAQ*. Or they can add the term *encyclopedia* to their topic to find an online encyclopedia article about it.

Another valuable wedge word for many issues kids care about is *law* or *legal*—Napster, student rights, censorship, filtering, are all issues being fought in court. Some other wedge words that can be added to any topic: *expert*, to ask for a high level of authority to answer questions; *forum, discussion,* or *bulletin board* to find a place to listen in on a discussion, to review archives of discussions, or to ask questions about the topic; *textbook* or *demonstration* to return a searchable online teaching tool; *database* asks for searchable data files. That's not an exhaustive list, but once we show students the trick, they'll be able to think of other wedge words themselves.

Show them how search engines are ready to help students narrow overly broad searches. Vivisimo, for instance, divides search results into smaller subject folders. MSN Search and Ask Jeeves both mention related search topics and sites that other users have found useful.

Teach them to use Google. Because it ranks sites according to how many other sites link to them, its top ten sites on any topic tend to be excellent resources. Furthermore, if we find a site there we like, clicking on "similar pages" finds more of the same sort.

What's NOT on the Net

Our pathfinders should not contribute to students' mistaken belief that they don't need the library anymore. We should point them to important resources in our own collections that are not available on the net: reference works, good books on the subject, important magazines, documentary collections, CD-ROM databases, videos, etc. Listing these specific resources on the pathfinder, not just a link to the OPAC, will help bring them into the building.

It's not hard to become a guru students will listen to—all we have to do is help them find quality sources faster and easier.

Link List

- Academic Info's Biology and Biological Sciences Gateway <http://www.academicinfo.net/biology.html>

- Ask Jeeves <http://www.askjeeves.com/>

- Documents in the News <http://www.lib.umich.edu/govdocs/docnews.html>

- Find Articles.com <http://www.findarticles.com/Pl/index.jhtml>

- Google <http://www.google.com/>

- Internet Public Library <http://www.ipl.org/>

- Librarians' Index to the Internet <http://lii.org/>

- MagPortal <http://magportal.com/>

- MSN Search <http://search.msn.com/>

- Multnomah County Library's Social Issues page <http:// www.multnomah.lib.or.us/lib/homework/sochc.html>

- Online Books Page <http://digital.library.upenn.edu/ books/>

- Polling Report <http://www.pollingreport.com/>

- Purdue University's Online Writing Lab <http://owl. english.purdue.edu/>

- Scout Report Archive <http://scout.wisc.edu/archives/>

- Statistical Resources on the Web <http://www.lib.umich. edu/govdocs/stats.html>

- Vivisimo <http://www.vivisimo.com/>

- X-Refer <http://w1.xrefer.com/>

Solution
Co-Opt Them: Let Them Teach Each Other

> We know from research that students would rather ask each other for help than go to adults. We can use that.

University Goes Back to Basics to Reach Minority Students

Elaina Norlin

A University of Arizona freshman from Korea said it all during a library-sponsored focus-group session: "I normally do not come into the library." Few of his friends did, either, he said.

After the UA Library conducted the focus groups of incoming students for three semesters, it emerged that many minority and international students found the library overwhelming and usually went, instead, to one of four student cultural centers on campus or the very crowded Global Student Center, which provides places for socializing and sometimes a small computer lab where they can write their papers or do research on the Internet. The trend was a major concern for the UA Library, whose mission includes being an inclusive place, especially for diverse populations. After several semesters of inviting minority and international students to a basic bibliographic instruction session and encouraging them—unsuccessfully—to return to the library soon, the library switched from passive to active mode by carrying its information-literacy message and technology expertise to the centers.

Program Moves in New Directions

To accomplish this, the library decided to broaden and improve its Peer Information Counseling (PIC) program.

Traditionally, the program coordinator recruited undergraduate minority and international students and provided them with training in information literacy and basic library research skills, the PIC students then worked evenings and weekends on the reference desk. The PIC program had been in place since 1993 but had become stagnant, with a high turnover rate both among PIC coordinators and among the student workers, who did not feel a sense of community at the library or of purpose for their work. Among other shortcomings, working on the reference desk did not provide a complete picture of what today's academic library professionals do, which usually includes bibliographic instruction, integrating technology to produce new Web products and services, and outreach to faculty and other campus constituencies.

In 1998, the library's Undergraduate Services Team expanded on the PIC program by developing partnerships with campus cultural centers and student service organizations. The team received more money so it could recruit more students, offer them more hours of service, and provide them with technology training. The training includes workshops in PowerPoint, HTML coding, Dreamweaver, and Adobe PhotoShop; most of these classes are available free at the library, which also has an Information Commons that allows students, staff, and faculty to use multimedia software programs and integrate them into their work or class assignments. The PIC students also work as assistants in some of the workshop classes to gain experience in instruction and in working one on one with a variety of technology users.

Finally, the students are also trained in marketing and presentation as a way to get them working as a team, developing products and marketing their services to the cultural centers on campus.

From Indifference to Acceptance

With the new technology training in place for the PIC students, I as the new PIC program coordinator began working with the four campus cultural and international centers, which target African Americans, Native Americans, Chicanos-Latinos, and Asian-Pacific Islanders. Being new to the university and the library, I assumed that these organizations would be thrilled to see their students receive free library assistance with research- and technology-related problems, but my initial attempts were often met with indifference or even hostility. The PIC students during this time made several presentations at the cultural centers, but we quickly realized that we needed to backtrack and try a new approach. In the meantime, the PIC students concentrated on creating Web pages that dealt with grants, employment opportunities, study abroad, financial aid, and graduate studies for minority and international students.

I did some research on why the centers were so resistant to the inclusion of academic programs, and I found that they were all under university pressure to incorporate educational programs into their strategic goals and objectives. UA's minority retention rates needed major improvement, so the university administration decided to reward the centers that could show strategic initiatives aimed at improving these numbers; but this was not a natural objective for the centers, which were established largely to give students a place to celebrate their cultural heritage through social activities.

Another problem was the computer labs within the centers. Each center worked independently, and since some were willing to incorporate educational programs and others were not, many computer labs did not have updated, working computers that were compatible with the library-networked computers.

At this point, I joined the campus-wide Diversity Action Council, where I met Lynette Cook Francis, the newly hired associate dean of students and director of the Department of Multicultural Programs and Services. I told her how I thought the PIC program would help the cultural centers show consistency in making positive strides toward initiating academic programs. Francis also supervises all the cultural-center directors, so after a few more meetings and a few compromises, the PIC program became a permanent addition to all the cultural centers. From there it was easy to get the Global Student Center involved because there was a successful collaboration in place that served as a model.

Accomplishments of First Year

The PIC students have worked at the cultural centers and the Global Student Center for more than a year now; here are some of the accomplishments and outcomes of the collaborations:

- PIC Web pages. The PIC home page is now linked to many of the cultural-center Web pages. The individual Web pages that were created for minority and international students were also linked to each center and to the online reference page on the library.

- Web gateway. Each page gets more than 2,000 hits each year. I also recommend cultural heritage-related Web sites and exhibits that will help students with their papers.

- English 101. One of our goals was to teach students about electronic resources they can use in writing papers instead of relying exclusively on the Internet. Every student has to take English 101, so we decided to create a "cheat sheet" listing some of the full-text databases students can use to write their papers. We discovered that many students did not even know that they could gain access to the library without actually going to the library. "Cheat sheets" like this are a starting place to help students use the library's electronic resources while still feeling comfortable in their own environment.

- Computer labs. To help the centers acquire updated computers, the PIC students worked with the directors to gather data on their current machines. Many of these were several years old and did not have enough memory to do basic word processing or use the Internet without frequent

crashes. We presented a report to Francis on the centers'
computer needs (based on how much memory it takes to
use the library's electronic resources, Microsoft Office, and
Dreamweaver), and today almost all the centers have new
computers and a network administrator to keep them up
and running.

- Technology as the carrot. At first, many students were reluctant to ask library-research questions—they felt they knew
everything because they used the Internet. However, they
still had technology questions, especially after Microsoft
Office and Dreamweaver were loaded onto the computers.
This is where the PIC students' technology training really
served as an icebreaker in developing a relationship with
the students. After the centers' students began relying on
the PIC students to help them with technology-related questions, the PIC students were able to refer them to the library
Web gateway, library subject specialists, and the library's
Information Commons. Also, the PIC students work on the
library's reference desk one night a week, and we eventually
found that some of the minority and international students
would come into the library to visit them.

- "Ask the Library." With the updated computer labs, the PIC
students were finally able to give presentations on the
library gateway and some of the unique services available at
the library. We also provide an "Ask the Library" e-mail link
for everyone so that the students could ask questions at the
point of need.

- Evaluation and assessment. After the first year of the PIC
student collaboration with the centers, we developed an
online assessment tool that the cultural-center directors can
fill out each year. So far, they have given the PIC initiative a
95% "excellent" performance rating, with very helpful suggestions on improvements for the future.

Our collaboration with the campus cultural centers has taught us how important it is that research into an organization's needs precede any attempt to offer realistic solutions. With this lesson under our belts, the UA PIC program has reached out effectively to minority and international students and ultimately brought more people to the library, both directly and remotely. The students also profited from the program. "Your help has opened many doors for me," said Marisa Duarte, a former PIC student now working toward an MLIS degree at Catholic University of America in Washington, D.C.

Finally, the third partner in this collaboration is also satisfied—which augurs well for the program's continuation.

"Having the PIC students working at our cultural centers has opened up more opportunities to combine social and educational programming," Associate Dean Francis said. "Each year the program gets better, and our cultural-center directors are enriched from the experience."

Reprinted from *American Libraries*, Aug. 2001. Copyright 2001, Elaina Norlin. Used with permission.

Working with, Not Against, Web-Savvy Users

Péter Jacsó

If you have patrons who think they're so smart about the Internet, fine: have them work with you to start new services or to maintain some Web pages. That way, everybody wins.

These days, librarians are often challenged by the savvy patrons who spend hours on the Web every day, exploring new services and products. They are the ones who come to the reference desk asking you if you have seen this new database or tried that nifty software, and want to ask questions about them, or—just as likely—talk about them, bragging about their latest discoveries. It can be taxing on the librarians who have their traditional work cut out for them, and who are also expected to know about anything that happens on the Web. Many of the savvy patrons are playing one-upmanship, and will go out of their way to prove that they know more than the librarians. Physicians and nurses face the same problems when patients come to them with information and misinformation acquired from the Web about the latest drugs that cure cancer, or that make you look 20 years younger. These are more difficult questions to handle, as they are very personal issues and often may have dire consequences, which is a serious burden on the healthcare professionals. Librarians are not under this kind of pressure, but they may still need some tools to ease the extra burden brought by Web-savvy users.

My suggestion (from the convenience of the ivory tower of academia, I admit) for taming the avalanche of input is to channel it in the right direction: Work with the savviest patrons, not against them (by dismissing their input), and show that their knowledge can benefit others while satisfying the Web-savvy patrons' ego at the same time.

Savvy Searchers' Corner

You can create a page that links from your library's home page where you can announce the latest developments in browsers, search engines, and digital resources. This would be a nice resource for those who have the interest and the attention span required to explore novel features, without handholding (aka bibliographic instruction) from librarians. This "Savvy Searchers' Corner" would include short blurbs about the most relevant new developments in the search arena. For instance, at the time I'm writing this, I'd note the extension of Google's search capabilities to 11 new word processing, spreadsheet, slide show, and PostScript files.

In most cases you may link the user directly to the developer's appropriate Help file for further information. Occasionally, it may be more efficient to illustrate how to use a new feature right inside the text of your announcement. For instance, "Use a query like this 'subject indexing' filetype.-ppt to retrieve PowerPoint documents about subject indexing."

Since such a Savvy Searchers' Corner might often announce a beta or brand new final version of software, I recommend that you add some warnings to minimize the users' frustration, such as this: "You may preview the documents in HTML format, but these converted formats are often difficult to read because of the scattered text or the color combination of the background and the fonts that Google generates for searching purposes. In this case you must click on the title field in the results list, which in turn will invoke the appropriate host software if it is installed on the computer you use." It would also be a smart idea to provide links in the announcements for lesser-known terms from the excellent PC Webopedia <http://www.pcwebopedia .com/>.

This Savvy Searchers' Corner could be updated weekly or fortnightly. Libraries that do not have the human resources for this might just provide a list of links to the list of new search products and services that are updated daily by the most informed and trustworthy search gurus, such as Gary Price <http://resourceshelf.freepint.com> and Chris Sherman <http://searchenginewatch.com/searchday>.

This could also be the place where the library announces digital resources that are certainly not for the faint of heart, such as the very powerful Surfwax service <http://www.surfwax.com>, which offers far more than the typical search engines even in its free version, but hardly provides instant gratification for the full spectrum of options. Similarly, in an academic environment where computer science courses are offered, this Savvy Searchers' Corner is the place where the library can notify people about ResearchIndex, formerly known as CiteSeer, which offers awesome citation indexing of free HTML, Adobe PDF, and PostScript documents of mostly computer and information science conference papers published on the Web.

Our Patrons Suggest

This could be a site to post your patrons' own Web site recommendations. However, you should moderate it to avoid surprises and liabilities, because a patron might post a raving announcement about a Web site that can do homework for the kids, and might slip in the URL of a site that's not really appropriate for a public library.

Before you start letting your users post recommendations, there should be clear guidelines about the types of sites, the format, and content of the description that they must follow. It must also be clear that it is not their constitutional right to make the library post any announcement.

Such a site can provide an outlet for those who want to share their knowledge, and indeed, quite often savvy patrons will have information about a good new site, or they might offer a search tip that the librarians are not yet aware of. In the print world, *PC Magazine* has followed this route by publishing short letters from readers that suggest solutions for common problems. Such cooperation may be encouraged by giving credit to the patrons who made contributions, and by giving some award for the savviest Web user of the year.

A Web Q & A Section

We know from studies that a majority of patrons don't like to ask questions face to face because they don't want to appear ignorant. We also know that almost none of the patrons come back to the reference desk if the first advice they got did not work. But think: Providing a Q & A service could eliminate the inhibiting factor of face-to-face communication. This Q & A section can be based on answers to actual new questions by patrons, and should be made searchable to allow others to see whether their questions have already been answered. Alternatively, the Q & A section can be set up as an FAQ section, anticipating the most typical questions that patrons would ask and providing the answers. FAQs are very common on many Web sites, so this would be a very natural forum to answer such questions as, "Which search engines can search for AIDS, without retrieving every site that mentions financial aids and hearing aids?" The right answer is

HotBot and AltaVista Advanced search (or Simple Search if you put your all-uppercase search term inside quotation marks).

Answering such questions can also provide a good vehicle to educate users about the more refined searching of such ultra-smart and ultra-polite search engines as Google (which, among other niceties, gingerly suggests correctly spelled alternatives for your misspelled query term). Even savvy searchers may not know how simple it is in Google to use the Advanced Mode to limit the search term to the title or URL field.

This is another area where some Web-savvy patrons might volunteer to help. Perhaps they can put in some time to maintain such a Q & A section. Even if this option is not viable, or not reliable, it would not take too much time to have competent librarians (who know how to find the good answers) respond to questions that are asked a zillion times at the reference desk.

You might feel that this sort of Q & A or FAQ service would not really help Web-savvy patrons who are, by definition, familiar with the Web. I don't think that is the case. Given the frequency of change in the syntax of search engines, and the appearance of new ones once or twice a month, I feel that a Q & A or an FAQ site would help even the Web-savviest library users.

Savvy Is as Savvy Does

By providing such services, you are likely to make your Web-shy patrons more comfortable, and you may even help some of them to become Web-savvy searchers, which in turn benefits the library. These are activities that don't have very high overhead costs, and in the long run you might reduce the time spent on routine Web-related questions, which now dominate the reference desk and make burnout set in faster than ever. One side benefit is that it may even help your not-so-savvy fellow librarians to become more knowledgeable if they consult these resources regularly, or if they're asked to research a question and provide an answer for your FAQ. Everybody wins.

Solution
Go Where They Are

Mobilize Your Instruction Program with Wireless Technology

Molly Susan Mathias and Steven Heser

From cataloging and inventory to circulating laptop computers, librarians are finding more and better ways to use wireless technology. You may want to consider whether your library could make a bigger impact by integrating wireless into its bibliographic instruction program, like we did here at the Milwaukee Area Technical College (MATC). Our mobile classroom is one example of how you can generate your own flexible training space and create a larger profile for your library within the institution, producing important partnerships with other areas on campus in the process.

MATC is a large 2-year institution that operates as one of 16 technical school districts under the Wisconsin Technical College System (WTCS). WTCS empowers all of the 16 local district boards to levy property taxes; these provide the majority of MATC's funding. The college is located in downtown Milwaukee, and its three outlying regional centers serve a three-county area. These different locales allow MATC to provide educational services for a culturally and economically diverse population that totals approximately 65,000 students. MATC administration endorses a philosophy that strongly emphasizes an institution-wide commitment to teaching and learning.

The libraries at each of these locations provide materials, services, and education to support the curriculum. Since 1996 the MATC library has nearly doubled the size of its collection and expanded its electronic resources from one command-based database to nearly 60 proprietary Web-based resources. Bibliographic instruction (BI) has always been a mainstay of our library and until recently was our primary means of outreach to the college. Despite our improved resources, our BI lacked space and standardization, and the technology was inadequate. We needed to turn our BI program around, and wireless technology provided the answer.

The Old Orange Couch Was Holding Our Library Back

Originally, we decided to upgrade our BI equipment to wireless in order to address space constraints in the library and the negative effect this had on our ability to present clear, organized instruction sessions. As the library's offerings were expanding, space to teach people about them seemed to be shrinking! None of MATC's four libraries has any training labs for bibliographic instruction, and expansion is not an option at the Milwaukee campus location. Until the fall of 2001, BI and library orientations took place on a centralized group of workstations within the library, which nearly always involved disrupting students who were studying. At the Milwaukee campus, library sessions were conducted on the infamous "orange couch," which could seat about eight students, leaving those remaining to stand or sit in chairs around a single computer. In general, library orientations were disruptive, awkward, and lacked effective demonstration facilities.

After some unsuccessful attempts to expand the library, we saw wireless technology as the most viable option for our space woes. This decision meant we would go from using a few stationary PCs in the library to 20 wireless laptop computers transportable via a cart. As we put our wireless plan into action, however, we discovered that in addition to offering a solution to the space crunch, our "mobile classroom" created the groundwork to partner with important groups on campus, and it eventually improved the library's image as a technology leader.

Details, Details, Details

In most cases, choosing to go wireless involves some knowledge of the capabilities of your own network in addition to the functions you'd like the wireless solution to provide. In our situation, some research was required to see if our network backbone would be sufficient to handle wireless technology. As it turned out, our college had a T-1 backbone that was more than sufficient to handle wireless communication. The challenge of choosing laptops, network cards, and hubs was not an issue because of MATC's service contract with the vendor Omni Tech. Choosing the wireless technology for the library involved checking a few boxes on a list provided by Information Technology (IT), so although we had some say in the make and model of the wireless laptops, the big decisions were made for us already.

The first order for the wireless classroom in April of 2000 included the purchase of 20 Simply Mobile Toshiba notebook satellite 2180CDT units, an outlet and extra battery for each notebook, and wireless 3Com communications cards and software. The order also included two mobile carts, two network access points (hubs), and 1 day of setup and training. Three wireless network/communication cards were also purchased to upgrade existing laptops. The entire cost of the wireless infrastructure was approximately $43,000.

The notebooks came equipped with a PC card that allowed them to exchange data with a Kom Wireless network hub. The hub, included with the cart, plugs into a data jack that allows a connection to the network backbone. Since these data jacks are available in virtually every classroom at MATC, almost any place on campus can be transformed into a high-tech computer lab or library training space.

Getting Everyone on Board

In March of 2001 we premiered the wireless cart in a workshop for faculty and staff with the help of two important and influential departments on campus, IT and Education, Research & Dissemination

(ER&D). The two of us conducted the majority of the workshop, which consisted of a hands-on demonstration of electronic library databases.

Our goals for the workshop were twofold. First, we needed to dispel some of the faculty's misconceptions about the library—it's not a book warehouse and librarians no longer conduct library orientations on the orange couch. Second, we needed to educate the faculty about electronic resources that libraries offer today. In retrospect, this workshop launched our mobile bibliographic instruction program. Not only did it get us in on the ground floor with wireless, but it also created a positive image of the library with respect to technology and generated interest in our bibliographic instruction that had not previously existed. In an exit survey conducted by ER&D, nearly 80 percent of faculty members attending the workshop stated that their level of usage for library databases would increase moderately or substantially in the future.

Our change to wireless was fundamental because it allowed us to bring library instruction to the students, not the other way around. But when our methods changed, we weren't the only ones affected. Instructors not only had to deal with the introduction of library services into their classroom environments, they also had to process this "new" electronic database information along with their students.

The workshop emerged from natural partnerships with other areas on campus, without which our experiment with wireless BI would have been considerably more difficult. ER&D is a union-based program that provides professional development to new and experienced teachers and has a solid reputation among faculty. ER&D also helps instructors to integrate technology and learning into the curriculum, so when the opportunity arose to collaborate with them and premier the college's wireless network within the workshop, we jumped at the chance.

We saw in this collaboration an opportunity to elevate the library's profile and help educate faculty about our electronic resources.

The workshop and wireless cart also strengthened our relationship with the IT department. The library is an ideal place for IT to promote emerging technologies because it has a natural client base of students and faculty. We think it's safe to say that without cooperation from both ER&D and IT, our wireless bibliographic instruction program would have been neither wireless nor instructional.

Our Instruction Process

The format we used to instruct faculty within the workshop strongly influenced the new instruction program we put together for students. In planning for the program, we had decided early on that we needed to create a "BI presentation template" using the form and content of the workshop as our guide. Every librarian at MATC can now follow this template when using the wireless cart. But even with this new standardization in place, getting a mobile session off the ground involves a little preparation time. First, instructors contact the reference desk to schedule a library orientation. Classes must be scheduled at least 48 hours in advance because our reference staff must find out what room the class is in. The librarian must then go to the room and write down the jack number for the IT Helpdesk to activate, since not all jacks are kept active at MATC in order to maximize network speed.

The laptops are charged as necessary for each session; up until this point, we have never scheduled more than one wireless activity during any given day. All of the laptops are battery powered and ideally have 2 hours of life, although we do have eight extra batteries in case a laptop begins to lose power. Fortunately, all MATC buildings are linked by skyways, so we can easily move the cart wherever we want. The network login process requires that we go to the classroom about 10 minutes before the session starts to plug in the hub and begin to set up the computers. The classroom may or may not be equipped with a teaching computer with display capabilities, but if there is no such computer, we hook up a video projection unit to one of the wireless laptops and begin the instruction session.

Wireless Changed Our Instruction for the Better

So far, the response to our wireless BI program has been positive. Since the library brings the computer lab to students in their classrooms, they are able to remain comfortable in their own environments, rather than being uprooted to go to the library or a computer lab. The wireless laptops also have a certain "wow factor," and most students express an interest in how the technology works. As a result, they seem to be more interested in the electronic resources we're offering them. Plus, the hands-on technology allows the library to incorporate more active learning opportunities for our students.

The mobile cart was also an impetus for us to standardize bibliographic instruction. Now the library has developed a core set of PowerPoint slides that we use for every instructional session, although databases and examples are customized for each class at the instructor's request. Whereas library instruction on the orange couch had seemed unfocused and haphazard, library orientations using the wireless cart deliver a clear and centralized message. This format does require some work for the librarian, since we must do more prep work and prepare for instruction outside the library, but we have adapted quickly.

Where Our Program Is Now

Overall, we love the wireless cart since it provides us with an instant computer lab. Two of our library locations now have their own carts, and the others can schedule time to use other mobile classrooms available at their campuses. We especially like the fact that we are increasing accessibility to library resources. The mobile classroom provides the library with a flexible training program that allows us to go wherever, whenever we're needed. We have also gained a great publicity tool for the library for campus outreach. Most importantly, our wireless cart helps us fulfill the library's commitment to and emphasis on teaching and learning at MATC.

That first cooperative workshop that we hosted in spring 2001 evolved into faculty workshops that were conducted at all four campuses last fall and a one-credit professional development course for faculty that is being offered early this year.

Since the inception of our wireless classroom, we've also joined forces with IT on a number of occasions. Presently, the library is working with IT on several projects, including redesigning our Blackboard services and beta testing Blackboard portals. This stronger relationship and gained trust has opened up the possibility for future collaborative projects between us.

Recently the college purchased Hewlett-Packard Omnibook XE3 laptops to replace the Toshiba models in our newer carts. We don't work for HP, but we can tell you that we prefer the Omnibooks mainly because of their longer battery life (1/2 to 2 hours in the Toshibas vs. 3 in the HPs) and the performance gains in reliability and speed. The Toshibas also take a lot longer to boot up and connect to the network. What we don't really like about the Omnibooks are the latches to open them—they get hooked on the matting within our cart, making them nearly impossible to close when we store them.

The change hasn't all been smooth going. Faculty members are very pleased with the change in library instruction, but we need to work on increasing their comfort level with the laptops. While they have been enthusiastic about the wireless technology for their students, we've discovered that they're less likely to embrace new technology for themselves. The IT department made the decision not to provide mice with the laptops, and users have to familiarize themselves with the track stick (pointer) on the Toshibas. If a faculty member is having a lot of trouble with the pointer, we will give him or her a mouse to use. Initially, we also didn't realize how much work setting up 20 laptop computers can be; now, if possible, we have more than one librarian work with the cart at an instructional session, particularly for setup and take-down.

Moving Toward the Future

Although we are pleased with how the mobile classroom has performed to this point, we still have a number of goals for our BI-on-wheels program. For one, we want to improve the technology on the carts themselves. At a recent conference, we noticed that many computer vendors are integrating the wireless communication hardware within the laptops, rather than using a slot on the side. We definitely want to investigate these new models, since the wireless cards we have now stick out of the laptops and are always in danger of being jarred loose.

We also have to tackle the printing issue; we don't have a printer networked to the wireless cart. Although most databases allow students to e-mail their results, students enjoy having some tangible result from their library instruction session. A new cart with more storage capacity, a networked printer, and some permanent wireless access points are all on our wish list.

We would like to increase use of the mobile classroom by going beyond library instruction to "network" with other departments. The library has maneuvered the cart to professional development meetings and campus-wide technology days, and we have attended occupational division and high school open houses to promote the library and our mobile classroom. Recently we've joined forces with the Continuing Education and Workforce Development and the Pre-High-School divisions to educate their staffs about a variety of information resources. One of our long-term goals is to obtain lab space for instruction, particularly at the Milwaukee campus. Even if we get training space, however, we believe wireless will remain a part of our BI program. Using the mobile classroom as a public relations and outreach tool has its own benefits for the library.

Our Recommendations

If you are interested in using wireless to mobilize your instructional program, we have a few recommendations:

- Before you invest a lot of time and money in a wireless solution, do some research on your institution's ability to handle wireless. Make sure that most if not all your traditional classrooms are wired with data jacks—despite the wireless technology, the mobile classroom is only as versatile as the existing wiring at your school.

- Get interested faculty on board right from the start; their support and interest will convert other instructors, and more importantly, they will request mobile library BI sessions for their students.

- Use the existing infrastructure at your school to work for you—you may realize you don't need to reinvent the wheel to go wireless by collaborating with other departments.

- Finally, marketing your mobile classroom is a must. Every instructor at your institution should be aware the library has wireless and know how the mobile classroom can benefit his or her students.

Wireless technology allowed the MATC Library to move its instruction program into the 21st century. Our mobile cart has improved the quality of our bibliographic instruction and fostered relationships between the library, faculty, IT, and professional development departments. The most satisfying development that has emerged from our experience with wireless is that we now feel the library is helping to propel the academic life of the college forward and into the future. The mobile classroom has provided a solid foundation to build on and to improve our service to students and staff. It has allowed us to create training space virtually anywhere and to leave the old orange couch behind.

The preceding was reprinted from *Computers in Libraries,* Mar. 2002. Copyright 2002, Molly Susan Mathias and Steven Heser. Used by permission.

Recommended Reading

Block, Marylaine. "What's NOT on the Net." *ExLibris* 2–9 Aug. 2002 http://marylaine.com/exlibris/xlib150.html

Burdick, Tracy A. "Pleasure in information seeking: Reducing information aliteracy." *Emergency Librarian* 25 (1998): 13–17.

Cahoy, Ellysa Stern. "Will Your Students Be Ready for College? Connecting K-12 and College Standards for Information Literacy. *Knowledge Quest* Mar.–Apr. 2002: 12–15.

Cox, Christopher and Stephen Pratt. "The Case of the Missing Students, and How We Reached Them with Streaming Media. *Computers in Libraries* Mar. 2002: 40–45.

Lenger, John. "If a Tree Doesn't Fall on the Internet Does It Really Exist?" *Columbia Journalism Review* Sept.–Oct. 2002: 74. *Even adult journalism students believe that if it's not on the Internet, it doesn't exist.*

Lightner, Brent. "ThinkQuest: Learning that Is Teamwork-Driven. *Multimedia Schools* Nov.–Dec. 1999: 18–22. *Another way to drive enthusiasm for high-level critical thinking in Web use is demanding teamwork for ThinkQuest competitions.*

The Shifted Librarian: Adapting to the Changing Expectations of Our Wired (and Wireless) Users

What IS a Shifted Librarian?

Jenny Levine

So I call myself "The Shifted Librarian," but what does that mean? I took the name from a presentation that I do called "Information Shifting" about how the change from pursuing information to receiving information is and will be affecting libraries. You can see the presentation at <http://www.sls.lib.il.us/infotech/presentations/info shifting/infoshifting.ppt>.

So back to the definition of information shifting. It comes from a *New York Times* article that discussed the history of consumer fair use and the entertainment industry's efforts to regulate use of VCRs and MP3 players. It referred to the 1984 Supreme Court decision in favor of VCRs in which the judges declared that these devices were okay because consumers were using them to "time shift." In other words, to record shows to watch them at their convenience.

Next up was a case in 1999 over the Diamond Rio MP3 player. Industry folk argued that consumers were illegally transporting digital files on it, but the judges decided that consumers were simply "space shifting," which meant they were just taking music they already owned and listening to it somewhere else. That's a very brief summary of the court cases, but what the article pointed out was that information in general was being shifted now that it was digital.

Take that to its logical conclusion, and you realize that people aren't going out to get information anymore. Instead, it's coming to them. Think about that for a second and you'll recognize the truth in it. After all, don't you feel information overload in your own life? That's because information is coming to you from everywhere now. Most of it may be noise, but focused information can come to you in new and more efficient ways than ever before.

If you read through my presentation, you'll see that I concentrate on how this trend will affect libraries in the future, mainly through its impact on the Net generation. Did you know that there are more NetGens than there are Baby Boomers? And you know what kind of an impact those folks had on our culture! If you're around kids at all today, you can see how differently they think and act about information and technology. I live with a six-year old and a seven-year old, and periodically I'll relate stories proving this point.

To my mind, the biggest difference is that they expect information to come to them, whether it's via the Web, email, cell phone, online chat, whatever. And given the tip of the iceberg of technology we're seeing, it's going to have a big impact on how they expect to receive library services, which means librarians have to start adjusting now. I call that adjustment "shifting" because I think you have to start meeting these kids' information needs in their world, not yours. The library has to become more portable or "shifted."

Therefore, a "shifted librarian" is someone who is working to make libraries more portable. We're experimenting with new methods, even if we find out they don't work as well as we thought they would. Sometimes, we're waiting for our colleagues, our bosses, and even the kids to catch up, but we're still out there trying. And please don't think I don't love books and print, because I do. No amount of technology will ever replace them, and libraries will always be a haven for books. It's the extras that I'm concentrating on, especially as we try to serve our remote patrons.

So welcome to the online life of a shifted librarian. I'm glad you're coming along for the ride, because it's going to be fun. I promise.

Solution
Use Your Web Site to Attract New Users

Catching (and Keeping) E-Patrons

Jeanne Holba Puacz

Luring people to the library requires more than dropping your bait and waiting to reel patrons in—thanks to the Internet, it's become a competitive sport. E-commerce has empowered average customers. No longer are they relegated to choosing from only local goods and services. The Web provides them access to a virtual marketplace where they can browse the world, comparison shop, and find the best deals. Many businesses have recognized this shift and are working hard to improve the capabilities of their Web sites in order to lure in and keep e-customers.

We in libraries need to realize that we are in a very similar position. Thanks to the Internet, libraries are no longer the only information game in town. Just as customers can now shop for the best deal on goods and services, they can shop for the best deal on information. If the online presence of a library is not informative, innovative, and service-oriented, there is little to stop e-patrons from surfing on to different sites that better meet their needs. We need to take a lesson from big business and focus on making our Web sites as effective and patron-friendly as possible. Attracting people to Web sites, offering them great deals, providing excellent service, and encouraging them to make return visits are some of the biggest challenges in the digital economy.

The Vigo County Public Library, in Terre Haute, Indiana, is trying to determine how best to meet these challenges now, and how to plan for future improvements. I would like to share some of our ideas on luring empowered patrons to our library's Web site and convincing them to keep coming back for more!

Start by Choosing the Right Lure

Marketing your Web site is vital to its ultimate success. Marketing will drive visitors to your site; if those visitors are impressed by the content and services of your site, chances are they will not only return to the site at another time, but they may also recommend the site to their colleagues, friends, and family. Never underestimate the power of word-of-mouth advertising! Additionally, those visitors will generate usage statistics; you may be able to present those statistics to your administration to justify a higher budget or additional staff for Web development. More money and more staff should, in turn, help to further develop and improve the site, thus attracting new patrons.

We at the Vigo County Public Library (VCPL) try to capitalize on any opportunity to advertise our Web address. We put the VCPL Web address on everything we can, even on the staff! The backs of the Summer Reading Club T-shirts are emblazoned with the library Web address; the staff is encouraged to wear these shirts to advertise both the program and the Web site. We have also created "business cards" for our Web site. They look like normal staff business cards; however, instead of a staff member's name across the top, the card invites patrons to "Visit our Web Site" and provides the address. Traditional contact information for the library, as well as our logo, is also on the card, as is the e-mail address for the "Ask a Librarian a Question" service. We try to include the URL on all library fliers, newsletters, and pamphlets; many staff members include the Web address in their e-mail signature files too. We have even had pencils printed with the library name and Web address; we hand these out during library classes. This way our students can take notes, take home a fun bonus, and it's all good advertising. We are still hoping to convince our administration that we need bumper stickers!

Publicizing your site's content is another great way to attract visitors. Articles in local publications about the library and its 24/7 e-branch are a great way to start. In addition to general articles about the site, be sure to capitalize on specialized publications and groups. Try to advertise the young people's page in school newsletters and during your children's programming; push the history room's page to local genealogical societies. Don't forget to stress any special local history sources available from the library's Web site, like digitized historical documents or indexes to local events, newspapers, or documents.

Classes designed to showcase our Web site and its features also seem to be helpful in attracting and retaining visitors. The VCPL offers a variety of free computer classes that are available to all interested patrons. We begin all Web classes on the library's home page. This way we can show the class participants how they can obtain valuable information from our site. If the class is a basic introduction to the Web, we use the library site to teach class members how to follow links, scroll, and use navigation buttons. If the class focuses on how to find subject information on the Web, we use the library's "Useful Web Sites" links to lead the students to relevant sites that have been chosen and reviewed by subject specialists.

We also encourage our staff members to discuss the Web page when they are giving talks or presentations to local community groups. Whether hosting a book club or speaking to local businesspeople, mentioning the Web site (and its address) is a great way to generate new traffic. Taking a supply of URL "business cards" may also be helpful when presenting to community groups.

Learn How to Set Your Hook

Remember, no matter how great the advertising for your site, if the content is incomplete, chances are good that visitors will not be hooked. The library's hours, policies, branches, events, and, of course, the library catalog are basic items that should be included on a site. In addition to the basics, however, try to include some special information that may not be available to your patrons anywhere else on the Web. The greater the number of unique and helpful services and sources that you can offer from your site, the more likely you are to develop a loyal e-patron base for your online branch.

Offering remote access to databases is an excellent way to entice and serve your Web-savvy patrons. In today's wired world, there is no reason that patrons should have to visit the library's physical location to use an online source; coming to a Web branch should be an alternative. At the VCPL, we were anxious to offer remote database access to our patrons; however, we were having difficulties acquiring the service through our library automation vendor. Luckily, we found an easy and reasonably priced solution in EZproxy. Our database vendors approved it as an acceptable means of authentication and we have had a great deal of success with the software. Our patrons are continually impressed and pleased that, with the library's help, they are able to research reliable sources from the comfort of their own homes.

Another feature that is very popular with patrons is one that comes standard with many online databases: Patrons can e-mail articles and citations to themselves from the database. Although this is a common feature, many people, even those who are technologically advanced, are not aware that it is available. Prominently advertising this service would likely garner even more happy patrons. In addition to traditional magazine and journal databases, the VCPL is now offering access to a database of e-books from netLibrary and a database to assist with test preparation from learnatest.com.

Virtual reference is a service that the VCPL has been providing successfully for quite some time. Currently, questions are accepted via e-mail or via a simple Web form at <http://www.vigo.lib.in.us/ref/ask.htm>. The questions are reviewed by our reference librarians and addressed quickly; we try to ensure a maximum turnaround time of 24 hours from the receipt of the question.

We encourage patrons to send us their suggestions for new library services they would like to see offered or materials they would like us to acquire. Again, these are accepted via e-mail or via a Web form at <http://www.vigo.lib.in.us/suggest.htm>. Additional e-request services offered to patrons by the VCPL include the ability to place holds on items via the Web catalog and the opportunity to request copies of local obituaries via e-mail or Web form. We are actively investigating the possibility of offering real-time reference service and are anxious to begin implementing this feature. We have been able to generate some excitement for online real-time reference thanks to a helpful article in the April 2001 issue of *Computers in Libraries* that explained HumanClick software.

Making unique local history resources available to patrons on the Web has been an incredibly successful endeavor at the Vigo County Public Library. Our first project was to create and publish a browsable online index to local obituaries. The positive response was overwhelming, and it encouraged us to attempt other Web-based local history projects. Our latest effort is to make the actual digitized images of local marriage records accessible from our Web site. We are working to make both the marriage record database and the obituary database searchable in order to better serve our interested patrons.

In addition to these projects, we are planning to make several important local history books Web-accessible. We are continuing to increase the number of archival finding guides that are available from the VCPL Archives Web page and are working with a local historian to complete a Web-based timeline of local history. Special Web displays are another great way to showcase unique local history resources; we have created and posted Web pages, which include images and text, highlighting local celebrities in honor of Black History Month, Women's History Month, etc.

Reeling the New Patrons In

As many businesses have learned, nothing can take the place of efficient and friendly service. Libraries need to grasp this, but they also need to consider that in the electronic world we may need to broaden our definition of service. Prompt, informative, and friendly responses to e-mail questions and suggestions are necessary for good service, but what other services can we provide? We feel that the overall design of the Web site is a key way to try to provide exemplary service. The site should be informative, easy to navigate, and visually appealing, and you must pay careful attention to design issues. Remember that regular review and evaluation are also necessary for the continued success of the site.

One service that is simple to supply is to include the name, address, telephone number, and e-mail address of your library prominently on your page. Many patrons (and many librarians!) get very frustrated when they are unable to locate contact information on company or organizational Web sites. Making your site searchable is an excellent capability that some librarians make available to their patrons. It is a service that we at VCPL have been investigating and are hoping to add in the near future. If site search software is not an option for your library, a simple home-grown site index or map is a viable alternative.

Good site design, however, is not just making the site easy to navigate or visually appealing. You also need to pay special attention to the technical aspects of the design. Remember, just because patrons are Web-savvy does not necessarily mean that they have advanced computer systems. A number of our techie patrons, many of whom are students, have older, slower systems at home. So, when designing your site, try to make it visually attractive but not so graphic-intensive that it is slow to load, and try to make slow-loading items, such as sound and video, optional. Pay attention, as well, to whether the site is compatible with ADA (Americans with Disabilities Act) requirements. For instance, how does it respond to a screen reader? Talking with your disabled patrons can teach you much about making your Web site a useful resource for all users.

Practicing good Web site maintenance, like ensuring that there are no broken links on your site, is a simple yet effective way to offer good service to your patrons. A variety of free link checkers is available for download on the Web, as is similar software that can be purchased if that is preferable in your library. Here's another design tip that you should not overlook: Check that your page is functional and displays correctly in a variety of Web browsers and browser versions.

We have been able to configure the VCPL Web catalog to provide our online patrons with some helpful services. Many traditional OPAC services, such as placing requests, specifying pick-up locations, reviewing accounts, and renewing items, are available from our Web catalog. We also provide access via the catalog to the online databases to which our library subscribes. We have recently begun to add reviewed and cataloged Web sites to our OPAC with Brodart's DartClix service. Although these cataloged Web sites sometimes confuse our technophobic patrons, our techies seem very pleased. The latest upgrade we have added to our catalog is the inclusion of jacket photos, reviews, and tables of contents for our new titles. This information, provided by contract with Syndetics, was reasonably priced, fairly easy for our systems department to implement, and has made our catalog more dynamic, more interesting, and more informative.

The online environment has provided the VCPL with the opportunity to provide some additional services to our patrons. We are now able to offer them the option of receiving e-mail notices when requested items become available. We are investigating expanding that service to also provide patrons notification of new programs and materials in which they might be interested. Our patrons also have the opportunity to apply for or renew their borrowers' cards online. Although these services are available to the patrons via traditional methods, i.e., waiting for notices to come in the mail or coming to a library branch to renew a card, we feel that offering the choice of utilizing these expedited Web options is a service our patrons deserve.

Netting Your New Catches

The good advertising, great deals, and excellent service are obvious means of ensuring return visits to your site, but are they enough? We feel that, although these are vital aspects, we should do more. Thus, we are constantly looking for ways to upgrade and improve our Web presence. Updated links and information are continuously being added to existing pages on our site, and new pages are regularly in development. We are currently preparing for a site redesign in order to improve and ensure access to and usability of our site. Some of our new services, such as real-time reference, enhanced e-mail notifications, an online book club, and continued expansion of the digital local history archive, are in process and should be implemented very quickly. Some services, such as providing improved access to the library's collection through a more effective Web catalog and including personalized "my library" accounts, similar to "My Yahoo!" pages, are additions that we hope for, but that are still in the planning stages. A Web address that is easier to remember is another item that periodically comes up for discussion.

Your Web site is an important part of your organization. It is the only part of your library system that patrons can access regardless of their physical location, and it is often the only part of your library that they can access 24 hours a day, 7 days a week. Your library's Web site should be as innovative, informative, intuitive, and attractive as possible. Remember, regardless of the size of your library or the budget you have to work with, there are reasonable ways that, with a little effort, your site can be improved. The best advice we can give is to try to strive for kinetic thought, planning, and development; do not allow your site to become static. If your site is constantly developing and always offering great deals and excellent service, your regular patrons are sure to come back and you are sure to attract new patrons as well.

Solution

Weblogs

As noted in Chapter 2, a number of libraries are now operating Weblogs as a way of sharing library news, book reviews, and interesting new Web sites with their patrons. As Darlene Fichter shows us, some libraries are also using them on their intranets as part of their knowledge management strategy.

Blogging Your Life Away

Darlene Fichter

A Weblog is an online journal—a Web page with a series of short entries in reverse chronological order, so the newest is always at the top. Weblogs are frequently updated and contain a mix of links, commentary, personal thoughts, and individual opinions, often with some humor thrown in as well. They are an unusual blend of the personal and the public, published on the Web for all to see.

Some people believe Weblogs represent a revolutionary new means of communication, comparable in some ways to the creation of the World Wide Web itself. Others call them a new "genre" of incestuous and vain self-publishing, an electronic vanity press. Still others regard them as just a plain old list of links with commentary and wonder what the fuss is all about.

By now, you've probably cottoned on to the fact that Weblogs are not Web logs—the line by line recording of every request served by your intranet Web server, and this column is not about statistics and analysis. There's more vocabulary to learn: Bloggers are Weblog authors; a blog is another name for a Weblog.

The History of Weblogs

As recently as 1998, there were just a handful of Weblogs. They provided links to new Web sites, as well as to obscure but interesting pages that most people were unlikely to come across on their own. These early blogs often included short descriptions or commentaries, helping readers decide which sites were worth visiting.

While that may have been the genesis of Weblogs, they have evolved into an interesting hypertext format. In addition to the original "link and comment" blogs, today we find news or "read it here first" blogs, and personal journal or "what I had for lunch" blogs. There are also distributed discussion blogs, where several authors carry on a time-lapsed conversation cross-linking to each other's comments and responses.

Some Weblogs, such as Doc Searls <http://doc.weblogs.com> are the product of a single author, while others are collaborative efforts. On Slashdot <http://www.slashdot.org>, many authors create "news for nerds."

Part of the attraction of Weblogs lies in the fact that they offer an independent, often sarcastic and funny, individualistic point of view. In a world of "marketese" and mass communication doublespeak, the authenticity of this personal voice is appealing.

As Weblogs became more popular, naturally everyone wanted a way to automate the drudgery of coding content by hand and creating archives. Sites with automatic blogging tools popped up, such as Pitas.com, Blogger.com, and GrokSoup.com. Suddenly, everyone had a blog. It's a bit like everyone having a Web site. Some only a mother could love!

Due to the hype in the media, Weblogs have attracted rave reviews, as well as critics. Steve Bogart, quoted by Julia Keller in her *Chicago Tribune* article "She Has Seen the Future and It Is—Weblogs" (September 7, 1999), sums up the best and worst of Weblogs when he says: "At their best, Weblogs are both content providers and context providers for the mass of information available on the Web. At their worst, they're exercises in vanity, giving us the illusion that we've done something valuable by copying and pasting a link."

Weblog Relationships with Intranets

Many organic bottom-up intranets have Weblogs and may have even started this way. There are Webmasters, librarians, and other staff members who regularly update and comment on news of note or point out good stuff that other members of the company might not otherwise find! In fact, a good Weblog on a company intranet is probably read more often and has a more loyal following than the "official news" page.

During the planning process for intranets, clients often ask for advice on how they can get their staff to use it. Taken at face value, the answer to that question is simple—make it necessary. The real question that is being asked is much more difficult. How can we make employees want to use the intranet? That's harder. The intranet has to be useful, easy to use, and interesting. Monotone corporate talk puts most of us to sleep, so it's no wonder that intranets written in this way and composed with this type of information put people to sleep, too. Maybe Weblogs are part of the answer; where individuals can add content and commentary not deemed "official."

Practical Applications

Intranet Webmasters can make use of Weblogs in many ways. Some ways are the following:

1. Produce a daily news page about particular products, industry sectors, or competitors' activities. You can incorporate free external, commercial, and internal sources. Providing commentary and a context for the stories or links can be very useful to your readers. With the right software, intranet users can subscribe to the Weblog and receive updates as email alerts. They also can visit the Weblog at anytime and search the archives or, using the calendar, view articles by date.

2. Maintain an online journal recording the progress toward new Web development or other new information product introductions.

3. Create a FAQ blog for various products and services regularly adding new questions and answers.

4. Create a weekly list of the best "free" Web tools for searching for information or for publishing.

5. If you really want to be adventurous, consider installing Weblog software so any intranet user can be a blogger.

There is a lot of buzz about creating intranets that help workers share knowledge. Weblogs might be one approach to take within the knowledge management initiative. Imagine teams and departments creating individual or collaborative Weblogs that post sites, files, notes, and commentary. Weblogs can keep everyone in the loop and allow ideas to flow within the team and among teams. Ironically, one of the chief criticisms of "public" Weblogs is their incestuous nature, where everyone is linking to everyone else. This would be a boon to intranets where we want to encourage knowledge to spread and employees to forge more connections and share knowledge with each other.

By producing a Weblog, a library can showcase expertise on a particular topic to enhance the library's reputation as a source of authoritative information. Josh Duberman, from Pivotal-info LLC, believes Weblogs offer an excellent marketing vehicle for the independent information professional.

Blogging Sites and Scripts

There are many automated tools and scripts that you can use to create your blog. These programs greatly accelerate the work of gathering, organizing, and publishing your blog.

One of the most popular sites for creating blogs is Blogger.com, which gives you complete control of the look of your blog. Blogger allows you the option of publishing the blog on your own Web or intranet site. To do this, Blogger needs to be able to FTP files to an account on your own system. For security reasons, you will want to create a separate captive account that is used only for this purpose.

Handy browser add-ons like Blog This! enable you to blog any Web page that you happen to be viewing. Just right click on Blog This!, and the title of the Web page and its URL are automatically added to your Blogger.com update form. NewsBlogger is another add-on that allows you to review Moreover's news headline service <http://www.more over.com/> and select items that you wish to capture and edit. NewsBlogger also supports keyword searching of news stories, which can be very useful.

Remote Weblog Services

Blogger.com is just one of many remote Weblog services. Each service has unique features. GrokSoup <http://www.groksoup.com> has a strong focus on providing tools for blogging the latest news. It offers automatic syndication of your content using XML standards. There are also Slashdot-style discussion groups for every article, automatic archiving, Quick-Sites for loading multiple news sites, and mailing lists.

Pitas.com is a popular Weblog creation and hosting site. Your Weblog is hosted at "yourname.pitas.com." The software is easy to use and the site offers a choice of default design templates. The adventurous designers can also create a custom look.

LiveJournal.com is another site that provides client side tools that help with gathering and editing blog entries. One nice feature of Live-Journal is the ability to integrate your blog with your own Web site by using various scripting options. Various options for embedding Live-Journal are described on their Developer Info page. One of the scripts they provide is a Perl program that will grab your journal behind the scenes so you can display it on your local site.

Reliability and Confidentiality

Remotely hosted Weblog services have their pluses and minuses. Many of them offer their services for free. This is certainly a plus. However, there is no guarantee of reliability or access to your archive over time. Occasionally, these services run into financial difficulties. Blogger.com made the headlines in January 2001 when they asked for contributions toward the purchase of a second server in order to keep up the exploding population of new bloggers. Their appeal was successful. Blogvoices.com, a popular add-on discussion service for Weblogs, announced in January 2001 that their service was discontinued. If you are keeping a copy of your blog on your own Web site, it is probably just fine to use a remote service. If it runs into trouble you know that you have a copy of your archives while you're shopping around for another service.

Reliability is not the only factor. Some Weblogs must be restricted to your intranet users, or you may require a high degree of confidentiality. In this case, remotely hosted solutions may not suit your needs. There are free Weblog scripts that you can install and run locally on your intranet server. Three scripts are:

Open Journal (OJ) <http://grohol.com/downloads/oj/>
Features: Automatic updating and archiving on a weekly or monthly basis without having to use FTP, able to customize the design
Requires: Perl, cgi-bin directory

Master WebLog <http://willmaster.com/master/weblog/index.shtml>
Features: Automatic updating and archiving, able to customize the design
Requires: Unix or Linux, Perl version 5+

Squishdot <http://squishdot.org>
Features: Allows multiple posting and creates a Weblog similar to slashdot.org

Requires: Installs a plug-in module for the Zope Application Server

For a more complete listing of other remotely hosted Weblog sites and Weblog scripts to install locally, see the Open Directory <http://www.dmoz.org/>.

Weblogs by Librarians

Are you wondering what information professionals are doing with Weblogs? Take a tour of a few blogs about libraries, librarians, and information science:

The AcqWeblog <http://acqweb.library.vanderbilt.edu/acqweb/ms_acqs.html>
Ms. Acquisitions, Anna Belle Leiserson, has a Weblog focusing on library acquisitions.

'brary' blog <http://chickeninthewoods.org/brary/index.php>
Stephanie Davidson gives her Weblog this byline—"just a little semi-regular dose of bookish stuff from your friendly neighborhood librarian."

Liblog: A Library Weblog <http://www.rcpl.info/services/liblog.html>
Liblog is produced by staff of the Redwood City Public Library and looks at the libraries and new technologies.

Library News Daily [Now called Peter Scott's Library Blog] <http://blog.xrefer.com/>
This blog, published by Peter Scott, focuses on news about databases, conferences, services, software, and vendors.

LISNews <http://www.lisnews.com/about.php3>
LISNews was set up by Blake Carver and presents news about library and information science.

Neat New Stuff I Found on the Net This Week <http://
www.marylaine.com/neatnew.html>
Your "librarian without walls" Marylaine Block creates
this blog.

Newsresearch.weblogs.com— "A Resource Guide for News
Researchers" <http://newsresearch.weblogs.com>
In his weekly blog, Bill Lucey identifies research sites related to
the news. News hounds will love this one.

Research Buzz <http://www.researchbuzz.com/news/
index.shtml>
Tara Calishain who produces the Research Buzz newsletter
also has a Weblog.

Is There a Weblog in Your Future?

Weblogs are not for everyone or every intranet. If you're doing this
already by hand, then using a remotely hosted Weblog service or
installing local scripts will certainly speed up and make the work
easier.

Information professionals are bound to feel a natural affinity to
Weblogs. Selecting, critiquing, and illuminating the best or the worst
of the Web in a particular area is just part of what many of us already
do on a daily basis. Now we have a new set of tools that makes it a
whole lot easier!

Some librarians don't just post information like their Weblogs. They use push technologies, automatically sending content to users, like the Morton Grove Public Library's MatchBook program, described in Chapter Two, or notifying them of new content through news syndicators by "RSSifying" their Weblogs; i.e., putting them into XML so that rich site summary syndicators can notify their readers whenever content on the site is updated. What is RSS?

> RSS is an XML format designed to let content providers share headlines and content with other sites without having to create a completely new Web page. In essence, RSS defines specific criteria about a story including the headline, the URL, and a brief summary. When a content provider makes that information available in the form of an RSS feed, anyone can grab the information and put it on their Web site. The best part is since the URL points back to the originator's site, traffic isn't lost. (Bannan, par. 2)

If you want to try this yourself, Steven Cohen has written a simple step-by-step tutorial on "RSS for Non-Techie Librarians" in the June 3, 2002 LLRX (http://www.llrx.com/features/rssforlibrarians.htm), and the Utah State Library has also created an online RSS Workshop (http://gils.utah.gov/rss.html).

Solution
Use Their Tools of Choice: Chat

Our Experiment in Online Real-Time Reference

Kelly Broughton

When we first started using "chat" at the reference desk, it was weird—really weird. It was scary. The computer bonged at us whenever someone hit the chat Web page, and I had a tendency to jump immediately to the screen that told me what IP address this visitor was coming from and what browser he was using, not that any of that mattered. Then I'd just sit there, staring in anticipation at the screen, hoping he had a real reference question, yet fearing how to deal with it online.

On chat, you can only type things and you just know someone is on the other side, also sitting there and staring and waiting for an answer, which not only should be completely correct, it should be there right now! You can only type so fast, and in many instances, you also actually have to find an answer. Unlike the telephone, you can't say, "I'm doing this and looking there" while you are actually doing it. Also, unlike when the person is standing there in front of you, they can't observe you diligently trying various keywords in the catalog. Maybe more importantly, you can't see them. You can't tell if they're angry and impatient. You can't tell if they're desperate. Like D. Scott Brandt said in his column [November/December 2000 *Computers in Libraries*, p. 66], these types of communications "are more demanding than e-mail. They tend to put pressure on you to respond right now...." That is the whole point of integrating real-time communication into a Web site: Users can conveniently communicate with you at their time of need.

That is precisely why some form of an easy-to-use, online, real-time communication method will inevitably be integrated fully into reference services. It is why we decided to give it a try at the main reference desk here at the Jerome Library at Bowling Green State University (BGSU) in Ohio. BGSU is a residential university offering bachelor's, master's, and doctoral degrees, with about 16,000 full-time students. Last spring, we began experimenting with using online chat for remote reference. We certainly have found it exciting, and we think it offers huge potential for serving our users. It also brought up some surprising and interesting issues for us to struggle with as librarians and managers.

Save the Remote Users!

It only makes sense that since we spend hundreds of thousands of dollars making resources accessible remotely, we now need to serve the people who use them. Providing users with access to remotely available electronic resources without providing assistance and instruction on how to use them is like telling them which airport they are scheduled to depart from, but not giving them a flight number, airline, or gate number. They might be able to figure it out eventually, if they know their destination and approximate departure time, but only after considerable effort and frustration. Our patrons are increasingly using our remote resources. Statistics for searches and downloads continue to grow as our in-person reference contacts decline.

As reference librarians, one of our struggles has been trying to make the difficult and complex process of conducting research as easy as possible. Sure, interfaces have improved over the past few years. At BGSU, we even have the advantage of being in OhioLINK, a consortium that provides a single interface for nearly 40 of our most popular databases, all with easy one-click access from the bibliographic citations to local paper holdings information and electronic full text! But the truth is that research is complex. There's no getting around it. It's hard. It can be frustrating, even for us. Imagine what it must be like for people who don't do it for a living. On top of all that, not only are we offering users greater access, but we're also offering them more variety, too. Here at BGSU, we now have over 120 different databases from which to choose. Throw in the information available on the Internet and the subtleties of using Web search engines proficiently, and there is no doubt about the need to assist users remotely.

Finally, consider this: If we don't do it now, someone else will. Now is the time to take advantage of this opportunity to prove our worth. There are plenty of non-library-oriented "ask-a" services out there on the Internet, and not all of them do things nearly as well as we could. New products such as Questia and XanEdu, which market research content and assistance directly to students and faculty members, are also something to keep your eye on. They claim to be assisting classroom faculty and students by adding pre-selected, relevant, scholarly content to online courses or offering easy, one-stop access to research materials for a fee. They give the false impression that research can be made easy. Additionally, most, if not all, of the content has already been purchased by the libraries that serve the very same students and faculty! Certainly, for OhioLINK institutions, the content is not only already available; it is much better packaged and serviced, albeit in a more complex package. But it's a truthful package. So we need to be doing what we can to make that complex package work for users. Answering their questions online, in real time, only seems logical.

How Can We Help?

Here at the Jerome Library, we started out just wanting to see if our suspicions were right—that users, especially students, needed and would use a service that would enable them to interact with a librarian in real time over the Internet. For that reason, we needed to choose something with a minimum of expense, both in purchasing dollars and labor. One of our systems staff members volunteered to help us with software and technical issues, and all the librarians were willing to try, a few even enthusiastically. No one had much time to spend on it.

First, we considered instant messenger applications, but they presented one large obstacle. In our reference area, we have a bank of iMac computers that allow downloads onto the hard disk that remain there until the computer is re-booted. During high-traffic times, you can find at least three different instant messenger applications on these computers: AOL, Netscape, and MSN seem to be the most popular. If we chose just one of these applications and the user didn't use that one or any one at all, he or she would have to download it before asking a question. That barrier seemed to defeat the whole purpose.

We found free software on the Web from a company called HumanClick. It had lots of other advantages, in addition to its price. It required nothing but a Java-enabled browser for the user. It required very little on our end, too. We loaded a small piece of software on all of the workstations we wanted to use to answer queries, and we put a short Java script into our Web page. It ran off the company's servers and only when we turned it on at our end. If we had it "off-line," it allowed the users to send us an e-mail instead.

In May 2000, we loaded the HumanClick application and tested it with a couple of librarians and staff. Then we had a very short training session on its use. It took less than 20 minutes. We then asked librarians and staff in other departments and branches to give it a try. About a week later, we added a link to the library's home page and a link from our e-mail reference page. We decided to try it while we were at the reference desk over the summer and see what happened. We kept statistics using hash marks on a clipboard, and eventually we started to cut and paste the entire transactions and print them out, noting a few items like the length of the interaction, and the time and day.

A Few Points on 'Chat'

Observing my teenager chat online, I finally began to understand a few things about communicating this way. She was multitasking. She was listening to music, chatting in two or three different conversations, and surfing the Web. The time lag didn't bother her at all. She was doing other things in between thoughts in one particular conversation, and if she had another thought before she received her friend's reply, she just went ahead and sent it. Our colleague, Carol Singer, called this "curiously disembodied." There's no better way to explain the feeling. It certainly is not natural to us, but many of the students don't seem to even notice.

Despite the strangeness of communicating via chat, it didn't take long to get accustomed to it. We discovered that users tended to send many short messages rather than one long paragraph. The transcripts don't make complete linear sense, but while you're in the conversation, it's understandable. It certainly eases the anxiety of empty waiting time. The users didn't seem to be as bothered by the length of time it took (to send, have the other person read, and then reply and send back) as we were. Eventually, we got used to doing something else too (like directing someone to the pencil sharpener, looking up items in the catalog, etc.).

However, we encountered a major technological problem in that we could not make the system reliably work for our users on Macintosh computers. One of the main disadvantages of using free software is that you have no technological support. We of course made the company aware of the problem and received assurances from them that they were working on a solution. About 50 percent of our campus desktops are Macs, so this became a rather large concern for us. Unfortunately, as we investigated other free products that provided chat, we couldn't reliably make them work for our Mac users either.

Late in the summer, HumanClick added two features that really changed how we communicated and how we felt about the potential of this communication method in reference services. First, we could now "can," or store, messages. After a short discussion, we added about a dozen preset messages that we hoped would help ease the time lag and save us from carpal tunnel syndrome. These were accessible to the librarian from a simple pull-down menu.

The second and more important feature that HumanClick added was the ability to "push" Web pages. By simply selecting a pull-down menu option and pasting in a URL, we could send any Web page we wanted. This is an enormous advantage. It is extremely difficult to teach someone by using only the written word. Nothing to point to. No facial expression to discern. No way to observe if they really could do it on their own. In academic libraries, we already struggle with this in using e-mail for reference. For example, someone e-mails us about how to find articles for a paper about antioxidants in wine and heart disease. It's really not all that great to send an e-mail back saying, "Try the keyword search '(antioxidants or wine) and (heart or cardiovascular) disease' in the research databases Biological Abstracts, CINAHL, or Periodical Abstracts," with a statement about how to get more assistance. You never really know if that's enough. But now at least we could send them Web pages.

Of course, this technological advance begged a new question: Which page do you send? With this cut-and-paste-the-URL method, it certainly isn't practical to send the users every page that they would see if we were helping them in person—the library home page, the research database's home page (and why), the subject or alphabetical list of research databases, the main menu of the selected database (and why we chose it) ... We haven't even gotten to the search yet, and that's already four Web pages and a lot of explanation. It doesn't take too long to say, hear, and see, but it sure takes a lot of time to send and read. The other option is to do the searches ourselves and send them the results list with a short explanation of where to check holdings and look for full text. In an academic library, our mission is to teach, to make it so that they can do at least some of it on their own next time. This sure doesn't help much at all with our goals in helping our users become more information literate and self-sufficient.

Time to Try a Better System

When HumanClick added the canned messages and pushing features, the company also announced that these features would not always be available for free. By this time we knew that we had a valuable service, so we began looking for funding opportunities. We also decided to stick with the best we could offer at the moment, hoping that we wouldn't have to go back to a service with fewer features if we failed. We also decided to go for the gold—to try to find the best possible product for our situation, knowing we may have to settle for less.

Our statistics showed that we were already receiving more reference questions on chat than we were on our e-mail reference account, and we didn't think it would be too difficult to argue that an improved product would greater enhance the service and improve our teaching capabilities. Additionally, our university was coming close to completing a multimillion-dollar project that included an entire new network. To that end, dollars, in the form of competitive grants, were being awarded for projects that had the potential to take advantage of the new network. Three of us co-authored a grant proposal asking for $10,000 to partially fund the purchase of a commercial product that would allow us to offer an improved online reference service. This improved service would not only include the features we had become accustomed to with HumanClick, but many more, as well as promise the potential for future enhancements.

We looked at a variety of fee-based customer service products. The product we chose is called Virtual Reference Desk (VRD), and it is available from Library Systems & Services, LLC. The VRD product stood out, despite its rather large price tag ($8,000 for setup and training, $500 per month for maintenance). First and foremost, it is a product aimed at libraries, not commercial enterprises. A few other libraries were in the process of making it available to their patrons and reported that the company worked diligently to make it work with their proprietary databases. The company's product developer is Steve Coffman, who is a librarian. Finally, we would be able to make it available almost immediately, without major hardware upgrades and with very little work needed by our already overloaded systems staff.

The VRD product is powered by eGain, a Web-based customer call center application. It offers many features over and above simple chat. Some of these are transcripts that include URLs sent to both the user and the librarian via e-mail after each interaction, statistical reports for the library, queuing and customization features, and 2 full days of in-person training by company representatives. It also offers co-browsing and other collaboration features that will allow us to escort users around the Web and improve our ability to teach online. Additionally, as the university switches over to the new network, and we and our users upgrade our desktops, VRD also offers voice and video features that we hope to integrate into our online reference services.

Our interim dean of the libraries agreed to make up the $4,000 cost difference if we were to receive the $10,000 grant from the university. We received notice in early December 2000 that we would be getting our request, and we began the process of purchasing the VRD product.

Since then, our training process has gone well, and our experience with HumanClick really paid off because as we're writing, it's February and we're ready to go live with our new product at the end of this month. We're busy preparing canned messages, slide shows, and completing our customization. Also, two of us are beginning to work with a committee in our consortium, OhioLINK, to determine how OhioLINK can help its member libraries begin delivering remote reference services. It promises to be an exciting and challenging end to our academic term.

We Can Make It Work

One of our major concerns is the impact this is going to have on our workload. Luckily, we are learning this new product during a semester where we are not only fully staffed, but we also have a returning faculty member on supplemental retirement and 16 hours a week from a graduate assistant. We'll be more concerned with staffing the service as it grows in popularity. Funding for continuing and expanding the service will also continue to take effort and concentration.

Many libraries have been trying to effectively accomplish real-time online communication for quite a few years in a variety of ways using multi-user domains, Net-conferencing, instant messengers, and other applications. For a variety of reasons, I don't think users or librarians really found any of these communications methods to be ideal. With the dawn of Web-based customer call center software, there may be a solution at hand.

Further Reading

For more information about all types of virtual reference services offered by libraries around the world, visit the ELITE Project Web site from the University of Leicester at <http://www.le.ac.uk/li/distance/eliteproject/elib>.

Bernie Sloan has compiled a comprehensive bibliography on this and related topics and has made it available at <http://www.lis.uiuc.edu/~b-sloan/digiref.html>.

The summer 2000 issue of *Reference & User Services Quarterly* (vol. 39, no. 4) is a special issue on "Digital Reference Services."

To join the discussions of hundreds of librarians and others in all phases of implementing and providing similar services, try the DIGREF listserv (more information at <http://www.vrd.org/Dig_Ref/dig_ref.shtml>) and/or the livereference e-group at <http://groups.yahoo.com/group/livereference>.

Solution
Use Their Tools of Choice: PDAs

Information @ Your Fingertips: Porting Library Services to the PDA

Ken Varnum

Corporate information centers are constantly struggling to find ways to get the attention of the higher levels of their organizations.

For some, it's a matter of survival—if you do not provide a high-value service to those who are making funding decisions, you might as well close up shop. For others, it's more a matter of service—delivering information to those who need it, when they need it, how they want it. For still others, it's a combination of these two drivers.

Our library provides a range of information services to Ford Motor Company—general reference and research services, customizable alert services, automotive news, and so forth. While a good portion of our specific reference and research requests come from senior management, our more generalized news and alert services have often gone unnoticed, or at least underutilized. We offer a range of personalizable Web and email information services to the company. While these products are widely read, their readership as a proportion of population grows smaller the farther you go up the corporate ladder.

We thought a great deal about how we could more effectively reach these people, and concluded that the problem was more in our delivery means than in our product. The group we want accessing our materials is a group that, as a whole, does not surf the intranet, and prefers printouts of email messages over the on-screen version. These are not technophobes or fuddy-duddies who don't "get" the Web; these are very busy people who are rarely at their desks. They get their correspondence and their reading done between meetings, on airplanes, waiting in offices, and anywhere or anytime they have a few minutes to spare. How to reach this group?

It turns out that this same cohort has also adopted personal digital assistants (PDAs) such as the Palm Pilot, in a big way. They carry them in their pockets everywhere they go, using them as calendar, address book, and notepad. We figured that if we could somehow deliver information to users on their PDAs, we could get people's attention and quickly build a new user community. Our information services would be at the executive's fingertips, quite literally, all day long. The stumbling block, of course, was taking our Web and email content and making it available to these managers on their handheld devices.

How the System Works

The core of the system is software written by AvantGo <http://www.avantgo.com>. The AvantGo software translates Web pages into a format that PDAs can understand by converting complex HTML pages into a simpler text-and-image format (think of what you would see if you were still using the original Mosaic to browse the Web). The AvantGo software has three components. The first component is the AvantGo server, a computer that resides on the Internet (or on an intranet) and does the heavy work—taking Web pages and preparing them for display on a handheld device.

The second is software on the desktop PC that communicates with the server and with the handheld. The third is "MobileLink," software on the handheld device itself that manages the Web documents that have been downloaded and displays the pages.

A user downloads and installs the desktop and handheld software, and selects the "publications" he or she wants to subscribe to. In other words, they are downloaded to the user's handheld each time the handheld and the desktop PC talk to each other. These Web pages can then be read on the handheld PDA. Not only can they be read, but any forms on the site—for example, checkboxes to order full-text articles, or a survey that asks the user to enter their name, address, and so forth—can also be duplicated on the PDA. Information entered into the form is transferred to the PC the next time the user synchronizes the PDA, and from there it goes to the AvantGo server, and back to the original Web site—just as if the user were using Netscape or Internet Explorer.

Unfortunately, the AvantGo server is outside our firewall, and cannot see pages on the inside. The corporate firewall stood between users and the information on the intranet. Another group in Ford installed AvantGo software on the intranet just as we were beginning to examine the issue, so we were able to take advantage of the installation. The only difference from the Internet AvantGo server is the addition of a plug-in tool on the AvantGo server and on the PDA to allow users to authenticate themselves to the internal security system. This means that users can only download information they are permitted to see, without having an extra password. Their PDAs are also password-protected; users cannot access the information on their PDAs without first entering their password on the PDA itself. (Oddly, Palm PDAs do not "hide" passwords as they are entered—so when you key in your password, you see it on the screen, rather than the asterisks or dots commonly seen on most Web browsers. You have to be careful nobody is looking over your shoulder, or your password will no longer be secret!)

What to Put in People's Hands

With a way to get information into the right hands, we were faced with the decision of what information to put there. The two products we decided on for the launch of the PDA service in April 2000 were both automotive news publications. The first of these is World Auto Highlights, a weekly compendium of published automotive news from the world's press. We get the content from a major news service, and select articles about automotive-related events outside the United States.

The second service is Weekly Highlights, which is developed inhouse by a small team of abstractors who read the world's automotive press—particularly publications that are not indexed in the major databases—and write abstracts of the articles. Both of these publications have wide and devoted readership throughout the company, and seemed good choices for our PDA service.

We discussed several other possibilities before settling on these two. For example, we thought about adding a feed for RLIS Select (an email alert service that notifies users when new papers, books, or news articles in their areas of interest are available through the library) or our Information Systems Bulletin (a monthly summary of key articles written by the various information technology consulting groups). We decided against using RLIS Select since it does not provide content directly, but provides links to content elsewhere (including things that are not on the Web).

We likewise decided against the Information Systems Bulletin because the monthly newsletter we produce to spotlight the most important trends would not be frequent enough for users to get in the habit of using their PDAs to get the information. Conversely, if we simply published everything these services provided us, the volume of reports—numbering in the hundreds per week—would overwhelm users.

Another service that we have not yet added, but likely will soon, is our document request form, which allows users to enter citations for articles, books, etc., that they want copies of. These items are either photocopied or charged to the customer, as appropriate.

Design Issues

As a product designer, it pays to make low use of images on the Palm output. This is so because users can decide whether or not to download images at all. Aside from taking up scarce memory on the PDA and rarely serving anything other than an esthetic function, few graphics render well on the tiny screens built into PDAs. And with most Palm devices, which have monochrome displays, everything gets turned into shades of gray and green. In fact, to make the Palm version as simple to read as possible, we created a low graphics version of the sources (with just a small, two-tone version of our site's logo). The rest is plain old ASCII text, with no formatting.

Even after eliminating graphics, there is precious little screen space available. Several lines of text in an HTML header, such as <h1> or <h2>, almost fill up the screen. Making sure there is something other than titles and credits on the first screen becomes even more important on the Palm; users should not have to scroll to find the opening sentence of a story or the first link in a table of contents.

One of the publications we ported to the PDA is dynamically generated by a series of computer programs (written in PERL).

Customizing the output to work on a PDA was relatively simple. When the AvantGo server, acting as the intermediary for the hand-held device, requests a specific Web page, the scripts that generate the Web site can recognize the request as coming from AvantGo (based on information in the request's header). This means that the output from the back-end database can be tailored for a PDA rather than for a desktop monitor. For dynamically generated publications, no extra work needs to be done once the scripts are modified. The PDA output is automatic. It should be noted that while the PDA can handle complex Web layouts, such as those created using tables, simpler pages use less memory and render faster. Again, if the data being displayed is stored separately from the template, it is simply a matter of using a different, PDA-specific, output template.

We ran into a problem with one of the publications, which resides on a server we do not control, and for a variety of reasons were not able to alter the publication's programming so the AvantGo server could access it. In this instance, we decided to create a second copy of the publication on our server that would be PDA-accessible. While not the optimal solution—as it involves weekly intervention to copy the data from one server to another—it works.

One of the nicest surprises is that Web forms do not need any special treatment—so the document request forms for the full-text of articles that we do not have permission to reproduce electronically can be ordered by the user by tapping checkboxes on the screen. These requests are emailed to the library the next time the user synchronizes the PDA, and are then treated as if they came from the Web directly. This is a particularly nice feature in light of the fact that "mail-to" URLs—which allow users to click on a link on a Web page and send an email message—do not function in the current version of AvantGo. A simple Web form for the user to fill in provides an alternative way for users to provide feedback to the site owner.

Other Issues

Aside from the design of the site, there are several other issues to consider. The first is that of the intellectual property rights of the data provider. Does the service allow multiple copies of this information in multiple formats? If the license does not allow email distribution of the content, it may not allow PDA distribution. If the license is for unlimited distribution within the site, then PDA distribution is likely permissible.

A second issue is the security of the information itself. While we are not making any proprietary information available to users of PDAs, it is something of which we are aware. If proprietary or confidential information is made available to PDAs, it is important that users are aware of this and turn on their PDA's security. While it's unlikely the company business plan would find its way onto a PDA, it is quite conceivable that daily financial information could be uploaded. PDAs are small and easy to misplace, so it is important that users understand the risks. Furthermore, many PDA users keep their handheld device synchronized with a personal computer at home, in addition to work (I do, so that I have just one address book and one calendar to maintain); information could find its way onto a less secure home computer. When setting up a system like this, it is important to consider the kinds of information that will be made available. It may require developing a program that requires PDA users to authenticate themselves before synchronizing their PDA to the network.

The third issue is cost. If you control the back-end database that generates the Web content, and can make a few modifications to the code, cost for adapting content to PDAs can be very low. If the back-end database is not easily altered, this, of course, becomes more problematic. As a rule of thumb, though, if a document "lives" at the end of a static URL, it can be reached by the PDA. And, once these basic modifications are finished, very little maintenance is needed to keep it going. The largest infrastructure costs are the AvantGo server software and the computer it is installed on.

Where Next?

We are exploring other content areas to add to the PDA service. One component of RLIS Select we are thinking seriously about is the table of contents alert service. With this service, we make the tables of contents for major business and technical journals available as order forms on the Web, and notify subscribers when a new issue is published. Users get the email message, go to the Web site, and order the specific articles they want to read. We photocopy these articles (after paying copyright fees, of course) and send them to the customer by interoffice mail or fax. And we are looking at ways to turn the torrent of IT research publications into a more manageable, selective stream.

Providing information to PDA users is surprisingly easy, and has been quite successful, at a relatively low cost (a total of a couple days' programming time and a few hours' Web development time to build the site's home page, along with half an hour every week to update content that cannot be updated dynamically). We aim to expand the content included in the site, and spend a bit more programming time to create a form so that users can customize their subscription via the Palm.

Solution
Personalized Services Through Your Web Site

News Brief: brarydog.net Launches Web Portal for Students

The Public Library of Charlotte and Mecklenburg County (PLCMC) has announced the launch of brarydog <http://www.brarydog.net/, a gateway to the Web that's designed especially for students.

"We think of brarydog as your personal library and Web companion," said Helene Blowers, PLCMC's director of Web services. "Students in middle school through college are brarydog's target audiences, and it's a great resource for students who need homework help."

According to the announcement, PLCMC is the first public library to develop a customizable Web site like brarydog. Although similar Web pages originated with search engines such as Yahoo!, developer of MyYahoo!, brarydog is different in one distinctive way.

"The customizable pages provided by search engines typically are specific only to the computer you use to customize your page," Blowers said. "But you can access brarydog from any computer that has access to the Internet—Mac or PC. With brarydog, people can get to the library's subscription-only online resources, and can add their favorite links from anyplace on the Web to create a page with the resources and sites they like and use most. They can do this because each person will select a user ID and a password to gain access to his or her own brarydog page. Wherever they are, at whatever computer with Internet access, they use that ID and password to sign on, and their individual brarydog page will appear."

To make searches and customization easier, Blowers and the library's Web services team built several "desks" that students can use to easily organize sites and resources:

- Reference Desk—Through this feature users can ask brarydog a question, access dozens of online and homework help resources, and add their own reference links.

- Reader's Desk—Access the library's online card catalog or locate hundreds of reading recommendations. Add your favorite readers' items and links.

- News Desk—Use this desk to add your own News Desk items and links.

- Children's Desk—Search online databases to locate great reads for young people.

- My Desk—Add your own personal desk items and links.

All the information resources available on brarydog are free to residents of Mecklenburg County with or without a library card. In addition, there are 10 premium resources on the site that require a library card number, including Grolier's Multimedia Encyclopedia, Electric Library and Electric Library Elementary (with full-text access to magazines, newspapers, pictures, maps, and television and radio show transcripts), Health Reference Center (offering topical overviews and full-text access to over 100 medical and health periodicals), Business ASAP (with investment reports, company profiles, and full-text access to more than 450 journals), and NoveList (reading recommendations for adults, young adults, and children).

"If you don't live in Mecklenburg County, you can apply for a brarydog card online," said Blowers. "If you live in Rock Hill, Chicago, or even London, you simply pay a $25 library fee, which gets you a card and access to all the library services, including the premium services on brarydog."

brarydog is a member of the family of Web sites developed by the PLCMC. The library also has developed such sites as StoryPlace <http://www.storyplace.org>, a story-telling site for children in English and Spanish; BizLink <http://www.bizlink.org>, an online business-information research tool; and HealthLink Plus <http://www.healthlinkplus.org>. See a complete list and description of the sites at <http://www.plcmc.org/sharedPages/PLCMCwebSites.htm>.

Source: Public Library of Charlotte and Mecklenburg County, Charlotte, NC, 704/336-2725; http://www.plcmc.lib.nc.us.

Reprinted from *Information Today*, Oct. 2000. Copyright 2000, Information Today. Used by permission.

Recommended Reading

Coffman, Steve. "Distance Education and Virtual Reference: Where Are We Headed?" *Computers in Libraries* Apr. 2001: 20–5.

Drew, Bill. "The Wireless Student & the Library." *Library Journal* NetConnect 15 July 2002. http://libraryjournal.reviewsnews.com/index.asp?layout= article&articleid=CA232340/

Fagan, Jody Condit and Michele Calloway. "Creating an instant messaging reference system." *Information Technology and Libraries* 20.4 (2001): 202–212.

Foley, Marianne. "Instant messaging reference in an academic library: A case study." *College & Research Libraries* 63.1 (2002), 36–45.

McGlamery, Susan and Steve Coffman. "Moving Reference to the Web." *Reference & User Services Quarterly* 39.4: 380–386.

Sloan, Bernie. Digital Reference Services Bibliography: A Supplement. August 7, 2002. http://alexia.lis.uiuc.edu/~b-sloan/digiref.html

___. Digital Reference Question Logs. http://www.lis.uiuc.edu/~b-sloan/ log.htm

Spivey, Mark A. "The vocabulary of library home pages: An influence on diverse and remote end-users." *Information Technology and Libraries* 19.3 (2000): 151–156.

Trump, Judith F. and Ian P. Tuttle. "Here, there, and everywhere: Reference at the point-of-need." *The Journal of Academic Librarianship* 27.6 (2001): 464–466.

Chapter 5

Access Issues

The Internet was such a wonderful new toy that it maybe took us a bit longer than it should have to realize that not everybody could play. We were ahead of the curve on the digital divide, of course, because providing free learning opportunities for minorities, immigrants, and the poor is what we've been doing for more than 150 years. But there are also patrons whose disabilities make them unable to use our computers, patrons who are unable to read our English-language Web page text and instructions, elderly patrons who are intimidated by the machines, and patrons with inadequate phone lines and outdated equipment who can't download Web pages full of bandwidth-eating graphics. We've been promising the joys of the Internet, but not always delivering them equally. Not only do many of these problems constitute bad service, they are now violations of law as well.

Solution
Accommodating Disabilities on Our Workstations and Web Pages

Providing Equitable Access— From Ergonomics to HTML

Cheryl H. Kirkpatrick and Catherine Buck Morgan

Everyone in the library world is familiar with the vast storehouse of information at our fingertips. The Internet has become a part of our everyday lives. However, we seldom hear about the people who can't even get to the Internet without special equipment or software—people who are challenged in vision, hearing, motor skills, and cognition. These people have the same need for access to information that we all have, but how can we provide that access in a public environment?

Located in the heart of the state capital, the South Carolina State Library supports the state's government employees, public libraries, and citizens. Among its many services to the population of South Carolina, the State Library has a history of providing services directly to Carolinians who are blind and physically handicapped.

In 1996, the State Library gave one computer to each public library headquarters in the state for use by visually handicapped patrons. Then in 1998, we focused attention on ourselves and installed a public workstation dedicated to accessibility for the visually handicapped. This workstation was equipped with JAWS, VERA, and ZoomText software, and a scanner. (See Figure 5.1.)

JAWS for Windows 3.7 by Henter-Joyce, a division of Freedom Scientific, Inc.-JAWS (Job Access With Speech) uses a voice synthesizer to output the contents of the computer screen to the sound card.

OPENBook: Ruby edition by Arkenstone, Inc., a division of Freedom Scientific-OPEN Book is a scanning and reading software. The user scans text with this application, which then reads the text back to the user. It includes a built-in editor, bookmarks, a dictionary, a thesaurus, and a spell-checker. IBM's ViaVoice Outloud speech software is included in the package.

WYNN (What You Need Now) by Arkenstone, Inc.-This is a reading program for individuals with various reading challenges, dyslexia, and learning disabilities. It uses a bimodal method of presenting the written word by highlighting each word as it reads it. The software allows the user to adjust the amount of space between words, the speed at which it reads, and the background and foreground colors. WYNN also includes an editor with bookmarking, highlighting, and note-taking features.

ZoomText Xtra Level 2 by Ai Squared-This screen reader features synchronized magnification. It was designed for the low-vision user, and includes two speech synthesizers.

Gus! Word Prediction Software by Gus Communications, Inc.-This software will predict the current word that the user is typing, and prompts the user with a pop-up dialog box full of selections. The user indicates the correct word and the program inserts it. The software can be programmed so that "hagd" becomes "have a good day," saving the user numerous keystrokes.

Duxbury Translator by Duxbury Systems, Inc.-This product creates Braille output from WordPerfect and Word documents. It is capable of multi-language translation for grade-one and grade-two Braille. It also features interline printing, producing ink and Braille on the same page.

Microsoft's Windows Accessibility Options-These are used on each workstation.

Additional software includes MS Office 2000, Adobe Acrobat 4.0, MS Internet Explorer 5.5, and McAfee VirusScan.

Figure 5.1 Specialized Applications on Our Workstations

In the summer of 2000, the State Library added two workstations in the new reading room at its Department for the Blind and Physically Handicapped (DBPH). These workstations were equipped with WYNN, Duxbury Translator, ZoomText Level 2, OPENBook 5.0: Ruby edition, and JAWS software.

We thought we had done all our upgrading. Then last fall, the State Library's director, James B. Johnson, was appointed to the South Carolina Access to Information Technology Coordinating Committee (SCAITCC). This committee was created by a proviso from the South Carolina General Assembly, and was charged with studying and providing "on a pilot basis, information technology access to South Carolinians with functional impairments."[1]

Catherine Morgan attended the meetings with Johnson as "technology interpreter." Cheryl Kirkpatrick, the State Library's Web administrator, was invited to join the SCAITCC's Web Accessibility Workgroup, where she chaired the training subgroup.

When the State Library itself was selected as one of five pilot sites for the SCAITCC study, we discovered that there was much more involved in offering equal access for all. Up until this time, our efforts had been focused on providing software to aid the visually challenged. Now it seemed that we had only been looking at a very small part of the problem.

We decided to upgrade the two workstations at DBPH and to begin a concerted effort to make our Web site fully accessible. During our renovations, Catherine concentrated her efforts on the workstations while Cheryl focused on the Web site.

Knocking Down Barriers:
Choosing and Using New Hardware and Software

The SCAITCC developed a "shopping list" that detailed what accommodations we'd need to meet the standards in the federal Section 508 of the Rehabilitation Act Amendments of 1998, and the additional assistive technology that would support accessibility.

Using this shopping list, we determined how we would modify our setups to meet the recommendations of the committee. The committee funded our expenses.

Renovating the Workstations

There is a wide range of functional impairments: vision impairment/blindness, hearing impairment/deafness, deaf/blindness, ergonomic/mobility impairment, and cognitive impairment. To help people who face those challenges, we started upgrading two workstations. The base workstation was a standard Pentium III with an 800-MHz processor, 128 MB RAM, a 15-GB hard drive, a CD-ROM drive, a sound card with speakers and headphones, and a 10/100 PCI network card. We made certain to have enough expansion slots for the various peripherals, including USB ports. Each workstation had a 21-inch monitor, a scanner, and a printer.

To meet Section 508 standards, we needed to address the physical setup of the workstations. We began by adding an adjustable work-table (from DBH Attachments). The model we selected uses a remote control to adjust the height of the workstation, and features swinging arm mounts for the scanner, printer, and keyboard. This allows the user to have each peripheral within easy reach. The table height adjusts with the touch of a button to accommodate a child or an adult, as well as wheelchairs. We also added an ergonomic, adjustable chair. The final touch was the addition of ErgoRest forearm rests. These armrests attach to the workstation and support the forearm. They are jointed, so that they move with the user.

An oversized trackball aids users who cannot manipulate a mouse. We chose the Roller Trackball, which features a 2.5-inch roll ball, and separate buttons for clicking and dragging.

The shopping list indicated that we needed keyguards for the keyboards. (A keyguard fits over the keyboard, preventing involuntary keystrokes.) We did purchase these, but found that, for individuals who did not have mobility impairments, they were extremely difficult to use. And, we discovered that visually impaired users would not be able to feel the Braille keycaps. We remedied this by providing two keyboards, one with the keyguard and one without. The standard keyboard is always available; staff will supply the one with the keyguard when requested by the patron. We affixed Braille labels with large-print letters to the keys of the keyboards.

Universal add-on touch-screens with antiglare tint (from Troll Touch) were attached to each 21-inch monitor. The touch-screens are another input device. We found, however, that the antiglare tint made it difficult for low-vision individuals to see the screen, so we decided to use the touch-screen on one workstation only.

Each workstation has an inkjet printer and a color scanner. Both are networked to a Blazie Braille embosser.

Installing Nifty New Software

The software that's available to assist functionally impaired users is amazing. Screen readers include JAWS for Windows (JFW) by Henter-Joyce, and Window-Eyes by GW Micro-the two top contenders. A lower-priced alternative is the IBM Home Page Reader. These are widely used for accessing information on the Internet. Other software allows the user to scan in text, which the software then reads aloud. Word prediction is a different type of software. It offers a word choice based on the first letters keyed in, and the user can select the appropriate word; this is especially useful for people with mobility impairments. There is also software that translates the written word to Braille, and software that transcribes the spoken word.

Some of the software we describe in the sidebar may appear redundant, but while there are commonalities, each has an additional feature not offered by the rest.

In addition to our major software packages, we also purchased a bifocal illuminated folding magnifier and a cassette recorder for each workstation. The magnifier is simply a large magnifying glass that the low-vision patron can fold down to view the monitor—a low-tech, inexpensive solution. The cassette recorder allows the patron to capture what the screen reader produces. For labeling equipment, we have a hand-held Braille labeler, which uses vinyl tape.

Fixtures That We Didn't Buy

The shopping list committee recommended a HeadMouse for users with severe mobility impairments, and a refreshable Braille display. A HeadMouse is one of several hands-free input/pointer devices available for users who cannot use their hands. The technology ranges from apparatuses such as sensors that follow head or eye movement, to a stick-like pointer attached to a band that fits around the head, which allows the user to physically tap a keyboard or screen.

A refreshable Braille display is an electronic device attached to the PC by a serial cable that translates screen text. The device displays Braille to a series of small pins set in eight-dot cells. Computer Braille uses eight dots rather than the six-dot Braille we generally see. But our patron base has not indicated the need for these items, and other agencies in our area serve these populations.

Our committee discussed voice recognition software such as Dragon Speak. But this software must be "trained" by the user and, in a public setting, the user would not have the time to train with his or her own voice. Therefore, we didn't include voice recognition software on the shopping list.

While we were making sure that people could physically access information using our equipment, we also needed to make certain that the information on our Web site was in a format that could be accessed.

Updating Infrastructure: Our Web Pages' HTML

We actually began making our Web pages accessible in June 2000, before our involvement with the SCAITCC. However, in the fall, when our library became a test site for South Carolina, accessibility became an urgent priority. Our goal was to have the Web site completely accessible by June 30, 2001.

Listening to our Web site with a screen reader was an eye-opening (or should we say ear-opening) experience. We highly recommend it. These tools read from left to right, and across columns. This can make for amusing listening for us, but for a visually challenged listener, the experience can be frustrating, to say the least. We discovered that changes needed to be made, and they needed to be made quickly.

Understanding the Challenge

We went into high-gear learning. As this was a relatively new area, we had to hunt for resources. Books on Web accessibility were difficult to find and the articles we did locate were very general and often did not go beyond using the <alt> tag. Our primary sources of information were Internet sites. Three sites we found especially helpful were CAST's Bobby, the Web Accessibility Initiative (WAI) of the World Wide Web Consortium (W3C), and WebAIM (Web Accessibility In Mind).

Well into our project, we located two good books: *Adaptive Technology for the Internet: Making Electronic Resources Accessible to All*, by Barbara T. Mates, and *Web Accessibility for People with Disabilities*, by Michael G. Paciello. Mates' book is written for libraries and is a good starting point. Paciello's book is very detailed and includes more HTML code.

In order to evaluate training sources for South Carolina Webmasters, SCAITCC funded several formal training opportunities. We took an online course from EASI (Equal Access to Software and Information), a well-known organization that tells people about access-to-information technologies. It provides seminars, online workshops, Webcast interviews with experts in this field, an electronic journal, and discussion lists. Cheryl also took the WX online tutorial and attended training from WebAIM. This is a project of Utah State University that is funded by a grant from the U.S. Department of Education. It has an excellent Web site that provides a wealth of information on accessibility.

While these training experiences were very valuable, none of them affected us as much as actually working with a blind professional. Scott Brennan, of the South Carolina Commission for the Blind, was a member of the training subgroup. Scott taught us how blind users make use of assistive technology and how layout, word choices, and navigation affect a blind person's ability to gain information. More importantly, he showed us the impact that this technology can have on people's lives. This was an invaluable experience.

Undertaking the Challenge

Once we had an understanding of accessibility, we evaluated our Web site and made a plan for change. We had to decide which standards to follow. We considered Bobby compliancy, the recommendations of the WAI of the World Wide Web Consortium, and Section 508. These standards are very similar and following any of them would have made our site accessible. We decided our site must, at a minimum, meet Section 508 standards; but we wanted to go beyond the minimum requirements as we rebuilt our electronic library.

However, our site consists of over 700 pages—a daunting challenge. We decided that, first, all new pages were to be created as accessible, and any pages that were being routinely updated would also be coded for accessibility. Next, Cheryl studied the usage statistics of the site and chose the top 20 pages by number of hits. After the top 20 pages were finished, Cheryl worked through the site one section at a time. We were very fortunate to have an intern, Lin Zhang from the University of South Carolina's College of Library and Information Science, assisting us in this process during the spring of 2001.

It's not difficult to make your Web site accessible. In Figure 5.2, we list 15 things you can do to make your site readable to most people with disabilities.

Welcoming New Tenants

Our deadline of June 30, 2001 has come and gone. We have purchased and installed all the hardware and software that were a part of

- At the top of your document before the <HTML> tag, include a Document Type Definition. This provides information about the page to a screen reader, such as which language is being used. Example: <!DOCTYPE HTML PUBLIC"-//W3C//DTD HTML 4.0 Transitional//EN">.

- Have a clear color contrast between the background of your page and the text. Similar colors and graphic backgrounds make reading your page difficult for people with low vision.

- Use <alt> tags that describe images, animations, and Java applets to the user. Screen readers will read an <alt> tag, so the tag should contain a short, meaningful description. This is particularly important for images that are used as links.

- You can use empty <alt> tags <alt=""> for images that serve a purely decorative function. Screen readers will skip empty <alt> tags.

- If you have an image that cannot be described in a few words, such as a chart, use a D link. This is a recent development on the Web that you may not have seen. Beside the image, place [D] and link this to another page that contains the information in text format.

- Use client-side image maps instead of server-side image maps and supply an <alt> tag that describes the hypertext link for each hotspot. Wherever possible, also provide a list of the links contained in the image map.

- When creating links, use words that describe the destination page to the user. Because screen readers can take a long time to read a page, blind users often tab quickly through the links on a page. They need links that describe the destination. A link name such as "Click here" and "http://www.infotoday.com/cilmag/ciltop.htm" is not descriptive. Link names such as "User Guidelines" or "Computers in Libraries" tell the user exactly where he or she will be going.

- Use a <title> tag to identify the link. Some screen readers read <title> tags instead of the link name. Example: <A href="http://www.infotoday.com/cilmag/ciltop.htm" title="Computers in Libraries">Computers in Libraries</A>

- Provide a transcript of any audio files you use, and include captions for video files.

- Tables can be accessible if you are careful with the code. Use <TH> for table headers on tables that contain data. Do not use <TH> in tables used for layout. If tables are used for layout, avoid using multicolumn layout. Screen readers read from left to right. While a sighted person can read one column down the left side and then read the column down the right side, a screen reader will read straight across both columns. When using tables for layout, enter your text in the order that it should be read.

- Within your code, text within tables should be laid out in order so that it makes sense when read.

- Colorblindness is common, so be careful how you use color. Do not communicate information by color only. For example, a form that shows required fields in red won't convey any meaning to a colorblind person. Use an additional method of conveying the information.

- Avoid blinking and flashing images. These can cause seizures in people with photosensitive epilepsy.

- Avoid frames whenever possible.

- If you must use frames, there are a couple of things you can do to make them more accessible. Give each frame meaningful name that describes its function. Use names such as "navigation. html" or "content.html" instead of names such as "side.html" or "frame] .html". Use the <title> tag to provide a description of the function. Use the <noframes> tag to provide a text equivalent of the information presented on the page. Do not use the <noframes> tag to simply inform the user that a frames-enabled browser is needed to view the page. If you provide a "noframes" version, be sure you update the information on this version whenever you update the primary page. + Use a text-only version of your page as a last resort only. If you do, as with frames, be sure you update the information on the text version whenever you update the primary page.

Figure 5.2 Coding Tips for Making Your Web Site Accessible

our project. At the time of this writing, our Web pages that are frequently used are accessible but some of our older pages still need to be adapted. You can see our progress at <http://www.state.sc.us/scsl>. This is an ongoing process. As we continue to learn, and as technology continues to develop, our site continues to evolve.

The SCAITCC was not able to fully complete its activities within FY2001, as directed in the proviso. So it created a new committee, the South Carolina Access to Technology Executive Committee/Partnership (ATEC). ATEC will continue training state agency Webmasters, and will complete the setup of the other pilot sites. When the remaining sites are operational, the committee will promote and advertise the pilot centers, and begin collecting usage statistics and other data.

Because of our participation in this project, both of us are more aware of the needs of these special populations and the solutions that technology can provide. We are glad our state took the initiative to provide this kind of assistive technology to our residents, and we are pleased we had the opportunity to participate.

While it is possible to spend a large amount of money to make information accessible to the functionally challenged, you can make improvements with a small amount of money and a willingness to think creatively. It costs nothing to make Web pages accessible, and there are assistive technology devices that will fit any budget. In any case, the goal remains the same—meeting the challenge of providing access to information for everyone.

To Contact the Companies

Ai Squared <http://www.aisquared.com>
P.O. Box 669
Manchester Center, VT 05255
802/362-3612

DBH Attachments, Inc. <http://www.dbhattachments.com/>
P.O. Box 734

158 Sunrise Dr.
Adamsville, TN 38310
800/852-3026

Duxbury Systems, Inc. <http://www.duxburysystems.com/>
270 Littleton Rd., Unit 6
Westford, MA 01886-3523
978/692-3000

Freedom Scientific <http://www.freedomsci.com/>
(for Henter-Joyce, Blazie, and Arkenstone)
11800 31st Ct. N.
St. Petersburg, FL 33716
800/444-4443

Gus Communications, Inc. <http://www.gusinc.com/>
1006 Lonetree Ct.
Bellingham, WA 98226
360/715-8580

Troll Touch <http:/www.trolltouch.com/>
25510 Avenue Stanford, Suite 106
Valencia, CA 91355
800/201-1160

Reference

1. Access to Information Technology Status and Fiscal Impact Report: A Report to the Legislature. South Carolina Access to Information

Technology Coordinating Committee; http://www.scstatehouse.
net/reports/penny/itreport.doc.

Solution
Provide a Helping Hand Across the Digital Divide for Young Adults

You would think young adults wouldn't need help crossing
the digital divide, given the attraction computers have for
kids. But that requires getting them in the library, and making
your library a place that welcomes young adults can be a
challenge.

Wiring Teens to the Library

Michele Gorman

Every day we welcome between 50 and 60 teens to the Carver
Branch, one of Austin Public Library's (APL), TX, ten Wired for Youth
(WFY) centers. They come in to use the computers for e-mail, do
homework, or read the latest graphic novel or most current issue of
Computer Gaming Magazine. Sometimes they come to Carver to
socialize, get help with a school project, take a class on web development, or ask questions about anything from how to publish their own
poetry to how to find information on the Internet about summer jobs.
They feel that they belong here. They know someone is here to help
them. They also come to the library because it is a better alternative to

hanging around the neighborhood. They have a say in the development of the program, and they are always encouraged to share their ideas on how they envision "their" library.

The WFY program, made possible with funding from the Michael and Susan Dell Foundation, serves young people between the ages of 8 and 18. Dell offered APL a $500,000 challenge grant to develop the program, with a one-to-one match for every dollar raised by the library. So far, $350,000 has been raised. The target population for each WFY center is dependent on its location. At the WFY center at Carver, programs and classes are developed for and geared toward young people between the ages of 11 and 14, owing to the library's proximity to a junior high school. Through WFY, Austin's young people learn and practice an array of electronic information literacy skills that will assist them in their formal education, developing future goals, and ultimately becoming productive adult members of their communities as well as lifelong patrons of the library.

In the last year, WFY librarians report that more teens and preteens than ever before are using the library and its resources for homework, research, and net surfing for school and for fun. Statistics also show that a record number of teens and preteens have participated in computer classes in WFY centers throughout the city, with almost 100,000 young people using them since May 2000. Classes range from beginning-level word processing and Internet navigation to more advanced classes involving graphics editing and manipulation, animation, and web design.

Getting Teens Wired:
Suggestions for Libraries on a Budget:

- Designate and promote a time of day when one or two terminals can be set aside for teen use.

- Invite members of the local technology community to teach classes for teens on searching the Internet, word processing, or simple computer programming.

- Seek out college students who need to earn volunteer credit for educational coursework. Many of these students are well versed in computer software and will trade volunteer hours for credit by working after school with teens.

- Recruit teens to help develop and maintain lists of the most popular Internet sites for homework, games, e-mail, teen chat, advice, and teen zines—online magazines for teenagers. Post these lists and make print copies available for all teen users.

- Have teens with younger siblings create lists of sites for younger Internet users, such as homework help sites designed for younger children, kid-friendly games that are easy to navigate, and coloring sites.

- Seek out and download freeware and shareware (see suggested sites for getting teens "wired").

- Recruit teens to create their own print or online zine—have them check out <http://www.zinebook.com> for inspiration and more information.

So what makes APL's Wired for Youth program different from other programs around the country, like Youth Wired in San Antonio or Teen Central in Phoenix? WFY centers are located in ten libraries throughout the city to reach as many kids as possible, rather than in one central location. Setting up technology in ten locations puts it within the reach of all Austin kids, rather than just a few. We can also build better relationships within the local communities through the development of individualized programs and the fostering of one-on-one connections between young patrons and the WFY librarian. Each of the ten locations is staffed by a full-time WFY librarian.

Although all of the WFY centers are equipped with the same computer hardware and software, they are each different, depending on the patron base they serve. For example, the Manchaca WFY center offers a Colleges and Careers program for teens at the high school located across the street from the library. The Southeast WFY center has programs and classes for a variety of ages, since it is located near an elementary and a middle school. Each center is also greatly influenced by the language and culture of its surrounding populace. The WFY centers at both the Terrazas and Cepeda branches serve a bilingual (Spanish/English) community and feature bilingual computer classes, including introduction to computers and introduction to the Internet, desktop publishing, introduction to Spanish databases, photo imaging, and basic web design.

The WFY librarians have found that meeting together weekly as a team helps avoid any fragmentation of the program. These meetings give us a chance to share, brainstorm for future programming, and solve problems.

Programming

The WFY center at Carver, located in an African American community, has served a growing clientele of teens and preteens since it opened in March 2001. For many of the kids, this is their first experience with a public library. In the year that the Carver WFY center has been open, it has provided technology and technology-oriented programming to approximately 9,000 young people. In the hopes of meeting the educational needs of our young patrons while fostering the strength of the culture and the community, we continually try to develop new educational activities so that the kids learn about themselves, one another, and their community. Computer classes cover topics such as web design, graphics manipulation, audiovisual production, Internet usage, word processing, and desktop publishing.

We also have various groups and ongoing monthly activities that are not technology-centered but focus instead on the development of a community of young people in the library.

Youth Advisory Committee: This group comprises more than a dozen young men and women who accurately represent in age, gender, and race a cross-section of the teens and preteens who use the Carver Library, allowing the target audience to have a say in the development of the WFY program. The committee meets once a month to help plan and implement current programs and classes and to brainstorm for future programs and special events. They also spend time each month creating the Wired at Carver! Newsletter, a document published monthly in both print and pdf format [no longer extant].

Sister Soldiers: This group of young women meets once a month for both planned activities and informal social interaction. The development of self-esteem and self-advocacy is its focus. The goals for these young women include increasing self-awareness, self-respect, and self-confidence. In the past year the group has been involved in journal writing, mural painting, creating wisdom rocks, and making self-collages.

Cool Careers: Each month a guest speaker visits the Carver WFY center, spending time with the kids and talking about his or her profession. The guest often presents a brief overview of his or her job, educational background, required education, degrees, or certification, and a look at salary (both today and prospects for the future). In addition, there is usually a Q&A session and a hands-on demonstration or activity. We have highlighted both traditional and nontraditional professions aimed at both young men and women, including television camera operator, forensic scientist, comic bookstore owner, and playwright.

The Future of WFY

The WFY program has attracted thousands of new users to the Austin Public Library. WFY has helped fulfill the library's mission of promoting lifelong learning, and has attracted a new generation of patrons who might not have otherwise ventured into a public library between story time and adulthood. We have received an additional $50,000 grant from the Dell Computer Corporation to provide extra summer help (cyberlifeguards) to increase the hours the WFY centers are open and to provide additional classes and programs. We will be adding additional equipment to increase the capabilities of all WFY centers. We also have been awarded grant money to improve the technology and YA collections and to add more library materials to entice teens and preteens to read.

The cyberlifeguards are library school graduate students who will be working 20 hours a week to provide one-on-one assistance and to help the WFY librarian with summer classes and programs. "Just like lifeguards at area swimming pools, the cyberlifeguards are there to ensure that kids use the Wired for Youth center computers safely and effectively," says Youth Services Manager Jeanette Larson.

Wiring Teens at Your Library

Money and staffing are most likely the two biggest challenges you will face if you decide to develop a "wired" program for teens in your library. In the current economy, not many library systems can allot $1 million to create a brand new, state-of-the-art computer lab with adjoining space for teens. Also, chances are if you don't have a YA librarian currently on staff, you will not be hiring one any time soon. If you do have someone on staff who does have the time to work with teens, it is unlikely that he or she has the requisite background in computers and technology.

This gap in staffing often leads to the following scenario: your only children's librarian attempts to throw a teen book club into a schedule already overflowing with story times for toddlers, library tours, after-school fun clubs, and outreach programs for the neighborhood day-care center. Your library's circulation staff is already overworked and feels that teens just loiter and talk too loudly in the library. While this may not be how things are unfolding in your library, the sad reality is that many libraries don't have the necessary resources or staff to create a comprehensive library program for teens and preteens. While this is discouraging—and will continue until funding authorities realize that today's teens are tomorrow's taxpayers—it is still possible to develop a simple technology program for young people.

Another frequent problem is teens playing games on library computers. Although homework is always a priority in all WFY centers, we allow kids to play games on the Internet. We also let the kids chat on sites that have been approved by our filtering software management team. Through experience we have learned that computer games are often a gateway activity for kids who frequent the WFY center. We have witnessed that a majority of our users begin by playing games. Once they feel comfortable with the computer and within the library environment, they gradually begin to sign up for various computer classes and branch out to using software applications for both schoolwork and fun.

Setting Your Sights on Wired

If you have your sights set on the development of a more elaborate technology program for teens, including new computers and the most up-to-date software, seek out public and private sources such as grants from the government and national and neighborhood associations that support libraries and technology. Also, your library's foundation or Friends group may be able to help you secure financial support for the development of a wired program for teens through corporate donations, grants, and other fundraising opportunities. Look for funding within your community, such as partnerships with local technology companies, computer stores, and other Internet-related businesses. Corporations, organizations, and independently owned businesses that support technology and education can be your greatest allies in locating funds for the development of a wired program for teens.

The most successful programs for young people are the ones that let kids take the lead in developing their own program. Ask them for help and honor and respect their opinions and expertise. Allow the teens and preteens in your library to help build a wired program, and chances are good that they will return with their friends, not only to use the technology but also to check out a book or two.

Best Sites for Teens

Free e-mail:

<http://www.hotmail.com>

<http://www.yahoo.com>

Free Web Page Hosting

<http://angelfire.lycos.com/>

<http://www.tripod.lycos.com/>

<http://geocities.yahoo.com>

<http://www.fortunecity.com>

<http://www.freewebspace.net>

Web Design Tips and Tutorials

Webmonkey for Kidshot <http://hotwired.lycos.com/webmonkey/kids/>

A great introduction to making web pages. It's easy to navigate and understand and filled with practical information.

WebKIDS <http://www.webkids.info/html.html>

A complete tutorial on basic and advanced HTML, with tips and tricks for web design. For both beginning and advanced web designers.

Web Genies <http://www.webgenies.co.uk>

A colorful, interactive site that is especially good for novice web designers. The language is easy to understand, all lessons are easy to follow, and a glossary is available.

Web Graphics and Images

Cooltext.com <http://www.cooltext.com/>

Allows users to create their own banners and logos that look great and require little or no previous experience in web graphic design.

html Gear <http://www.htmlgear.lycos.com/>
Sponsored by Lycos, this site has free add-ons for a web site such as guest books and counters to enhance a site and make it more interactive.

Free Software and Shareware

Rocketdownload.com <http://www.rocketdownload.com/default.asp>
A comprehensive archive of reviewed shareware, freeware, and demo software.

CNET's download.com <http://www.download.com.com/>
An exhaustive resource of more than 40,000 software programs available for free or trial that can be downloaded via the Internet.

The Internet Movie Machine <http://www.16color.com>
Animation software to download for free that is a lot of fun for beginning animators of all ages.

Solution
Help Seniors Cross the Digital Divide
Surf's Up for Seniors! Introducing Older Patrons to the Web

Jeanne Holba Puacz and Chris Bradfield

The Vigo County Public Library, located in Terre Haute, Indiana, had been getting an increasing number of calls and visits from distressed senior citizens. "My kids bought me this thing for Christmas and now I don't know what to do with it" and "What is a dot-com?" were becoming all-too-familiar refrains. Our seniors were baffled by the Web addresses popping up in newspapers, magazines, and on television. Many were desperate to e-mail their grandchildren, but were even more desperate to find out what this mysterious e-mail was.

Although our library has long been offering computer-training classes, many of the seniors seemed hesitant to sign up for them. It was becoming apparent that we had a real need for senior-oriented computer classes. We, the reference/systems librarian responsible for much of the public training and the associate manager of one of the branches, respectively, decided to put our heads together. It was past the time to develop a series of free classes specifically designed to turn our techno-phobic seniors into "techies."

Afraid to Get in the Water

During the past year we had been listening to the various reasons our seniors gave us for not attending the regularly scheduled computer classes held in the library computer lab. Some were concerned about being in classes with significantly younger classmates, as if the younger students would be impatient with their basic questions. Others seemed intimidated by the class setting itself; all of the library classes were hands-on and held in the computer lab. Even the most basic classes required the students to work hands-on with computers. Another complaint we heard from many seniors (including one of our grandmothers) was that they had tried taking computer classes elsewhere and had been disappointed: The classes advertised as basic were too advanced, the teacher geared the class toward those that already had experience, most classes were very expensive, etc. Many felt that if they signed up for another class, they would just be disappointed again.

Rather than risk having disappointed patrons, we took their concerns to heart and incorporated them into the structure of a new program with classes that would be tailor-made for senior citizens. When planning our classes, we were torn. We didn't want to overload our timid seniors, but we did want to give them enough information to make them feel somewhat competent with a computer. We felt the classes needed to include, at the minimum, an introduction to the basic parts and operations of a computer and an overview of using the World Wide Web.

We decided to divide the material into four separate sessions in order to keep the amount of information presented at each class manageable. Instead of having all of the classes be hands-on in the "scary" computer lab, we opted to have a mixture of teaching styles and locations. Classes one and three were to be presentations and discussions in a "non-computer" location, and classes two and four were to be hands-on with computers. The presentation sessions would be to the whole group of students and were designed to be approximately an hour in length. The hands-on sessions would be for small groups, and would be approximately a half-hour in length. We also agreed that the senior students should have an opportunity to come in for extra practice if they lacked confidence in their new computer abilities. In addition to the four classes, we would also make one-on-one appointments, lasting approximately 20 minutes, available to any interested students.

Luring Them to the Edge

We chose to hold the first series of classes in association with the East Branch of the library, which is very popular with seniors. Additionally, the branch is located in a shopping mall where many seniors "mall walk" for exercise. We hoped to attract not only our regular senior patrons who were anxious about computers, but also the "mall walkers" who were not yet regular library users. In an effort to make our topic less intimidating, we created lighthearted posters and fliers, posing the question "Want to know how to surf without water?" and promising that the "Vigo County Public Library Life Guards will teach you to surf!" We placed the posters in front of the library and also at several points around the mall. Fliers were passed out at the branch, and several mall businesses were also kind enough to help distribute the fliers.

The seniors' response to the proposed classes was incredible. Within 5 days we had 30 seniors signed up for the first series. We ran out of fliers and took down the posters well before the series was scheduled to start. Even though we stopped advertising, word of mouth worked wonders for us; before the first series was over, we had a waiting list of more than 40 seniors anxious to sign up when a new series would be offered.

Come In, the Water's Fine!

In an effort to make our seniors more comfortable when attending the classes, we decided to have the presentations not only in a "non-computer" location, but also in one that was extremely senior-oriented. Therefore, we chose to have classes one and three (the presentations) at the community center of a local retirement village, which is located approximately one block from the East Branch of the library. In addition to this being a non-threatening location for our somewhat-hesitant students, we hoped that having the presentation in a retirement community would help to advertise the library's services to the residents who were not yet regular patrons.

This alternative location also enabled us to further change the atmosphere of the class. Since the seniors would not be sitting at computers, we could serve coffee and cookies, which would give the class the more-relaxed feel of a social event.

Getting Their Feet Wet

We focused the first presentation (class one) on the basics of using a Windows-based computer. We chose to focus on Windows PCs since they are the computers used in our library and the computers the seniors would be using during the hands-on classes. Using PowerPoint, we developed the first presentation. It included an overview of hardware, software, mousing, opening and closing programs, and turning the computer on and off. Presentation two (class three) was an introduction to the Web. Again using PowerPoint, we presented the basics of the Internet and the Web, touching on how a computer communicates via a modem through the phone line, what an ISP is, and what a Web browser does. We used slides to show what links look like on a Web page, how to use navigation buttons, how to type in an address to go directly to a Web site, and how to perform simple searches.

Throughout the presentations we attempted to include humor (including several bad "mouse" and "spider web" puns) in hopes of lightening the mood and making the whole concept of computers seem less intimidating. To help the seniors get acquainted with the parts of a computer, we passed around keyboards, mice, and a variety of computer disks. This all helped to demystify the concept of computers for our students.

We made handouts of the PowerPoint presentations and distributed them along with pencils to encourage note taking during the presentations. We also gave handouts defining some of the more intimidating computer jargon. At the end of each presentation, we included a slide "warning" the class of what they would face during the next session. Finally, we had the seniors sign up for their hands-on, small-group sessions in one of the library branches. In order to accommodate their busy schedules, we offered a variety of times and a choice of locations for the hands-on sessions.

We brought a large assortment of books and videotapes on computer topics to each of the two non-computer presentations. At the end of each presentation we encouraged the seniors to browse through the materials and to check out any items of interest. We brought borrower card applications with us in case a senior new to the library was interested in checking out some of the resources. Checking out materials and processing library card applications manually might seem a little cumbersome, but we considered the comfort of our new patrons and the added circulation statistics, so it was well worth the effort.

The first hands-on session (class two) covered basic computing. We opened and closed programs, practiced mousing (by playing computer solitaire), put a floppy disk in and took it out of the disk drive, and shut down the computer. We tried to point out some possible pitfalls before they happened, such as right clicking instead of left clicking and moving the mouse while clicking, so the seniors would not be as flustered when these things happened to them. In the hands-on Web class (class four) we, by default, reviewed mousing and opening programs. Students then opened Internet Explorer and checked the library's home page for links. After locating some links, the students were encouraged to follow them for practice. We reviewed the location and function of the navigation buttons such as Back, Forward, and Home; demonstrated how to use the scroll bar or the arrow keys to view an entire page; and then had the seniors practice using these items while moving about in the library's Web site. Next we tackled the address line and had the seniors go directly to a Web site by typing in the URL, and we also had them do a very simple subject search by typing a subject into the address line.

Raising the Comfort Level

Although we did not set a minimum age limit to define who qualified as a senior, we did feel that advertising the classes as "seniors only" was a key to our success. The seniors seemed much more comfortable and willing to ask questions when surrounded by their peers. They weren't threatened by the other class members but, rather, seemed encouraged to see that they were not the only ones that felt out of the technological loop.

Also, even though the seniors were more comfortable asking questions when surrounded by their peers, we also gave them an added incentive: We bribed them! We informed them at the beginning of the first presentation that any student willing to ask a question would get a piece of candy. Of course many of them didn't actually want the candy, but they understood the underlying meaning: We really did want them to ask any questions they had, and we were happy to try to answer them. We stressed that they should "ask a librarian," and reminded them that answering questions is part of our job!

Honing Our Initial Ideas

We feel that the first series of senior classes was quite successful; however, we are continually working to make improvements. We have found that our initial timeline of one class a week for 4 weeks allowed too much time between the presentations and the hands-on sessions. Our revised timeline has all the classes occurring within a 2-week period, with the hands-on session following the presentation by no more than 2 to 3 days. This shorter timeline allows for more immediate reinforcement and practice of the concepts presented, and it seems to be much more effective. We also found that changing locations from the retirement community to the library, plus the sign-up for times for the small-group sessions, confused some patrons. In an effort to eliminate this confusion, we began bringing reminder slips to the classes so the students could immediately write down the time and place of their hands-on sessions.

We originally encouraged the students to take notes during the presentations (classes one and three), and even brought them paper and pencils with which to do so. However, we did not think to do the same during the first set of hands-on sessions (classes two and four). The few patrons who brought pencil and paper to the hands-on classes were taking notes throughout the session. Therefore, during our second senior series, we decided to try providing writing materials for the hands-on sessions as well, and were pleased to see many of the students happily taking notes.

A totally unexpected problem that we encountered involved solitaire. We believed solitaire to be an easy way to practice mouse skills; unfortunately, several of the class members informed us that they did not know how to play the game. So, we have decided to include a set of solitaire rules in our future handouts!

Besides the solitaire rules, there are several other additions we hope to make to future classes. We intend to make "crib sheets" for our seniors to carry when they come to the library to practice with the computers. We would like to provide laminated index cards including such information as how to open and close programs, how to access the Internet at the library, how to use the address line in the browser, and a reminder that one click plus the Enter key will open a program if they have trouble double clicking. We feel this small card would give them added confidence when using the library computers—they could subtly check their cards and get started without having to immediately ask for help. We also hope to be able to include such helpful tips as how to enlarge the size of the icons or change the mouse click speed during future basic hands-on sessions.

Riding a Wave of Excitement

The response of the seniors before, during, and after the classes was very positive and wonderfully enthusiastic. They were very pleased that the library had recognized their needs, and they appreciated our attempts to help them catch up to their grandkids technologically. Most were disappointed when the series came to a close, and some previously intimidated seniors were now brave enough to sign up for the more advanced classes held in the library's computer lab. We had excited patrons who wanted more, and we thought it would be wrong for us to deny them! So, we have begun taking names of those interested in joining a library-sponsored computer club for seniors that would cover such topics as email, word processing, and how to buy a home computer.

We feel that the benefits of this program are multifaceted. By holding the presentations at local senior centers and retirement communities, the library is reaching out and helping to foster goodwill in the community and thus meeting a goal of its mission statement. This effort at community outreach has been well-received, and we are getting requests from additional community organizations hoping to sponsor a series of classes. Many of our seniors are more comfortable with the new technology available in the library, and many are coming back on a regular basis to practice and to improve their skills. They are happily sharing the news of the classes with their friends. We're getting an increasing number of calls from excited seniors eager to learn, instead of the calls from wary and intimidated seniors that we were receiving just a short time ago. The library is not only better serving some longtime patrons, but it has also gained some new ones. We are starting to see increased circulation of computer materials, particularly immediately following the presentations, and are thrilled to see an increased use of our electronic resources by this important and loyal group of patrons.

Solution
Partnerships Within the Community to Reach Across the Digital Divide

Partnerships That Support Public Access Computing

Mary Stillwell

The U.S. Library Program of the Bill and Melinda Gates Foundation makes grants to public libraries for computers, software, technical support, and training. Part of the training that is included in the grant is a four-day training strategies workshop at the training facilities in Seattle. During the workshop, class attendees focus on ways to develop staff and public training programs that utilize the Gates computers.

Library staff are enthusiastic about the contributions the granted equipment and support have made in their communities. As more libraries and community organizations develop mutually beneficial partnerships, it is likely that libraries will be better equipped to sustain and maintain their technology programs.

In order to find out how grant recipient libraries are partnering with community organizations to offer public training, I surveyed many of the past training strategies class participants. They sent me wonderful examples of how they are partnering with organizations in their communities to meet the demand for computer training.

What are some of the challenges to supporting and sustaining public access computing? Simply putting computers into a library does not ensure that they will be used or that the library can manage the expense and effort needed to keep them running. How does a library that has already stretched its budget to the limit accommodate the expense of maintaining several new computers? Not only that, how do they afford training and materials to ensure that patrons get the most use out of them?

Often grant recipient libraries have had computers, but not a computer lab. Sometimes they have not had any computers before receiving these grants. Receiving the new computers causes almost universal concerns for libraries. One of the biggest issues is that as soon as the public becomes aware of the computers, they demand computer training. Often the demand is so great that the library is unable to satisfy the public's needs. As an example of this demand for computer training, we received a picture from a recent grant recipient and training strategies class participant from Arlington, Texas, that captured the first day their library offered sign-ups for computer classes. The line of patrons extended from the information desk out the door of the library!

Reaching out to the community is one way to find needed support. Discovering organizations that are willing to provide supplies and materials in exchange for library service is a worthwhile effort that every library should investigate. Taking that kind of partnership a step further is something many libraries have done in order to offer needed computer training for children, young adults, and adult patrons.

Who benefits when a library partners with community organizations to support computer training? The library is able to reach new audiences, increase registered users, breathe new life into its programming, and use organization volunteers to relieve some of the burden on its own staff. The partner organization can benefit from the library's computers and other resources, the knowledgeable and well-trained library staff, and the ability to offer its members important and interesting programming. Other organizations that may not have considered that the traditional resources of the library would be valuable to them will perhaps take a second look now that the libraries can connect the community with resources that go beyond the traditional library landscape.

When I surveyed our former training strategies class participants, many provided examples of partnerships that illustrate extremely valuable and practical benefits to both the libraries and the partner organization, just as many libraries reported that the intangible benefits of effective public relations and the opportunity to reach out to the community were just as valuable as any benefit with a price tag. Several respondents to my request for information stated that partnering with community organizations was incredibly helpful in getting the word out into the community about services that the library offers. As Jennifer Dunham from the Statesboro Regional Library in Georgia told me, "We want an opportunity to promote our services to new people." She said that people view the library as a non-threatening venue in which to take a computer class.

The computers act as magnets, drawing in people who may not have visited the library in a long time. Several people mentioned that once people are in the door, they react with awe to the training and classes that are available in the library. "I didn't know the library did that!" is often heard.

Where can libraries find partnership resources? There is plenty of information available about establishing partnerships between libraries and community organizations. The American Library Association (ALA) has established this issue as a matter of primary importance and has partnering tips listed on its Web site <http://www.ala.org/celebrating>. These tips apply to any partnership situation and are certainly applicable if a library is considering establishing a partnership to support its public access computing efforts. Those tips suggested by ALA include:

- Have a clear vision of what your library stands for and what it brings to a proposed partnership.

- Research your potential partner to discover potential conflicts and mutual areas of interest, what it can offer the library, and how it can benefit from the library. Make sure your staff and library board understand the nature of the partnership, its requirements, and benefits.

- Appoint one person to coordinate and nurture the relationship.

- Don't undervalue the worth of your library. Its good name and visibility in the community are an invaluable source of goodwill.

Where are libraries finding partnership possibilities? There are plenty of youth-serving organizations that can be appropriate partners for libraries for offering computer training. Those libraries that I surveyed have established effective partnerships with many of these organizations, including Boys and Girls Clubs, YMCA and YWCA, Girl Scout and Boy Scout troops, church groups, 4-H clubs, school districts, summer day camps, and homeschool organizations. The partnerships with these groups focus on children and providing access to computers.

Organizations that serve adults can also benefit from the library resources and can help libraries reach the audience they need to serve. Consider literacy agencies, career centers, computer users groups, senior centers, and city or county service agencies.

The Gates library computers offer three main types of software—the Microsoft Office Suite, the Microsoft Encarta Reference Suite, and children's titles from several different sources. Many community groups would certainly make good use of these resources. Career centers need access to word-processing software, homeschool students can use reference titles for research, and the children's programs provide educational opportunities for all kinds of children's groups, like the Boys and Girls Clubs.

At the Escondido Public Library in California, Rosemary Tarenskeen reports that they have developed a very successful partnership with the Council on Literacy. The council has placed a full-time Americorps Volunteers in Service to America Program (VISTA) volunteer in the library's computer center. The VISTA staff member provides outreach for literacy and teaches computer skills as part of the literacy program. The VISTA volunteer also will be conducting a computer camp for seven- to fourteen-year-olds this summer. In addition to the outreach that the VISTA staff member provides for the library, this person has also procured equipment for the library, including a projector screen and a laptop through grants received on behalf of the library.

The Escondido Public Library also partnered with Education Compact, an organization that provides tutoring for students. Through this partnership, the library received a grant to create a teen center called the "Teen Hot Spot." Billed as the "coolest place to be" in the local newspaper, the Teen Hot Spot has overstuffed chairs, restaurant-style booths, and computers available anytime the library is open. The Education Compact provides materials and staff to assist teens with career-related and informational questions. More information is available on their Web site at <http://www.ci.escondido.ca.us/library>.

In Farmington, New Mexico, the library system established two "Power Libraries," one in the Boys and Girls Club and one in a senior center. These Power Libraries provide book collections and computers on-site at the community centers. The library provides staff to conduct computer training, and the centers provide space, publicity, and volunteers to maintain and staff the computers. The centers and the library also co-write grants to fund materials and equipment.

In Texas, the Victoria Public Library partners with the Victoria County Genealogical Society. A volunteer from the society visits the library at least twice a month and teaches a class for the public on genealogical Web sites and genealogy research on the Web. The society's members benefit from the partnership by having access to the library's resources, including a genealogy site on the Web that the library funds.

The Central Arkansas Library System in Little Rock, Arkansas, partners with the Shepherd's Center, an organization for senior citizens sponsored by local churches, synagogues, and mosques. The library staff teaches classes for the members with the help of volunteers from the center. The Shepherd's Center takes care of advertising the classes, registering the students, and calling to remind students about the classes. Lynette Jack, the manager of computer and network services for the library, says the partnership has been a great success due to the library staff's willingness to adapt the classes to the needs of the seniors and the Shepherd Center's help in handling all of the administrative details.

In Odessa, Texas, the Ector County Library has a longstanding partnership with the local junior league. The junior league had a goal of reaching at-risk individuals and lessening the gap in the digital divide. It provides volunteers who teach and give one-on-one assistance in the library's computer lab. They also contributed funds to help the library become automated. The junior league used the partnership with the library to help them achieve their goals while making important contributions to the library.

In McAllen, Texas, the library shares a building with the city parks and recreation department. The parks and recreation department supplies teachers for the classes offered in the computer lab, which include classes in Spanish. They also use the computer lab to conduct summer day camps for kids. In this partnership, the library supplies the computers and the parks and recreation department supplies the teachers.

In Mountain Home, Arkansas, the library has partnered with the local computer users group, which mostly consists of retired people. The group supplies a volunteer to monitor the lab every hour that the computers are available for public access.

In Tiffin, Ohio, the Tiffin-Seneca Public Library has an arrangement with Heidelberg College. The college places honor students at the library to teach computer classes. Karen Culp, assistant director, states that this partnership is valuable to the library because without it, the library would not be able to offer as many computer classes. It's also beneficial to the college because the honor students are required to perform community service in order to graduate. The students not only complete their community-service hours, but also they are mentored by library staff and learn to conduct themselves in a professional manor. Karen reports that the classes are full, and patrons keep requesting more!

At the Lewis and Clark Library in Helena, Montana, Candice Morris reports that county employees taught MS Word and Excel using the Gates Computer Lab, and all of the library staff members attended the classes for free. The library also held classes for seniors at a local senior-citizen center for a week. After the classes, the senior center provided volunteers to assist library staff with the public classes.

In Xenia, Ohio, the Greene County Public Library partners with the Greene County Career Center, which offers classes on the Microsoft Office Suite in the library's computer lab. This partnership prepares the library staff for teaching Office programs, and the career center can continue to teach classes that don't compete with the library's offerings. The career center benefits by having the opportunity to reach out to many more people than might have signed up to take a class through them, and they get to advertise their other programs as well.

At the Shasta County Library in Redding, California, the Volunteer Information Partner (VIP) Program creates partnerships with local organizations to bring volunteers to the library. VIP partners agree to provide volunteers in the computer lab for a set day and time to help library users sign on and off computers and to answer computer questions. Since the computer lab is staffed only by volunteers, this has been a great help to the library. VIP partners include the IBM/PC users group and the Redding Mac users group. The Mac users group also sponsors classes and currently teaches Internet classes. Large banners in the computer lab promote the name of the VIP partners, and the partners are allowed to place flyers about their organizations and events in the computer lab.

The Jackson District Library in Jackson, Michigan, has partnered with a community computer lab called the Ayieko Resource Center, which serves a low-income neighborhood through the Jackson Housing Commission. These popular classes are taught by library staff, and at one time involved a waiting list of more than one hundred fifty people. The library trained the center's volunteers, and now the center volunteers teach classes at the community center.

On a statewide level, Maine has a program called GOALS, Go Online with Americorps at Libraries and Schools <http://www.goals formaine.org> [no longer extant]. This program is a partnership between the governor's office, Americorps, and public libraries throughout the state. In six regional hubs, Americorps staff have offices in public libraries and provide training on the computers for library patrons. The goal of the program is to train ten thousand Maine citizens by the end of the three-year period. This is a great example of how this kind of partnership can work at a statewide level.

What are some of the ideas people have for future partnerships? Many of the grant recipients who responded to my request for examples said, "We haven't done it yet, but here is what we are thinking of!" So, I'm including a section here titled "good ideas—under construction."

At the Paulding County Library in Ohio, Director Susan Hill has a great idea for partnering with the local Ohio State University extension office and local 4-H clubs to have kids create projects using the computers. The kids can then submit the projects to be judged in the county and state fairs. What a great way to blend the new and the traditional!

In Rock Hill, South Carolina, the York County Library will be partnering with the City of Rock Hill's Hispanic Task Force to introduce library services to their Hispanic community. The task force and York County Regional Chamber of Commerce have already cosponsored a refresher course in Spanish for library staff.

In Virginia, the Montgomery-Floyd Regional Library System hopes to partner with Virginia Tech to offer some advanced training classes in the library's computer lab.

Several libraries also reported that they were seeking out opportunities to provide internships to local high schools and community colleges.

Conclusion

On the ALA Web site is a report titled "Public Libraries as Partners in Youth Development: Challenges and Opportunities." In this report, Urban Libraries Council president Eleanor Jo Rodger states, "Public libraries can become much more energetic partners in community development. They should be at the meeting table with other organizations and agencies that are interested in improving the quality of life for the people of that community. The challenge for libraries is to understand how their skills and traditional roles can be used in concert with those of other organizations." The full report is located at <http://www.ala.org/plpyd//dwtoc.html>.

Having computers may give libraries the opportunity to come to the meeting table within their communities, and to contribute to organizations and agencies that seek to improve the lives of their citizens in new ways that blend their traditional functions and new roles.

Recommended Reading

Bailey, Samantha and Sara Ryan. "Making Web Space for Young Adults: Issues and Process: A Case Study of the Internet Public Library Teen Division." 1996. http://www.isoc.org/isoc/whatis/conferences/inet/96/proceedings/ h4/h4_3.htm

Burwell, Lisa A. "Too old to surf? No way! An Internet course for seniors." *American Libraries*. Nov. 2001: 40–2.

Christensen, Susie. "How We Work to Make the Web Speak." *Computers in Libraries* Oct. 2001. http://www.infotoday.com/cilmag/oct01/christensen. htm *A librarian at the Danish National Library for the Blind shows you how they help organizations create online information that is available to everyone.*

Coyle, Karen. "Blueprints Needed for Information Highway On-Ramps: Librarians Have To Create A Standard for Exactly What "Universal Service" Means." *American Libraries*, Dec. 1997: 35–36.

Fialkoff, Francine and Eric Bryant, eds. "Movers and Shakers" Spec. Issue of *Library Journal*, March 15, 2002. *Includes profiles of several people who've done wonderful outreach programs, including Felton Thomas, of the West Las Vegas Library, Ben Ocón: Salt Lake City Public Library, Jennifer Chang of the Free Library of Philadelphia, and Veronica Myers: El Paso Public Library System.*

Chapter 6

The Techno-Economic Imperative

No question about it, buying technology for your library is like mowing the lawn—you can't do it just once and be done with it. Once you've got the computers and the fast Internet connections and the databases, you have to keep on buying newer faster computers, because no matter how many you have, your patrons will want more. You must continually buy new or upgraded software for all those machines. You have to hire expensive techies to make all the systems work, and spend money training staff on how to use them. You have to renew database subscriptions every year, often at the expense of books, newspapers, and other materials. (To get an idea of the extent to which costs have shifted from print to electronic resources, read Andrew Albanese's survey of library budgets in the September 1, 2001 *Library Journal*.) Is there anything we can do about the costs of our technologies? Well, yes, actually.

Solution
Build Your Own Systems

Can You Build It? Yes You Can!

Janet L. Balas

I am certain that when [*Computers in Libraries'*] editors picked this month's theme, Home-Grown Technology Solutions, they intended that this issue would inspire and encourage librarians everywhere to undertake their own projects. While the issue may have its intended effect for many, I am sure there are others who will become depressed while reading these marvelous success stories, believing that there is no possibility that they could ever have enough vision, enough technical expertise, enough time, and, yes, even enough money to attempt, let alone succeed, in developing an innovative, totally home-grown solution that would merit inclusion in a technical magazine.

A technology project doesn't have to be large in scope, nor does it have to chart unexplored territory, in order to be successful. I believe that a successful technology project is one that meets the unique needs of a specific library with its own particular population of users. When technology was first making its way into the library, employees and users often feared automation projects, believing that the new technology would be a great leveler, limiting services to only those that were routine and could easily be automated. In the early days this may have been true, and these first-generation systems seemed to demonstrate that a "one size fits all" solution could perhaps be more accurately characterized as "one size fits some." Information technology has grown more sophisticated, however, and librarians and patrons have grown more demanding, insisting that technology solutions have the flexibility to meet their libraries' unique needs. This is the promise of technology, and new applications are coming closer to achieving the ideal of providing "unlimited sizes to fit all."

This ideal still hasn't been achieved, however, in most current library technology applications, so many of us must turn to home-grown solutions to meet the needs of our users. Sometimes these projects are large and stunningly innovative, while others are smaller, focused on a particular gap in service. Both large and small projects can do a spectacular job of improving services—as long as they are the right solutions for the individual library and its users. Since many of you may still be feeling overwhelmed by all the enthusiasm for grand innovation, we'll look at some Web sites that point you to home-grown solutions—both large and small—that may help you find realistic ideas.

Innovation in the Library

When I was beginning my research for this column, I was astounded to find that there was a site that was tailor-made for this topic. The site is named, most appropriately, Innovative Internet Applications in Libraries, and offers links to the Web sites for projects that vary both in scope and design. The projects are divided into categories including Ages & Stages for those designed for special segments of the service population, Books and Reading Lists for Web-based reader's advisory services, Catalogs and Directories for examples of different formats for the old-fashioned library catalog, and Local Databases for local information projects. The "My Library" Personalized Interfaces section of links stresses customization, while providing electronic access to unique materials is the focus of the Special Collection & Online Exhibits section. Projects that provide online counterparts of familiar library services such as library instruction, guided tours, reference desk services, and well-known forms (such as those for interlibrary loan) are listed in the Tutorials/Guides, Virtual Tours, Virtual Reference Desks, and Web Forms sections. There are also links to sites helpful to librarians who are planning technology projects in the Site News & Evaluation and the Miscellaneous Helpful Sites for Cybrarians sections.

The authors of this site urge librarians to explore the various project sites, especially because some of them include narrative descriptions of the projects that are very helpful. My library has been making determined efforts to provide new services to teens, so I was very interested in the teen-related projects of other libraries, and I spent time examining each of those aimed at this population. I also enjoyed the virtual tours of many libraries. Particularly impressive was that of the Huntington Library in San Marino, California, with its use of QuickTime VR to provide panoramic views of its lovely botanical gardens. It might be reaching a bit to say that it is the next-best thing to being there, but seeing these beautiful gardens in this format has caused me to put this library on my "must visit" list for the next time I travel to the West Coast.

Best Practices in Canada

The Internet makes it easier for librarians to learn about exciting innovations in other countries. Canada has documented some of its library technology projects on a Web site titled "Best Practices" 2001—Innovative Internet Use in Canadian Public Libraries. The projects are divided into the following categories: community partnerships, supporting local economic development, electronic service delivery, and content creation. I was particularly intrigued by the proposed "Bookboat" complex of the Prince Rupert Public Library.

The Bookboat is not solely a technology project, but it would be just about impossible to design a library these days without information technology as an integral component of the plan. The project leaders are making use of the Web while Bookboat is in the planning stage in order to involve potential users in the design. Their vision is explained on the Web site, and interested parties are invited to submit their questions and observations through an electronic feedback form. Responses to comments from the public are included on the site. As I said earlier, I find this project intriguing and I plan to visit the Bookboat Web site from time to time to check on its progress.

Innovators Win Awards

Another way to learn about interesting projects is to visit library awards sites on the Web. LIANZA, the Library and Information Association of New Zealand Aotearoa, offers the 3M Award for Innovation in Libraries. This year's finalists and the winning entry are described in a press release available on the LIANZA site. It also had links to two of the three finalists, but, unfortunately, there was no link to the winning project. One of the projects, by the Manukau Institute of Technology Library, titled Get Ready Go, was a PowerPoint comic strip introduction to using library resources. Not a large project, certainly, but easily within the reach of many librarians looking for a new way to connect with reluctant users.

Consult with Your Library Automation System Vendor

Since most librarians lack the expertise to write their own automation systems but still know exactly what they want from a system, many have worked with their vendors to customize their automated systems to meet their individual libraries' needs. A good way to learn about these projects is to visit your library system vendor's Web site. It will often highlight innovative projects. The SIRSI Corp.'s Web site, for example, has a customer spotlight feature that highlights special achievements. Many vendors also sponsor electronic discussion lists for their customers, and customization questions and solutions are a frequent topic for discussion. Sometimes a small tweak to a system can make all the difference in the world to users, and these discussion lists can help you tweak successfully.

Is Linux Right for You?

I am sure that there are many technology enthusiasts who enjoy the challenge of a large project. While these ambitious types may not always have the opportunity to "go where no librarian has gone before," they would at least like to go where few librarians have gone before. A relatively new course in library automation is the use of Linux. Eric Sisler, of the Westminster Library, has developed a Web site titled Eric's Linux Information based on his experience implementing Linux in his library.

Another site for librarians interested in using this platform is the linux.in.libraries site. Linux-in-libraries is an electronic mailing list that covers its use in academic, public, and special libraries. Archives of this recently organized list are maintained on the Web site, as are the archives of the earlier mailing list, Linux4lib. A list of resources is also available, and the list owners encourage participants to send in any resources they find useful so they can be included on the site.

The Library of the Future

Planning a successful project involves looking ahead to possible new uses of information technology in the library. Research related to Internet resources and digital projects is featured on a special page on the Internet Library for Librarians site. The projects are described as "significant and special," so they could be characterized in many cases as broad-based research initiatives rather than specific projects. But the research results in many of these undertakings, such as the Cooperative Online Resource Catalog (CORC) from OCLC, which explores the cooperative creation and sharing of metadata, will have important implications for library technology in the not-too-distant future. Librarians who are looking ahead should be aware of current research in information technologies and its application in libraries.

I hope those of you who were intimidated by the thought of developing your own home-grown solutions are feeling a bit more confident now that you realize that not every project has to change the library as we know it. Yes, some home-grown technology plans do require significant technical expertise and an abundance of time, energy, and determination. Others, however, may be less ambitious in scope, but are no less successful if they meet the needs of the libraries and their users. Good ideas are out there to help us find solutions for our library "homes," and with the Internet we can share our innovative solutions with libraries around the world.

Resources Discussed

Innovative Internet Applications in Libraries <http://www.wilton library.org/innovate.html>

Welcome to the Huntington VR Tour <http://www.huntington.org/ VRTour/Welcome.html>

"Best Practices" 2001 <http://ln-rb.ic.gc.ca/e/about/bestprac/>

Waterfront Bookboat Complex <http://www.bookboat.com/>

Media release, 3M Award for Innovation in Libraries <http://www.lianza.org.nz/award_3m.htm>

SIRSI Corp.—Clients <http://www.sirsi.com/Sirsiclients/index.html#spotlight>

Eric's Linux Information <http://gromit.westminster.lib.co.us/linux/>

Internet Library for Librarians—Library Projects <http://www.itcompany.com/inforetriever/project.htm>

Reprinted from *Computers in Libraries*, Feb. 2002. Copyright 2002, Janet L. Balas. Used by permission.

Solution
Open Source Systems and Applications

Linux in Your Library?

Eric Sisler

Media coverage and general awareness of Linux has exploded in the past few years, but perhaps a short review is in order: Linux was created by Linus Torvalds, then a student at the University of Helsinki, Finland. It is an open source UNIX clone that aims at POSIX (Portable Operating System Interface) compliance. It is developed and maintained by many UNIX programmers and wizards worldwide via the Internet.

Linux itself is the core piece of software that allows other programs to communicate with the hardware. When most people talk about Linux, what they're really talking about is a Linux distribution, which includes the Linux kernel and a wide variety of software from other sources. Linux would not exist without major contributions from two other sources: the Free Software Foundation's GNU project and

Berkeley Systems Design (BSD) UNIX, one of the original flavors of UNIX. Beyond the Linux hype, these are the benefits and drawbacks to using Linux. What are the criteria for deciding if Linux is right for your library? If it is, how do you get started.

Advantages to Using Linux

First, the good news: there are many advantages to using Linux as your server's operating system. Linux doesn't have the overwhelming hardware requirements of other operating systems. It will run on nearly any of Intel's family of x86 processors and clones, which means getting started with Linux can be relatively inexpensive. Although my library's Linux boxes now live on server class hardware, they started out running on desktop PCs. One server was a recycled 486/66 with 16Mb of RAM and a whopping 300Mb disk drive! This may not sound like much by today's standards, but it was more than adequate for the server's duties at the time.

Linux can be purchased on CD-ROM from one of several Linux distribution vendors or downloaded for free from the Internet. Purchasing Linux on CD-ROM is a good way to get started because distributions typically include an easy-to-use graphical installer, a wide variety of commonly installed software, documentation, and often limited installation support. All the software packages included in the distribution have been checked and will, in most cases, work and play well together. Linux doesn't have any licensing issues, so one copy can be installed on any number of computers, a definite advantage over commercial operating systems.

Linux is open source, which means that all noncommercial software includes the source code. Although this may not be of interest to the average user, it allows those so inclined to make improvements and submit bug fixes back to the software's maintainer(s). These changes are often incorporated into the next release of the software, thereby benefiting all users.

Linux is an extremely stable operating system. Other benchmarks and testimonials aside, it has been astoundingly reliable at our library, Westminster PL, CO. There are only a few occasions when a server running Linux must be rebooted: to install/replace hardware, after an extended power outage, or when installing a new kernel. There are no regularly scheduled reboots, and the record for continuous uptime at our library stands at 201 days, with computers powered down only to install more memory, a redundant power supply, and a larger UPS (uninterruptible power supply). We have never experienced software-related downtime and frankly don't expect to.

Linux also doesn't suffer from software "bit rot," meaning that system performance doesn't degrade over time until the operating system must be reinstalled from scratch. Like many modern operating systems, Linux uses shared libraries, similar to Windows, called .dll files. These shared libraries reduce the size of compiled binaries (programs) and provide a standard set of functions and procedures. Unlike other operating systems, regular software packages do not arbitrarily overwrite these shared libraries or install their own versions. This greatly increases system stability and prevents newly installed software from breaking existing software. It also means that software doesn't have to be installed in a particular order to get everything to work correctly. The only time these shared libraries are upgraded is when installing a new release of Linux or when the libraries are intentionally upgraded.

The Linux Software Package

Most Linux distributions use some type of software package management utility, similar to the Windows install/uninstall wizard. This makes all aspects of software management much easier to live with by handling package installation, upgrading, verification, removal, and dependency checking. Verification ensures that all files originally installed are still present and reports any differences. Dependency checking verifies that all other required software is already installed and prevents new software from overwriting files already installed by another package. Software packages can also be digitally signed by the package's creator, ensuring that the package hasn't been tampered with.

With the recent attacks on servers running Microsoft's Internet Information Server (IIS) and the ongoing battle against Outlook-transmitted viruses, it's refreshing to know that Linux is immune. It is not completely free of vulnerabilities, but its overall design makes it difficult for viruses and worms to have any effect.

Linux Disadvantages

Now the bad news: as with any operating system, there are some disadvantages to using Linux. A big potential disadvantage is the steep learning curve associated with Linux. There just isn't any way around this except to grit one's teeth and get through it. However, once some of Linux's initial complexity has been conquered, things begin to make more sense and get easier.

Many libraries don't have computer support staff and either make due with technically minded library staff or, in some cases, support from their parent organization. A possible solution could include training library staff and/or a support contract from a distribution vendor, hardware retailer, or local consultant. Fortunately, the numbers of Linux-related training services and support providers continue to grow.

Because no one owns Linux, organizations considering its use get nervous. Often they feel that without "someone to blame" they risk being stuck with a problem they can't fix or with an obsolete operating system. Linux relies heavily on support from the community to report and fix bugs, often resolving problems much faster than traditional software vendors. With no single commercial entity owning Linux, there's no danger of it going "out of business," even though distribution vendors may come and go.

Is Linux Right for Your Library?

At Westminster PL, Linux evolved from a UNIX learning tool to the operating system on servers that provide access to virtually everything except the catalog. . . Linux isn't for everyone, so here are some things to consider before jumping into it:

- Does your library automation software run on a UNIX platform? If so, Linux can provide an inexpensive and safe way to learn more about it. During the learning process you'll probably discover a way to use Linux at your library.

- Do you have Linux/UNIX support staff available? This might be in the form of library support staff or your organization's Information Technology (IT) department. If so, you might be able to garner support and encouragement from them.

- Does someone on your staff have the desire to learn more about Linux/UNIX? If so, round up a spare desktop PC, purchase a Linux distribution, and let them experiment. The benefits of this may not seem obvious at first, but you'll reap the rewards later as you begin using Linux for everyday tasks.

- Are you looking to provide new services to patrons and staff? Perhaps you are already providing file, print, and CD-ROM databases via some other means but want to offer a new service. If so, chances are good that Linux has software to do just what you need at a price that's tough to beat.

- Are you about to retire older servers or desktop PCs that are too old to run other operating systems? Since Linux's hardware requirements can be quite minimal, consider putting it on an older server or desktop PC.

- Are you looking for an alternative to expensive commercial solutions? Linux can provide virtually the same services as a Novell Netware or Microsoft NT/2000 server at a fraction of the hardware and software costs. The technology budget for our new library was quite limited, so by using Linux we were able to purchase more computers for staff and the public.

- Are you looking for a more reliable operating system? As Joe Zelwietro of the Prince Rupert Public Library in Canada found out, sometimes NT servers begin acting up, requiring frequent re-boots. Faced with the prospect of having to re-install NT, he decided a better solution would be to use Linux as the library's Internet connection/firewall. Zelwietro replaced an ailing NT server running MS Proxy server with a Linux server running ipchains (native Linux firewall tools). After testing the new firewall with a few clients, he set up DHCP [Dynamic Host Configuration Protocol] and directed the rest of the library's PCs through the new firewall, pulling the plug on the NT Proxy server.

Adding Linux to Your Network

One of the best ways to get started with Linux is to pick a single task. The knowledge gained from configuring that first service will help with consecutive tasks and gradually things will get easier.

Most libraries have small connections to the Internet, which may be shared by a number of branches or even with the rest of the organization. Setting up an Internet cache server is a good way to take some of the load off the library's Internet connection.

Squid is a good, solid Internet cache and is included with most Linux distributions. Basic configuration is relatively easy, although a library with a lot of Internet PCs will probably want to run Squid on a server with plenty of RAM and fast disk drives. Our main branch has a 23-workstation instructional classroom, and the effects of installing Squid are quite noticeable there. As the instructor is demonstrating a site, Squid is busy caching many of the site's pages and graphics. Squid then serves these cached items as each student workstation requests them, resulting in faster retrieval time and a reduction in Internet traffic.

Although more and more databases are moving to the web, many libraries still have the CD-ROM version, often available at only a single PC. These standalone PCs often have changers attached to them that are slow to switch discs and can be a hassle to maintain. A Linux server running Samba can provide CD-ROM database access to multiple PCs. If the server has enough disk space, the CD's contents can be copied to the drive, eliminating the overhead of multiple CD-ROM drives or towers.

Apache is the most widely used web server on the Internet, and we use it to serve a variety of web pages: the public PC's homepage, staff recommendations, statistics, Linux information, and so on. A web server is a great place to put documents of all types that need to be easily accessible, regardless of whether they are regular HTML documents, PDF files, or even Excel spreadsheets.

If you have or are considering getting your own Internet domain, Linux can provide an inexpensive way to administer it. Providing DNS records for internal devices like PCs, printers, and network equipment aids in device identification and troubleshooting. DNS, or the Internet "phonebook," maps host names to their corresponding IP addresses.

Dynamic Host Configuration Protocol, or DHCP, provides centralized management of a client's TCP/IP settings-host/domain name, IP address, default gateway, DNS servers, etc. Once a network is up and stable, changes are generally pretty minimal, but DHCP can save you a great deal of time should an unexpected change occur. Although the "D" in "DHCP" means "dynamic," it can be used to assign static addresses to PCs, which we do for a couple of reasons. One, some of our web databases are authenticated by IP address, which would present a problem if IP addresses "drifted" from PC to PC. Two, by assigning static addresses to all PCs, troubleshooting is easier: we know that each PC always gets the same IP address. Matching a PC with its corresponding host name makes it easy to locate.

Linux can provide a wide variety of network services, all at a fraction of the cost of a commercial operating system. If your library is considering alternatives (to commercial operating systems), Linux is definitely worth investigating.

Resources

Westminster Public Library's Linux pages, where many of the following resources are also listed. <http://gromit.westminster.lib.co.us/linux>

The Free Software Foundation <http://www.gnu.org/fsf/fsf.html>

Google's Linux search engine <http://www.google.com/linux/>

Linux Online—general Linux Information <http://www.linux.org/>

The Linux Documentation Project <http://www.tldp.org/>

The Open Source homepage <http://www.opensource.org/>

O'Reilly publishing, home of the "Animals" & "Nutshell" series. <http://www.oreilly.com/>

Solution
Support and Contribute to the Free Online Scholarship Movement

A unique feature of our problem with expensive journals is that the scholars those journals are dependent on contribute their work for free, and yet libraries at the universities where those scholars do their work must pay exorbitant subscription fees to get the benefit of their work. Academic library budgets in particular have been distorted, with the costs of serials—including subscription databases—forcing reductions in purchases of books. This problem came to a head just as the Internet presented an interesting alternative—free online scholarship.

Where Does the Free Online Scholarship Movement Stand Today?

Peter Suber

There's a lot happening these days to create free online access to peer-reviewed scientific and scholarly journal articles. Here are some of the more significant trends:

- More disciplines are setting up preprint archives.

- More open-access peer-reviewed journals are popping up in every field. Most of these are online-only. But journals like *BMJ* [*British Medical Journal*] and *Cortex* show that even the costs of a print edition do not foreclose the possibility of free online access to full text.

- More universities are supporting institutional self-archiving for their research faculty.

- More priced journals are experimenting with ways to offer some online content free of charge, and experimenting with ways to cover the costs of providing this kind of free access.

- Editorial "declarations of independence" against publishers who limit access by charging exorbitant subscription prices are becoming more common. See my list at <http://www.earlham.edu/~peters/fos/lists.htm#declarations>. The most recent was last October, when 40 editors of *Machine Learning* issued a public letter explaining their resignation from the journal. One of the editors, Leslie Pack Kaelbling, then launched the *Journal of Machine Learning Research*, which MIT Press agreed to provide to readers free of charge. More scholars are demanding that journals offer free online access to their contents. The Public Library of Science, <http://www.publiclibraryofscience.org/>, has collected more than 29,000 signatures from researchers in 175 countries in the six months since its launch. More white papers,

task forces, projects, and initiatives are endorsing the Open
Archives Initiative. The two most recent are the
International Scholarly Communications Alliance,
<http://makeashorterlink.com/?A15D6226>, and the
Budapest Open Access Initiative, <http://www.
soros.org/openaccess/>. More initiatives are acknowledging
that progress requires the launch of new open-access
journals. Both the Public Library of Science (PLoS) and the
Budapest Open Access Initiative (BOAI) have come to this
conclusion.

One of the most interesting trends is for priced journals to experiment with free online scholarship (FOS). In the February [2002] issue
of *Information Today*, Derk Haank, the CEO of Elsevier, said that his
company has the same goal as the PLoS, <http://www.infotoday.
com/it/feb02/kaser.htm>. Even though this is a very misleading over-
statement, Elsevier is making some notable experiments in FOS. For
example, it owns ChemWeb and the Chemistry Preprint Server, which
both provide free access to all their contents. It allows authors to self-
archive preprints, even if not postprints. Its science search engine,
Scirus, not only searches Elsevier journals, but a growing number of
FOS sources such as Medline, BioMed Central, and arXiv. Finally,
Elsevier has started distributing science books through ebrary, which
allows free online reading of full texts, and charges users only for
copying and printing.

In general, *Nature* offers free online access only to tables of contents, abstracts, the first paragraphs of selected articles, and other
special features. Nevertheless, *Nature* hosted an important online
debate about FOS, <http://www.nature.com/nature/debates/e-
access/>, and of course it provides free online access to the contributions themselves. *Nature* has also agreed to be a partner in the
Alliance for Cellular Signaling [AfCS], <http://www.cellularsignaling.
org/>, which will put all the research discoveries that directly result
from its funding or reagents into the public domain. Papers that

survive AfCS peer review, will be considered—and be retrievable—as papers published in *Nature*. (AfCS will launch in the spring or summer of this year.)

Even though a growing number of journals like *BMJ* and *Cortex* offer FOS without half-measures or experiments, these experiments by Elsevier and *Nature* are nevertheless promising. They show a recognition that scientists and scholars are demanding open access and that this demand is legitimate and increasingly realistic. Moreover, of course, every journal or archive that moves to free online access for even part of its content is enlarging the absolute quantity of FOS, enlarging the proportion of FOS relative to the entire body of scholarly publications, changing the expectations of future authors and readers of research literature, and adding to the competitive pressure on journals that limit access to paying customers.

One of the most important FOS initiatives to date is the Budapest Open Access Initiative, which was launched on February 14. (Full disclosure: I am one of the drafters.) BOAI is important for several reasons. It endorses "parallel processing" or multiple strategies. It supports self-archiving and the launch of new open-access journals, two compatible and complementary approaches that have too often been pursued in isolation from one another. Second, it applies to all academic fields, not just to the sciences. Third, it is accompanied by a detailed FAQ, <http://www.earlham.edu/~peters/fos/boaifaq.htm>, no small thing for an initiative whose primary obstacle is misunderstanding (more on this below).

Finally and above all, BOAI brings serious financial resources to the cause. The long-term economic sustainability of FOS is not a problem. We know this because creating open access to scholarly journals costs much less than traditional forms of dissemination and much less than the money currently spent on journal subscriptions. The only problem is the transition from here to there. The BOAI is especially promising because it understands this and mobilizes the financial resources to help make the transition possible for existing journals that would like to change their business model, new journals that need to establish themselves, and universities that would like to participate in self-archiving. George Soros' Open Society Institute has pledged $3 million for this cause and is working to recruit other foundations that can add their resources to the effort.

There are three recurring objections to FOS initiatives, and all are based on misunderstandings. Because I've already heard all of them raised against the BOAI, let me run through them quickly. One is based on copyright, one on peer review, and one on funding.

1. The first objection is that we are advocating the reform, abolition, or even the violation of copyright. Not true. We want to use copyright to support open access. The copyright holder has the right to make access open or restricted. We want to put copyright in the hands of authors or journals that will use it to authorize open access. Copyright reform may be desirable for other reasons, but it is not at all necessary for the complete realization of FOS—and we are too busy to fight unnecessary battles.

2. The second objection is that we want scientists and scholars to post their research articles to their home pages and bypass peer review. Not true. The primary body of literature for which we want open access consists of peer-reviewed research articles. Peer review is essential for science and scholarship, and entirely compatible with open access to the papers it vets and validates. Again, peer review reform may be desirable for other reasons, but it is not at all necessary for the complete realization of FOS.

3. The third objection is that we think open-access publications costs nothing to produce, or that we have no way to cover these costs. Not true. We know that peer review costs money. Open-access journals will have expenses beyond peer review as well, though not many. Taken together, however, these expenses are far lower than for print journals and

far lower than for online journals that want to block access
to non-subscribers. But they are non-zero, and more costly
than simply posting articles to one's home page.

Here the misunderstanding is corrected once we acknowledge that
open-access journals will not be free to produce, and therefore will
need some revenue or subsidy in order to be free for readers.
However, once correcting the misunderstanding, we still face the
objection that we have no way to cover these costs. Our full reply to
this objection has several parts. Here's a sketch. First, the scope of the
FOS movement is limited to scholarly journal articles. We pick this
focus not because these articles are useful (as if everything useful
should be free), but because they have the relevant peculiarity that
their authors do not demand payment. Moreover, in most journals
and most fields, editors and peer reviewers do not demand payment
for their work either. Second, the costs of open-access publication are
significantly lower than the costs of print publication or limited-
access online publication. So the required subsidy is significantly
smaller than the budget of the average contemporary journal.

Third, we have a general revenue model for open-access journals.
The basic idea is to charge for disseminating articles rather than for
accessing them. There are many variations on the theme, depending
on who pays the cost of dissemination (which includes the cost of peer
review). A model that will work well in the natural sciences, where most
research is funded, is to regard the cost of dissemination as part of the
cost of research, to be paid by the grant that funds the research.
BioMed Central is a for-profit provider of FOS whose variation on this
theme is to charge authors, and let authors make whatever arrangement they can to obtain the funds from their grants or employers.

The economic feasibility of FOS is no more mysterious than the economic feasibility of television or radio. In both cases, funders pay the
costs of dissemination so that access will be free for everyone. In the
case of public television and radio, the funders are volunteers of means
and good will. In the case of commercial television and radio, they are

primarily advertisers moved by self-interest. The variations on the theme matter less than the general approach to pay for dissemination so that access is free. There are many successful and sustainable examples in our economy in which some pay for all, and those who pay are moved by generosity, self-interest, or some combination. Either way, those willingly pay to make a product or service free for everyone rather than pay only for their own private access or consumption. This funding model, which works so well in industries with much higher expenses, will work even better in an economic sector with the nearly unique property that producers donate their labor and intellectual property, and are moved by the desire to make a contribution to knowledge rather than a desire for personal profit.

Here are two trends that will guide the future of the FOS movement. On the one hand, the scholarly communication crisis (also known as the serials pricing crisis), which has long troubled and mobilized librarians, is starting to trouble and mobilize scientists and scholars themselves. On the other hand, this is happening much too slowly and incompletely. Most scientists and scholars are still oblivious to the magnitude of the crisis and even its existence. (A good introduction to the data and issues can be found [on the Create Change Web site], <http://www.createchange.org/faculty/issues/quick.html>.) This matters because the most important means to this very important end are within the reach of scientists and scholars themselves, and do not depend on legislatures or markets. One of the most effective ways that you can help the cause today is to educate colleagues about the seriousness of the problem and the beauty of the solution.

'Superarchives' Could Hold All Scholarly Output: Online Collections by Institutions May Challenge the Role of Journal Publishers

Jeffrey R. Young

Professors' office computers hold a wealth of original content: research articles, data sets, field notes, images, and the like. Some of the material will be published in journals months or years after it is created, but even then it will probably be available only to the journals' subscribers. The rest will never see the light of day.

Several colleges are now looking to share more of that work by building "institutional repositories" online and inviting their professors to upload copies of their research papers, data sets, and other work. The idea is to gather as much of the intellectual output of an institution as possible in an easy-to-search online collection. One college has called its proposed repository a "super digital archive."

Proponents say such superarchives could increase communication among scholars and spark greater levels of innovation, especially in the sciences. Some imagine a day when every research university gives its research away through the Web, allowing scholars and nonacademics to mine it for ideas and information.

"The whole power of science is the power of shared ideas, not the power of hidden ideas," says Paul Jones, associate professor of information and library science at the University of North Carolina at Chapel Hill. "Science advances when there's a free exchange of ideas. We move faster by being open. We know this, but we have disincentives right now to openness."

One of those disincentives, many scholars believe, is the scholarly journal system, which, critics argue, has a monopoly on scholarly output that leads to ever-soaring subscription prices. Institutional repositories could create an alternative to journals, fans of the archives say.

Journal publishers, meanwhile, say that such repositories are unlikely to supplant their publications. Journals, they argue, are still the best means of distributing and preserving research.

And even some of those supporting the new archives recognize the difficulty of getting professors to change their habits. To make the archives work, professors would have to take the initiative to submit their materials, and, in some cases, persuade journals they work with to allow them to place their articles in a repository.

Establishing a Model

The most ambitious and most closely watched superarchive is being developed at the Massachusetts Institute of Technology. It is called DSpace, and its goal is to collect research material from nearly every professor at the institute—though participation will be voluntary.

"We want to give faculty the infrastructure that supports alternative forms of publishing," says MacKenzie Smith, associate director of technology for MIT's libraries. Over the past two years, officials at MIT have been building a set of software tools to support the repository, and to make it easy for professors to submit material. Those tools are nearly ready, and four departments and programs at MIT will be testing them this summer.

Beginning this fall, MIT plans to open the archive to all of its professors. "We don't know how quickly it's going to catch on," says Ms. Smith, though she adds that professors have been enthusiastic about the concept.

The biggest obstacle may be inertia. Professors are busy, and they may not use the repository if they perceive it as more work, even if they like it in principle, says Ms. Smith.

"We've gone to a lot of trouble to make the submission process very simple for faculty," she adds.

Librarians don't plan to actively police what goes into the repository, though they do offer rules for what kind of work should be included. Among those rules: Work must be "scholarly or research oriented," and it must be "complete and ready for 'publication.'" Some departments might choose to have someone serve as editor of their department's DSpace contributions, to read over them before they are placed in the archive.

To make sure the new repositories don't lead to information overload, librarians are making sure that the materials are tagged with "metadata" codes to help search engines navigate the sea of data. Such tags include keywords, publishing information about the article (if applicable), or an indication of what language the article is written in, for example. Some departments may have graduate students or staff members handle the virtual paperwork for professors. The DSpace software will add the tags using information supplied by users.

"The time involved for preparing the metadata is a small price to pay for having these documents available for the long term," says Nicholas M. Patrikalakis, a professor of ocean engineering at MIT. Mr. Patrikalakis's department is participating in the pilot project and plans to upload its technical reports.

But new search tools would need to be developed to make full use of the metadata tags. So far, traditional search engines like Google aren't equipped to do that—though librarians say such tools would be relatively easy to create.

Professors who use the repository won't have to make all of their materials public. Researchers will be allowed to select access levels for each item they contribute. Some research may be made available only to those within MIT, while other materials may be free to anyone.

Why Share?

An incentive for making material available is that sharing research helps professors build their reputations, some experts say. Some research shows that the more professors open up their work, the more likely they are to get cited by their peers.

In computer science, for instance, articles that appear online are significantly more likely to be cited by other researchers than those that do not appear online, according to a study of computer-science research literature done by Steve Lawrence, a research scientist for NEC Research Institute Inc. "The mean number of citations to offline articles is 2.74, and the mean number of citations to online articles is 7.03, or 2.6 times greater than the number for offline articles," Mr. Lawrence wrote last year in *Nature*.

Different disciplines have different attitudes about how much sharing is appropriate, says Ms. Smith. Scientists often seek to get their research out as soon as possible, while scholars in the humanities might worry about someone stealing their ideas, she adds.

MIT officials say they hope institutional repositories will catch on across academe, and they plan to make the DSpace software available free to other colleges that want to use it. In fact, MIT plans to lead a "federation" of libraries that want to use the software, helping them with whatever policy issues arise, says Ms. Smith.

"We've had pretty serious interest in the system from about 30 major institutions," Ms. Smith adds. The DSpace project is supported by a $1.8-million grant from the Hewlett-Packard Company. Officials aren't sure exactly how much the archive will cost to maintain, though universities already have much of the equipment in place to run digital archives. Still, Ms. Smith estimates that DSpace could cost up to $250,000 per year, if all of the costs were added up. The hope is that free software tools will allow even small colleges to run repositories using their existing resources.

Early Adopters

Meanwhile, a few other universities have begun building their own superarchives, often at the urging of provosts or other administrators who want to showcase their professors' work and increase its impact.

One example is the California Institute of Technology, which has already built an institutional repository <http://library.caltech.edu/digital> with material from several departments. Much of the drive for Caltech's repository came from its provost, Steven E. Koonin, who is also a professor of theoretical physics.

"We do outreach and public education in so many different dimensions," says Mr. Koonin. "Why aren't we doing the same with the scholarly information we produce, which is the core of what the research institution does, most of which is funded by the public?"

Setting up the framework for an archive was the easy part, however. Getting professors to contribute is proving more difficult. "It's a slow process," says Eric F. Van de Velde, director of library information technology at Caltech. "We talk to people all the time" to try to get them to include material, he adds. "This is not foremost on the mind of any faculty member, and changing the work flow kind of takes time." So far, about 600 papers are in the archive, which has been in place for the past few years.

Another superarchive was recently created to serve the University of California system. The archive, called the Scholarship Repository, is run by the system's California Digital Library <http://escholar ship.cdlib.org>.

Colleges setting up repositories also have to set clear guidelines for who owns the copyright to the materials. At Caltech, professors retain copyright to anything placed in the archive, but they must sign waivers allowing the university nonexclusive rights to keep copies in its collection.

But professors don't always have the right to place their published papers in archives, or even on their own Web pages. Many journals require scholars to sign over all rights to works that are accepted for publication.

Several journals have recently changed their copyright policies, however, to allow authors to place copies of their papers in personal or institutional archives. But some publishers that have made such policy changes, such as the American Physical Society, don't make it easy for professors. Scholars must make their own Web versions of their articles by revising their own drafts to reflect editors' changes.

Librarians discourage professors from ever removing work from their repositories, so that once a paper is archived, it's there for good. "We don't want this to become like a bulletin board," says Mr. Van de Velde. "We want this to be a serious form of dissemination."

The repositories also encourage dissemination of materials that once remained hidden, including photographs and other multimedia.

"The more you go out and investigate what's going on in the faculty, the more you discover the rich, rich assets that are there," says Joseph J. Branin, director of libraries at Ohio State University, which is setting up the framework for an institutional repository called the OSU Knowledge Bank <http://www.lib.ohio-state.edu/Lib_Info/scholar com/KBproposal.html>.

Some professors have expressed concerns that universities might try to profit from the new repositories. Planning materials for super-archives at both MIT and OSU contain suggestions for how the university could charge a fee for access to selected materials.

But proponents of the repositories say that universities have an incentive to make the archives free to all. "The special literature that is at issue here ... is worth incomparably more to researchers and their institutions through its research impact than through any pennies that could be made from charging pay-per-view tolls," says Stevan Harnad, a professor of cognitive science at the University of Southampton, in Britain.

Changing Role for Journals?

The do-it-yourself, or self-archiving, approach by colleges establishes a new front in the struggle between colleges and journal publishers over how much research should be made available free online. College administrators have long been frustrated by the current academic-publishing system, in which colleges pay the overhead costs for the research and then must pay again to get access to the research results.

Since last year, more than 30,000 scientists have pledged to boycott journals that do not make their content free online no later than six months after initial publication. But despite the pledges, led by a group called the Public Library of Science, few scientists have actually withheld their articles, and few publishers have changed their ways.

Many of those who are active in the Public Library of Science boycott are now working to help spark alternative outlets for scientific publishing, such as institutional repositories. Even so, many who are working to build institutional repositories say they aren't trying to put publishers out of business. Instead, they say their efforts may change the role publishers play.

"Obviously, the information revolution is causing us to rethink how we do scholarly communication and dissemination," says Mr. Koonin, Caltech's provost. If colleges can handle distribution on their own, journals may focus on managing peer review and lending their seal of approval to the best scholarship, and charging authors rather than subscribers for their services.

"The print journals bundle together [several activities]—refereeing, editorial standards, dissemination and marketing," Mr. Koonin says. "What the technology starts to let you do is to unbundle those. You could have dissemination done by one organization or mechanism, but peer review done by another one."

Nice Idea, in Theory

"That will not work," says Arie Jongejan, chief executive officer of Elsevier Science and Technology, a division of Reed Elsevier, one of the largest commercial academic publishers. "You need publishers to organize that process."

"If I was a researcher, I would be scared to death to make myself dependent on that solution [institutional repositories]," adds Mr. Jongejan. Journals, he says, "do things very efficiently and very smoothly."

Elsevier does allow its authors to publish their papers in institutional repositories or other noncommercial archives, provided that the authors ask permission first. He says that fewer than 5 percent of authors ask.

Other attempts at widespread reform of academic publishing have fallen short. For instance, physicists have built a successful online archive of pre-prints—articles that are distributed before being reviewed by journals. That effort began more than 10 years ago, and some scholars predicted that other disciplines would soon build their own online pre-print archives. But few disciplines have even tried.

The reason is that disciplines are not the right agent for change, says Mr. Harnad, of the University of Southampton. "The right entity for all of this is the university," says Mr. Harnad, who is an outspoken proponent of nontraditional academic publishing. "There is no entity behind a discipline," he adds, but universities have an economic incentive to try to reduce the cost of scientific publishing.

"We are in this confusing stage where it's very difficult to say what it's going to be like 10 years out," says Lorcan Dempsey, vice president for research at OCLC Online Computer Library Center, a nonprofit library group. "The patterns of research and learning and communication are really shifting."

Most institutions are waiting to see how DSpace and other repositories develop before they join in, says Richard K. Johnson, enterprise director of the Scholarly Publishing and Academic Resources Coalition, an alliance of research institutions, libraries, and organizations that encourages competition in scholarly communications.

"A lot of institutions are thinking about this right now," Mr. Johnson says. "Over the course of the next year or so, we'll see quite a few of them beginning to deploy."

One way or another, colleges seem interested in collecting and showing off more of their scholars' work online. As Mr. Dempsey puts it: "I think there's greater attention being paid to the whole range of informational assets on campuses."

Tools to Build a 'Superarchive'

Several new free tools are available or under development to help colleges create "institutional repositories," superarchives of all research generated by the college's faculty members.

DSpace

What: Massachusetts Institute of Technology's project to develop a superarchive, as well as software tools for creating and maintaining the repository. The tools will be offered to other colleges that want to use them.

When: DSpace has been under development for two years. The university is testing it this summer, and plans to make the software available free to anyone in the fall, when the university will invite all professors at MIT to contribute to its archive.

Where: <http://web.mit.edu/dspace>

EPrints.org

What: Free software developed at the University of Southampton, in Britain, to help individual scholars, departments, or universities create archives of research papers online.

When: Available since 2000. An updated version was released this year.

Where: <http://www.eprints.org>

Open Archives Initiative

What: A series of "metadata" codes that librarians or others can attach to research papers to help search engines pull out desired information.

When: Available since 1999. An updated version was released last month.

Where: <http://www.openarchives.org>

One of the obstacles in the way of free online scholarship has been the lack of prestige accorded it because of the suspicion that peer review is inadequate. That's one reason to pay some attention to a project called MERLOT (Multimedia Educational Resource for Learning and Online Teaching, http://www.merlot.org/Home.po/), which provides peer-review of discipline-specific Web resources.

Solution
For the High Cost of Systems Technicians: Grow Your Own

A Course in Accidental Systems Librarianship

Rachel Singer Gordon

I never wanted to be a computer geek; in fact, I've been resisting the idea for years! In high school, I was the kid with the Atari, and while my fellow computer owners were cutting their teeth on BASIC programming, I was more interested in playing games and dialing up local bulletin board systems. In college, I graduated to using a monster of an IBM XT, on which I learned WordPerfect function keys inside and out, but neither wrote one line of code nor hacked into a single government agency. In the mid-1990s, when it became apparent that I would have to go back to school to earn a marketable degree, friends urged me to consider computer certification. Reluctant to lock myself into a future of dealing primarily with machines, I chose instead to attend library school with my trusty 486 by my side—and was introduced to the Internet for the first time. The rest, as they say, is history.

After graduating in 1996, I accepted an entry-level reference position at the Franklin Park Public Library District (FPPLD), which serves a population of 19,500 in Chicago's near-west suburbs. Like most smaller suburban libraries at the time, FPPLD was going through a period of technological transition. Internet access for staff had been enabled just months before my arrival. Although the card catalog had been closed in 1993, it was still available to and widely used by patrons. Our text-based online catalog was accessed through dumb terminals, some of which were hooked to noisy dot-matrix printers. The library possessed several stand-alone PCs for staff and public use, but maintained neither a Web site nor an internal network. Out-of-order signs abounded, purchased software stacked up for lack of someone to install it, and an environment without antivirus software or effective security made the use of public PCs treacherous at best.

Something needed to be done. Because I liked computers and was comfortable with some of the basics, I began to unofficially take care of some of the problems that were stacking up. Because I was willing to tackle some needed projects, such as hardware installation and setting up new PCs, I moved into the new role of reference/computer services librarian in 1998. As we acquired more machines, more software, and more demand for technology of all types, my systems responsibilities grew ever greater.

We implemented Internet access for patrons in 1998, and since then have offered public Internet training sessions several times a month. Our Web-based OPAC went online in late 1999, at which time we sold off the card catalog drawers and gained ourselves a lifetime supply of scratch cards. Since then, our internal Windows NT network has allowed the introduction of basic but useful functions, including laser network printing, file sharing, and intranet Web pages. Our Web site <http://www.franklinparklibrary.org> launched in the spring of 2000, and has developed to offer such popular features as an extensive local history section and home access to our OPAC and electronic databases. Our PC population has exploded to 36 (small by some standards, but sufficient for a library our size), and we recently said a less-than-tearful farewell to our last dumb terminal. Our security and antivirus software have been beefed up, and our planned migration to an all-Windows-2000 environment in early 2002 should further simplify security and workstation management.

All of these changes were necessary for a library that wished to remain technologically relevant for its community, but each required that someone take responsibility for project management, technical support, and the countless smaller steps that have enabled us to reach this point. I am now the head of the computer services department at FPPLD—a one-person department that was created in 1999. I still don't want to be a computer geek ... but I have come to accept that technology and librarianship are now intertwined to the point where many of us need to step into the more palatable role of systems librarian. Although I, along with many information professionals in similar positions, graduated from library programs that (at the time) lacked an emphasis on current technology, we are by personality and by training uniquely suited to adapt traditional library skills to the challenges of integrating and supporting computer technology in our libraries.

In this article, I'll be your instructor as you go "back to school" and learn to apply library class work and principles to real-world systems challenges. Each listing in the course catalog that follows is a required element for aspiring graduates of the School of Accidental Systems Librarianship. None requires previous experience or programming expertise; the only prerequisites are a background in librarianship, a willingness to learn, and an interest in technology. In the description of each area of study, I'll tell you how my experiences at FPPLD have inspired the necessity for that part of the curriculum—and hopefully impart advice that will allow you to learn from my mistakes. Although some course work may seem basic, remember the 80/20 rule: Those who absorb the lessons below (some 20 percent of what an IT person in a large institution may be expected to know) will be prepared to deal with 80 percent of the situations that normally occur in a smaller computer-dependent library organization. Those of us in smaller libraries without an IT department to call on can still keep those all-important systems up and running—most of the time!

Course Description #1: Organization of Knowledge

The organization of human knowledge is one of the basic tasks of librarianship, and learning effective organization is also a basic necessity for any successful library systems administrator. Computer services librarians are required to keep track of systems information, software licenses, vendor contacts, passwords, and each system's (and user's) individual quirks. Extra credit for those who collocate information on an institutional Web site!

Lessons in this course stem from personal experience. When I assumed responsibility for the computer systems at FPPLD, I inherited a jumble of manuals, disks, random computer parts, and software. The need for organization was soon made clear when one of our malfunctioning PCs took a trip to the computer store and came back with a new motherboard, having had the contents of its hard drive and all its settings wiped completely clean.

Problem one arose when Windows 95 declined to plug-and-play nicely with the existing graphics card. Windows decided that 16 colors were enough for any application, but several of our CD-ROMs had a differing opinion. Having no record of the brand and model of the video card, I had to take a screwdriver to the case, open the machine, and look at the card itself to see its type so that I could download driver software from the manufacturer's Web site. Lesson one, therefore, focuses on the importance of accurate record keeping of systems information. Students will learn to do a basic inventory of computer systems, assign each PC an identification number (or letter—Dewey is less than relevant here!), and print and keep systems information for each piece of library equipment.

Problem two followed soon after, when, video drivers safely in place, I began installing our CD-ROM programs back onto the hard drive. A number of products required a customer or serial number in order to function, but I had no record of such numbers. Resolving this issue required a call to technical support, a willingness to sit through a good 10 minutes of Muzak, and a chance to incur the scorn of the product representative who had to look up our records. Lesson two in this course, then, emphasizes the necessity of good record keeping of vendor and software information. Related topics include the necessity of maintaining good relationships with vendors and using your records to identify hardware and software in need of upgrading.

Whether you choose to keep your records in a database, in a 3-ring binder, or on little scraps of paper all over your desk, the need for effective organization and record keeping remains constant. Non-catalogers may take heart; this course differs from basic cataloging in that only you need to be able to retrieve the information, and only you decide how much information is necessary and in what format you'd like to keep it.

Course Description #2: Basic Research Techniques

Successful reference librarians know that they don't have to "know" everything—they just need to know how to look it up. As computer systems and software grow in complexity, few of us non-computer-geeks carry in our heads solutions to every situation or question. Previous experience, however, gives us a starting point, and information-seeking skills allow us to navigate the complexities of such misnamed resources as the Microsoft Knowledge Base.

In this course, aspiring systems librarians will learn strategies and starting points for finding solutions to the seemingly random glitches that plague any computer system.

Class exercises include the following:

- Searching the Microsoft Knowledge Base for an actual error and applying the solutions you find.

- Tracking down technical support phone numbers and e-mail addresses on the Web site of one of your major vendors.

- Locating alternate sources of tech support when a vendor's site lacks the answer and pay-for-support wants to put you on hold for 45 minutes.

The emphasis in this course will be on learning when and where to "look it up" when the answer to a computer-related dilemma is not readily apparent. A willingness to take the time to search for information before starting a repair can save hours of frustration. It took a number of times to beat this lesson into my head, but here is just one example: We'd purchased a new computer for our children's department, and after I had spent some time loading software, removing extraneous icons, and doing other basic setup, I went to install their UMAX scanner. This was an older scanner, so installation involved removing a SCSI card from their old PC, installing it in the new machine, and loading scanner drivers. The card installation went smoothly, the computer recognized the scanner, I installed the drivers from CD, and went to reboot. Big mistake. The system halted on boot up with a threatening "VMM32.vxd missing or corrupted, unable to load Windows" error.

I'll spare you the long version of this sad tale, but suffice it to say that quite a bit of time and energy could have been saved with a simple visit to the UMAX Web site. Their KnowledgeBase lists this as a known error and provides simple step-by-step instructions for its resolution. The lesson here? When in doubt, try looking it up.

Course Description #3: Learning How to Network

Even with the plethora of research resources available, you'll sometimes have to rely on others' expertise to help solve your technical dilemmas. Systems librarians appreciate the value of networking—in all of its senses. So in this lesson you'll learn how to interact with your online peers, whom to turn to when you need answers to your questions, and how to effectively manage your online networking to gain the most value from these connections. Participants in this course will be required to join at least one e-mail discussion list for systems librarians and to contribute at least one relevant post to the discussion. Topics include: locating and searching list archives to determine whether your question has been asked (and answered) in the past before posting, creating a professional e-mail signature file, and composing an effective question that includes enough information for readers to answer.

Over the past few years, numerous librarians have taken the time to help me resolve issues that they'd previously faced in their own institutions. One happy byproduct of joining pertinent e-mail discussion lists is that, just by reading, you'll find answers to questions you did not even know to ask, or ideas to try in your own library. Examples of useful items I've seen just in the past few months include free JavaScripts for library Web pages, virus warnings (arriving in time to download new virus definitions), suggestions on HTML editors and graphics software, discussions of Internet policies, and lists of current awareness sites for systems librarians. Participants on discussion lists also often post job ads, calls for papers, or conference information—all of which help you to keep track of what else is out there for systems librarians.

Course Description #4: Instruction Techniques

Librarians have always assumed a large number of roles, among them, that of teacher. Traditional bibliographic instruction focuses on giving library users the skills they need to locate and use library resources. In this Instruction Techniques course, you'll move beyond the bibliographic and learn to use those teaching abilities to deal with computer and electronic resources more effectively. We will cover a range of topics:

- The qualities of a successful technology trainer—These include patience, the ability to break complex lessons down into small steps, and a willingness to eschew jargon.

- The characteristics of an adult learner—We'll discuss how people learn, what motivates them to do so, and the need to make any computer instruction relevant to your learners by teaching them what they want to know.

- The responsibilities of a wired institution—If you provide public Internet access, are you obligated to provide training sessions? If you provide staff with updated office or automation software, how do you teach them to use these new resources effectively?

At FPPLD, I've been teaching public Internet and OPAC classes for several years, and I provide ad hoc training for staff whenever we complete a software upgrade (transferring our e-mail software from VMS mail to Eudora, for example). Although change can be disconcerting, having someone willing and able to provide training goes a long way toward keeping a library relevant in the Internet age. Participants in public Internet classes range from elderly who want to learn to find travel information or e-mail distant grandchildren, to younger trainees who want to use online resources to find a job or fill out a financial aid application. Some may have just purchased computers for their homes, while some may come back to log on at the library. Regardless of participants' reasons for attending, providing such classes allows us to expand the library's traditional interest in advancing literacy to promoting electronic literacy.

Phil Agre's "How To Help Someone Use a Computer" <http://dlis. gseis.ucla.edu/people/pagre/how-to-help.html> is required reading for this course.

Postgraduate Studies

Lifelong learning is a necessity for any effective information professional, but is an especially important concept for systems librarians whose responsibilities include keeping up with constant advances in technology. Unfortunately, many smaller libraries lack the funding to send staff to often-expensive computer classes and workshops. This makes it necessary for systems librarians to be proactive about educating themselves on the systems and software that are most commonly used in their environment.

Luckily, computer training is in such demand that a plethora of low-priced online classes and self-paced Web-based tutorials is available. For example, when I was preparing to install our Windows NT network, I enrolled in a $59 NT server administration class from ZiffDavis University (it's now SmartPlanet, and it no longer offers that class). You do get what you pay for and the course was basically glorified self-study, although an instructor was available to answer questions via online forums. The structure of being in a "class" and having to complete workbook exercises, however, forced me to spend some time learning basic server operation, which otherwise would have taken a back seat to my day-to-day responsibilities. I'm in no way prepared to take the Microsoft Certified Systems Engineer (MCSE) exams, but am able to move around the operating system, add users, assign permissions, share folders as drives, and carry out the other basic operations that comprise 80 percent of what needs doing to keep the network chugging along.

To earn extra credit in your independent study, take advantage of working in a library. Each month, scan one or two of the computer magazines your library subscribes to for new tips and tricks. If you receive solicitations for free computer weeklies such as *Network World* or *Information Week*, sign up. You won't have time to read all the articles, and some will be too technical or just irrelevant, but set aside an hour or so each week to skim through the articles that look pertinent. Sign up for free e-mail newsletters such as Information Today, Inc.'s NewsBreaks <http://www.infotoday.com/newsbreaks/breaks.htm> and *InfoWorld's* newsletters <http://www.iwsubscribe.com/newsletters> on a number of technology topics. Be liberal with the delete button, but make note of pertinent news and tips—this will often be your best way of keeping informed of virus alerts, software patches, and other timely technical topics.

Graduation and Beyond

Although the above lessons have been described as separate classes, the successful systems librarian will use these skills in combination. Mastering the organization of knowledge, for example, will help you learn where to research problems, while your independent study will give you the background to know when you need to do so. The patience and persistence you cultivate during your training sessions will be assets when the first five solutions you try for a computer glitch fail to solve the problem. Once you've completed the curriculum you won't be a full-fledged computer geek, but you will be better prepared to help your library cope with technological change. You'll be worthy of the title: systems librarian!

Further Reading

Wilson, Thomas. *The Systems Librarian: Designing Roles, Defining Skills*. Chicago: ALA Editions, 1998.

Recommended Reading

Albanese, Andrew. "Moving from Books to Bytes." *Library Journal* 1 Sept. 2001: 52–54.

Block, Marylaine. "Doing It Right: How Some Universities Encourage the Creation of Prime Research Web Sites. *Searcher* Sept. 2002: 42–47. http://www.infotoday.com/searcher/sep02/Block.htm

Computers in Libraries. Its articles are always useful and always readable.

Gordon, Rachel Singer. *The Accidental Systems Librarian*. Information Today, Inc., 2003.

Jacoby, Christopher. "How I built a failure-resistant web server for free." *Computers in Libraries* Feb. 2002: 24–28.

Mayfield, Kendra. "College Archives 'Dig' Deeper." *Wired News* 3 Aug. 2002. http://www.wired.com/news/print/0,1294,54229,00.html

Mickey, Bill. "Open Source and Libraries: An Interview with Dan Chudnov." *Online* Jan. 2001. http://www.infotoday.com/online/OL2001/mickey1_01.html

Poynder, R. "The Open Source Movement." *Information Today* Oct. 2001. http://www.infotoday.com/it/oct01/poynder.htm

Schaffner, Bradley L. "Electronic resources: A wolf in sheep's clothing?" *College & Research Libraries* 62.3 (2001): 239–49.

Troll, Denise A. "How and Why Are Libraries Changing? A White Paper." Presented to the Digital Library Federation 9 Jan. 2001. http://www.diglib.org/use/whitepaper.htm

Chapter 7

Running to Stay in Place: Continuous Retraining

Stop the World, I Want to Catch Up!

Marylaine Block

I have a question for librarians: how do you keep up with the changes in our technologies?

Perhaps, like me, you became a librarian because you love putting people together with the books and magazines and newspapers and children's literature and information they need, and now you find that you're expected to be expert at troubleshooting your computers, creating web pages, using scanners and PhotoShop and Power Point (all of which you have to keep re-learning as they add new features). Now, perhaps, you're learning chat in order to do virtual reference.

You may have learned HTML just in time to be told that you need to learn XML, or designed tip sheets on using a database two weeks before the vendor changed its interface. Maybe you taught a class on search engines and found within the next two weeks that one went out of business, one was no longer free, one came back from a near-death experience, and the others added new features.

AAAAAACK!!

How do you cope? How do you find out about new hardware, software, databases, web utilities, search engines, web sites, preservation techniques, and coding protocols? How do you decide which ones you have to learn and which ones you can ignore? Who do you trust to tell you which ones matter? How do you learn to use them?

How do you "learn the web"? Now there's an overwhelming concept—Google indexes over three billion pages now.

Traditionally we've kept up with changes in the profession through our professional associations, conferences, trade publications, and serious journals. Now, I suspect the mix includes, and maybe even favors, because of their immediacy, discussion forums and listservs, blogs, e-zines, and the web pages they refer us to.

I know that I rely on blogs for news and links to important sites and stories. I still attend conferences to hear speakers explaining new systems and ideas and to ask them questions. I also attend the exhibits, because the best way to understand new systems is to see demonstrations of how they work. I rely on e-zines and print magazines for lengthier explanations and research studies. [If you'd like to see what I read daily and weekly to keep up, check out my personal bookmarks page at <http://marylaine.com/home.html>.

E-mail subscriptions to Search Day <http://searchenginewatch. com/searchday/>, Search Engine Watch <http://searchenginewatch. com/> and Research Buzz <http://www.researchbuzz.com/> keep me up-to-date on changes in search engine capabilities. I regularly visit a few site review services to keep me up on new sites on the web <http://marylaine.com/netnew.html>.

I know what I do to cope with onrushing technological change. I DON'T know what you do. Please let me know your own strategies and sources.

> You can see what librarians told me about their keeping up strategies in part two of this article at http://marylaine.com/exlibris/xlib148.html.

Reprinted from *ExLibris*, 12 April 2002. Copyright 2002, Marylaine Block.

Solution
Individual Professional Learning

To Keep Up, Go Beyond: Developing a Personal Professional Development Plan Using E-Resources Outside the Bounds of Library Literature

Steven J. Bell

"How are you keeping up?" is a question that academic librarians are asking each other more frequently. It reflects our considerable efforts to cope with the deluge of information needed to keep pace with the rapid and turbulent change affecting the library profession.

Through its literature, conferences, and member interaction, librarianship offers multiple media for keeping personal professional skills current. But "keeping up," and, in fact, staying ahead on the innovation and creativity curve, requires academic librarians to go beyond the boundaries of their own professional development resources. This article identifies strategies for developing a personal current awareness program that draws from disciplines beyond our own.

The complexity of academic librarianship and the number of skills and technologies required for professional competency has radically altered the concept of "keeping up with change." It goes beyond being familiar with the latest library technologies or knowing the features in the latest version of an electronic database.

Change in fields once thought far afield or peripheral to our own, such as higher education, communications, computers, and instructional technologies, are today's innovation incubators. Keeping up with changes in those fields in addition to our own may seem an insurmountable task. The challenges are to find the sources that channel news of change to you in a way that requires minimal individual effort, and then to control your intake and digestion of information to avoid being overwhelmed.

Categories of Resources for Keeping Up

New technologies have changed the rules for keeping up, but also simplify the task. The old model depended largely on paper formats, while the new one relies on electronic publishing and distribution. Print is far from obsolete, but a thorough current awareness strategy must use electronic resources, especially for scanning diverse disciplines.

"Push" also characterizes these new literature formats. Either by subscription or other alerting technology, the latest information can be delivered to an e-mail inbox as easily as printed subscriptions appear in a physical mailbox. These new technologies fall into one of two categories:

- e-newsletters (sometimes called e-zines) and

- Web-based resources (magazines, journals and newspapers, Web sites, and Web pages).

As a mechanism for delivering concise and targeted information, newsletters are ideal. They cover a wide range of technologies and skill development. The migration from print to e-format increases their utility. The defining characteristics of the e-newsletter are e-mail delivery and hypertext. With their embedded links, the reader is often but a click away from discovery. If you don't mind advertisements, many are freely distributed.

E-newsletters themselves may fall into different categories. The most common type is an amalgam of text and links. Story items are usually brief and link to a Web page offering additional information. E-newsletters offering advice and commentary may often contain longer stories without links. There are no set boundaries, and the landscape abounds with hybrids.

Web-based resources can also be further divided by type. One subcategory includes magazines, journals, and newspapers. The other consists primarily of Web sites and pages that, when updated, report new information. Publications in the former subcategory typically provide full-text articles and industry news. The burden of keeping track of the release of new issues on these sites falls to the individual; though some publications are beginning to offer e-mail alerts of new issues, few offer such mechanisms. Tracking changes can be difficult.

Falling into the latter subcategory is the Web site or page that is periodically updated, but which is not intended to transmit information. These pages may have new, significant information two days in a row, and go static for weeks. You'd like to know whenever new information is added, but it is inefficient to check these resources on a routine basis. Taking advantage of Web-based publications and pages requires a device that provides an alert whenever a page has new information added, and does so via e-mail messages. Using a combination of resources in all three categories is a formula for a powerful and effective strategy for keeping up.

Delivered to Your Inbox

Relatively easy to publish and distribute, e-newsletters are becoming widely available in several areas of interest to academic librarians. The newsletters of greatest interest fall into four groups:

- higher education,

- instruction, teaching, and learning,

- Web technologies and design, and

- cool or new Web sites.

Here are some examples (URLs where more information is available are provided):

- *Chronicle of Higher Education.* While a subscription is necessary, some of the stories are provided free at the Web site of the *Chronicle.* The daily e-mail is divided into subject areas to facilitate honing in on sections of interest, such as information technology or distance learning. Go to <http://chronicle.com> for additional information. Higher education associations, such as the American Association of Higher Education or the American Council on Education, are other potential sources of news about developments in academia.

- *Online Learning News.* Free with advertisements, this newsletter combines text and links and is a rich source of ideas for bibliographic instruction and e-training. It focuses on techniques and products for electronic education, onsite and from a distance. Many of the items come from subscribers. It is published every other week. Access: <http://www.emailpub.com/lakewood> [no longer extant].

- *WebReference Update.* Reports on all types of Web site technologies, including JAVA, ASP, XML, multimedia technologies, and nearly any other cutting-edge technology that will help readers improve their Web sites. A recent issue included stories on using dingbats and clip art as Web graphics, and writing "friendly" HTML code. It is free, includes advertisements, is weekly, and has text and links. Access: <http://www.webreference.com/new>.

- *WebPromote Weekly.* Though clearly focused on the commercial Web site community, this free newsletter focuses on marketing and usability. What library can ignore information on how to improve a Web site? It is a good source for new ideas, covering topics such as statistics, user surveys, and multimedia Web technologies. It does contain advertisements, and features both text and links. Access: <http://www.webpromote.com>.

- *Internet Tour Bus.* Essentially a listing of cool and new Web sites that may be new additions to your Internet resource links or a potential source of new information for professional development, the Tour Bus is free and contains minimal advertising. It tends to give reliable information on viruses, hoaxes, and developments at technology companies. Access: <http://www.tourbus.com>.

Minding It on the Web

Web-based publications rarely offer a mechanism for update notification. That is why NetMind's Mind-It service is an essential tool for a keeping up strategy. Mind-It is simple and free. Anytime a URL in a subscriber's profile changes, the subscriber is alerted by e-mail. The message contains a link to the page, making it easy to then connect. One's profile can be modified at any time to add or delete URLs. To find out more, go to <http://www.netmind.com/>. A potential drawback is that some pages constantly are affected by minor change. Mind-It will not distinguish between important and inconsequential change. That may result in constant alerts of which few are of real value. There is a customization that can minimize this particular problem.

Web publications, sites, and pages tend to fall into the same categories as e-newsletters. Here are some additional examples of Web sites and pages that can be monitored with Mind-It.

- Alertbox: Jakob Nielsen's Column on Web Usability. Nielsen is a recognized expert on Web usability. Any librarian who manages or contributes to a Web site will benefit from Nielsen's insights into what makes a page work best. This is a free resource that carries no advertisements. Access: <http://www.useit.com/alertbox>.

- *New York Times Technology Page.* This Web page covers developments in computer and high technology fields. It is updated daily, but, to keep up, just follow the weekly digest, called the "seven day index." It's a quick way to stay abreast of cutting-edge technology, and follow the Web and Internet news. Access: <http://www.nytimes.com/pages/technology/index.html>.

- *Networking: The Node.* Just one example of the several pages devoted to the advancement of technology for teaching and learning. It disseminates news about activities and developments in distance education and learning technologies. Recent issues included stories on new interactive learning programs and innovative electronic classrooms. It is free and has no advertising. Access: <http://thenode.org/networking>.

- *Educational Technology & Society.* A free, full-text Web-based journal. Recent issues include topics such as lifelong learning and the ubiquitous use of technology in education. Issues also include Web site and book reviews and a column that explains new instructional technology devices. Access: <http://ifets.ieee.org/periodical>.

Avoid Getting Overwhelmed

One hazard in any keeping up strategy occurs when reading and reviewing alerts amount to an hour or more a day. Few of us can afford to allot that much workday time to this task. To prevent it from becoming a time-consuming burden, here are some strategies for minimizing the time devoted to keeping up.

- Be a browser. Many of the publications will be peripheral and you will want to follow up on only ten or twenty percent of the total. Get skilled at browsing. Do not attempt to read them in detail. Concentrate on spotting the one or two items you need to know.

- Use your e-mail client to get organized. Many e-mail software programs allow users to identify messages coming from specific addresses for routing to folders. Create a "keeping up" folder and set aside 15 minutes each day to scan its contents rather than stopping other activities throughout the day to read materials just arriving in your inbox.

- Print or capture and review later. Many "keeping up" resources primarily identify Web sites, and considerable time is spent visiting sites of interest to determine if they can be of further use. Avoid making those determinations online. It can be more efficient to make a quick site visit to print that page or use your browser to capture the page for offline viewing. Use your offline time to determine those sites worth a return visit.

- Share the load and tackle it as a team. Develop a list of all of the e-newsletters and sites you follow. Ask co-workers to join in a "keeping up" club. This distributes the load and reduces the likelihood of any individual getting over-whelmed. Participants can easily share important items by forwarding or cutting and pasting news into e-mail mes-sages. My staff and I quickly and simply alert each other to significant news items, and we provide proactive service to faculty and other administrators by sharing important news items we know they will want to see.

Conclusion

To discover new ideas and resources that could lead to innovation, librarians need to explore other fields. Our own literature communi-cates the latest trends in the theory and practice in librarianship, and it makes possible the ongoing dialogue needed to advance the pro-fession. But we need to go beyond this. We must be conversant with our colleagues who are instructional and computer technologists, and be able to understand the realms in which they operate. Others in our organizations respect our expertise and look to us for leader-ship and guidance in navigating through these turbulent times of fast-paced technological change. So what we know about the land-scape of the information age must be more than what we learned in our own profession.

Efforts to keep up will expend your most precious commodity, time. But consider the value of discovering one new piece of information, software product, or Web site that could save time, increase produc-tivity, provide better service, or simply raise the library's profile.

Time is the resource we must trade off to keep up, and there is no certain payoff. In that sense, keeping up is an activity not unlike an investment. It is risky because there is something to lose and there is no guaranteed return. But like an investment, if done cautiously, wisely, and with a clear strategy, there is no limit to what might be gained.

More "Keeping Up" Sites

There are more "keeping up" resources from within and beyond librarianship than can be contained in this article. For more information visit the "Keeping Up" Web page at <http://staff.philau. edu/bells/keepup>.

Solution
An Adequate Dedicated Library Training Budget

Of course the other question is, whose time and money are you learning on? Are you expected to learn this in your multitudinous spare time, or does your library give you time off to attend conferences and workshops? Do you have to pay your own expenses or does your library pay for travel to conferences and for staff tuition for coursework at local colleges?

The 1.6% Solution

James B. Casey

During my 29 years as a librarian I have noticed that our profession and the public library boards that govern us tend to be amazingly "penny wise and pound foolish" when it comes to investing in the very thing that libraries are supposed to promote—the growth of human knowledge. To an overwhelming degree, the intellectual growth of library staff and trustees enables a public library to be successful and brings about lifetime learning possibilities for many thousands or even millions of patrons. Yet, in the area of providing budgetary support for continuing education and professional involvement of librarians and trustees, great opportunities are often overlooked or rejected outright.

In virtually every case, the largest part of any public library budget is invested in staff salary and benefits. Of our Oak Lawn (Ill.) Public Library's total 2002 budget of $3.79 million, a full 52% ($1.97 million) is designated for salaries and an additional 16.3% ($618,261) for benefits. The total of 68% devoted to salary and benefits is close to the overall average for public libraries within the United States according to the 2001 Public Library Data Services Statistical Report issued by ALA's Public Library Association (PLA). It is fair to say that the overwhelming majority of all public-library dollars expended in the United States are devoted to compensating library staff. On the other hand, how much is invested by public libraries in the growth and development of the staff for whose services taxpayers have had to pay so dearly? Quite often the answer is, not enough or absolutely nothing at all. That is just about as crazy as spending $30,000 on a new car and then failing to pay for regular oil changes, tune-ups, and an occasional car wash. It just doesn't make any sense.

A Wise Investment of Public Money

How much would it cost to provide continuing education and professional growth opportunities for both library staff and board members? Oak Lawn Public Library expends only 1.6% of its total budget (about $61,000) per year in a category generally called "Dues and Meetings." Out of that 1.6%, professional dues for the Illinois Library Association and ALA as well as several other professional associations are paid in full for interested librarians and trustees; all expenses are covered for those librarians and trustees who attend ALA's Annual Conferences and Midwinter Meetings, and PLA Conferences; tuition reimbursement is provided in the amount of $1,000 per year for full-time staff and $500 for many part-time staff; in-service day programs are funded up to $5,000 per year; and funds are available for other staff incentive and morale initiatives. These funds also include recruitment money that pays for travel expenses for those coming to interview at our library for professional positions. That 1.6% goes a long way and the overall budget line has yet to be exceeded.

What about libraries with lesser budgets? With a small public library possessing a total annual budget of $300,000, 1.6% would represent $4,800 and might well cover all of the expenses noted for Oak Lawn, but reduced in amount to serve the needs of a proportionately smaller staff. In fact, the need for expertise and new perspectives might be even greater in a small public library where few people have to do much more varied work and respond to so many different challenges in the course of an average work day. In such cases, affording the time for staff to participate in professional growth opportunities might be an even more difficult challenge than setting aside the 1.6%. Nevertheless, finding the time and allocating the money are essential. This is especially true for those small libraries that hope to overcome the inertia and lethargy of the "We can't afford it" mind-set.

Professional development budget lines should not be seen as perks or as a fringe benefit of employment or trustee service. The expectation should be to develop human resources and thereby improve the library's overall performance. Traveling to conferences and participating in a substantive manner, taking courses to improve knowledge and professional ability, and belonging to and participating in professional organizations—all of this is quite often very hard work.

It takes a significant investment of time and energy to reach out for new information and for a broader perspective. That is precisely why 1.6% of the library's budget will probably never be exceeded by demand. Not everyone on a board or staff is likely to be both able and willing to get away for professional trips or night classes or to undertake homework assignments on weekends. At least, they may not be inclined to do so regularly or every year. Quite often it will be among the most creative, dedicated, and diligent trustees and staff who will want to use the professional development monies. Reimbursement for these expenses is not typically considered a benefit. The practical reality is that such considerations can possess considerable weight in the decisions of talented, creative people to join or continue to serve your library as "low pay" librarians or "no pay" trustees.

Knowing and learning more about what is going on in the library profession are only some of the benefits that accrue from investment in professional development of staff and trustees. Quite often, success with grants, levies, and public perception aren't just a matter of what you know but of who you know. Active involvement in professional organizations, traveling to conferences, publication in professional journals, taking classes, and broadening of one's contacts in the profession and in the political and/or academic spheres can greatly enhance a library's public profile. An increasingly influential library is also more likely to be a winning library when it comes to fundraising and passage of levies. The investment of that 1.6% in professional development can eventually leverage many thousands or millions of dollars.

Accountability Is Important

Even 1.6% of a budget can be considered excessive if it is perceived to be a perk for the staff and trustees. Alas, some of the horror stories of lavish expenditures of public money on various junkets and indifference to professional concerns are all too true. The waste of tax money can also be accompanied by horrible press coverage and possible litigation if expense accounts are used for illegal purposes. Accountability for the expenditure of both public monies and staff time is of the utmost importance.

Along with investing funds for support of professional development, it is equally important to invest time to develop policies outlining expectations for participation and parameters for the library's support. Oak Lawn Public Library has set policy guidelines and basic ground rules for both professional travel and continuing education (see below). In addition to such understandings, staff and trustees should prepare written reports describing their attendance at professional conferences and share any articles, speeches, or committee assignments undertaken as part of professional growth and sharing.

In terms of financial management, attendees should always keep receipts for conference expenses and make full, clear, and accurate reports since reimbursements are made with tax dollars and thus subject to audit. It is also possible that some expenditures that are not reimbursable by the library might be tax deductible.

To succeed in the Information Age, libraries have to invest more dollars in developing their human resources. This isn't an impossible quest. The often-repeated phrase "We don't have enough money" will have to be countered by creative thinking that looks at budgets from the perspective of problem solving rather than hand-wringing—from the perspective of where the library needs to go in the future rather than "doing what we have always done in the past." The future belongs to those who prepare for it.

Staff Development:

- Is an investment in a library's most expensive asset, its staff.
- Does not need to be a large budget line item.
- Raises your library's profile, helping with fundraising and passage of levies.

Creating a Staff Development Policy: Topics to Address:

- Length of employment required to qualify for funds.

- Reimbursement for use of personal auto, taxicabs, or other ground transportation.

- Standard mileage for frequently visited destination.

- Maximum reimbursement for round-trip airfare.

- Spouse travel.

- Parking, car rental, and tolls.

- Conference registration fees.

- Association membership dues.

- Rooms and meals: The limits per day for meals can be based on 75% of the per-day, single-occupant room rate.

  Breakfast = 15% Lunch = 20% Dinner = 50% Miscellaneous = 15%.

  Sample calculation if the room rate for hotel is $100:

  Total for meals = $75 Breakfast limit = .15 x $75 = $11.25 Lunch limit = .20 x $75 = $15.00 Dinner limit = .50 x $75 = $37.50 Miscellaneous = .15 x $75 = $11.25.

- Tuition reimbursement:

  Amount reimbursed as either a set amount or percentage of tuition.

  Grade or certification requirements for reimbursement.

Expectation of continued service after completion of reimbursed coursework.

Solution
Systematic Ongoing In-Service Training

The Learning Systems Approach to Staff Development and Training at Multnomah County Library

Janet Kinney

Multnomah County Library, with a history that reaches back to 1864, consists of a central library, 14 branch libraries and a collection of almost 2 million books and other library materials. As Oregon's largest public library, we serve over one-fifth of the state's population. Today our staff numbers 301 full-time, 201 part-time and 128 on-call employees.

The library has a long tradition of supporting staff training and development. In early 1998, the library had many elements of a "learning infrastructure" in place. The system had technology trainers who offered formal and informal instruction on technology topics; several committees were responsible for presenting training (the Reference Committee, for example); Multnomah County offered classes for staff; and outside vendors provided network training. Staff also participated as presenters and attendees at local, regional and national conferences and workshops, and supported each other through on-the-job training. But it was never enough, and with all of the changes happening in our work environment the challenges of keeping up-to-date were daunting.

One such change in our environment was the passage of a $37 million levy in 1997 and the funding of an extensive program of branch renovation. This new funding dramatically increased the number of public service hours and the number of public access computers and staff computer workstations. Public services hours increased 64 percent, including open hours every Sunday at Central and all branch libraries, and the computer count went from 604 to 1,008.

To help cope with this change, library management and staff identified training as one of the top organizational priorities and began to establish a more sophisticated, integrated approach to staff training and development. In early 1998, we decided to create the Learning Systems group to strengthen the learning environment and to help develop the processes and tools that would be required to distribute training and development throughout the library, and integrate learning into all library initiatives.

The Library, as a unit of county government, had also begun to integrate a quality program known as RESULTS (Reaching Excellent Service Using Leadership and Team Strategies) and was participating in the Oregon Quality Assessment process. A quality improvement council had been formed and the organization was beginning to move toward team-based initiatives.

The theoretical background supporting this decision was the work on learning organizations and chaos theory. For a useful mediagraphy on learning organizations see: <http://www.albany.edu/%7Ek17686/learnorg.html> [no longer extant.]. For information on Dr. Peter Senge's work see: <http://www.fieldbook.com>, and for a quick overview of the publication Why Learning Organizations? see: <http://world.std.com/%7Elo/WhyLO.html>.

This article reports on some of the first year's activities as we began implementation of the learning systems approach. Although these activities have been developed in the context of a large metropolitan library, we think the approach and some of the specific activities could be beneficial to libraries of all sizes and types.

The New MCL Approach

The learning systems approach was formally begun in July of 1998 and is just now beginning to emerge. This new kind of thinking and acting requires risk-taking and patience. It requires dialogue and discussion; revision and redesign.

Management

One of the first steps was to hire a Learning Systems Manager at the senior management level. This position was created to provide a "choreographer" to help direct the many already existing training activities toward the accomplishment of broader organizational initiatives, to help identify and fill in any missing pieces in the system's infrastructure, to reallocate resources as needed, and to help pace and prioritize the many training opportunities available to staff.

Staffing

Decisions regarding staffing have proven to be among the most difficult. The vision is to have a small number of positions allocated to learning systems, and to integrate learning and teaching into virtually every job description. Within this vision, learning systems staff are the coordinators and communicators, while staff from throughout the system are called on to help create curriculum and deliver the training.

In the first year the Learning Systems staff included a full-time senior manager, a supervisor (expanded from .5 to 1 FTE), a senior support staff (expanded from .5 to 1 FTE) and a trainer at the Librarian II level (decreased from 2 FTE to .5). In addition, over 100 staff participated in the direct delivery of staff training during the year.

We are currently reviewing the level of staff assigned to the group. Consideration is being given to establishing an adult learning specialist position to bring more expertise to curriculum development and design. The definition of this role will be a high priority in the next year.

Budget

A first-year imperative was to begin to assess the budget implications of distributed training. Each department has begun to analyze the cost of staff time spent developing, delivering and taking training as well as out-of-pocket expenses such as registration and travel costs. The Learning Systems budget included funds for unexpected training opportunities and team travel. Data collected this year will be used to improve our budgeting methods and to establish annual goals expressed as a percentage of total personnel budget.

Communication

Trying to keep everyone informed about the new learning approach presents a real challenge. An already existing intranet site and newsletter have been expanded to include broad coverage of learning opportunities. The Learning Center is the intranet site that attempts to provide one-stop access to a wide variety of learning related resources including lists of classes for staff, classes for the public, conference and workshop information and registration, independent learning resources (online tutorials, online learning opportunities), and professional development links.

Learning Systems also publishes the Learning Link, a newsletter of learning opportunities for MCL staff members. Published about every six weeks, this online newsletter announces forthcoming classes, features a popular column by the NT Server Manager, and generally tries to keep staff informed.

Individual Learning Plans

With so much going on in the organization, we needed to focus on the individual and his/her own learning needs. Adopting the "individual development planning" model often cited in human resources literature, we are deploying Individual Learning Plans (ILPs) for all staff. Prototyped by supervisors, managers and by staff at three branches, the ILP is now being rolled out to all staff. The ILP includes a self-assessment tool that allows staff members the opportunity to examine their own training/learning needs and to decide how to integrate this learning into day-to-day responsibilities. This emphasis on the responsibility of the individual to take charge of their own learning is an important component of learning organization approach.

Currently over 150 staff have begun to develop ILPs. The deployment of the plans is being staggered to help the system develop the capacity to provide the type of training and development activities that staff identify during this process.

New Staff Survival Training

On July 1, 1998, the MCL libraries increased public service hours by 60 percent. This called for a bold approach to training the new pages, clerks and library assistants that were being hired in large numbers.

Circulation Staff

We calculated that approximately 40 new circulation employees would have to be trained and ready to take their places at circulation desks throughout the system on July 1. Traditionally, such training would take place in each library or section one-on-one between the supervisor and the new employee. To integrate the large number of new staff, we needed a different approach.

In a bold new initiative, six clerks who had demonstrated the skills to be good trainers (and knew how to figure out the details to accomplish this) were selected from various branches to create a peer-based training program. As described by the supervisor who helped put this program together: "Some came willingly, some not so willingly; some had concrete ideas of how this could be accomplished; some didn't have a clue. Their charge was short: 'Go forth... train these new clerks not to work at the branch they are assigned to, but to work for Multnomah County Library.' "

This team created a five-day program that addressed various learning styles and used a variety of training techniques, including lectures and hands-on experiences. This intensive training was supplemented by updated training manuals and the establishment of a mentor program. The mentors developed a time line and checklist of tasks to be learned over the first three months of employment.

The program has been very successful and very well received by both trainees and supervisors. It has also established the precedent for peer-based training. Unfortunately, we seriously underestimated the number of people who would need the training. The original program, or a condensed version, has now been presented to over 185 people, including new clerks, library assistants, librarians, supervisors and on-call staff. The training is now being offered once a month and all new circulation staff must take this training before being assigned to a branch or section.

Library Assistants

The library assistant curriculum was prepared collaboratively by over 25 library staff members and delivered in an intensive two-week time frame. The training included an overview of the library system, basic reference skills training, technology training (including equipment troubleshooting), introduction to the Library's online catalog Dyna, and an introduction to Multnomah County Library's electronic reference environment. This last component has proven to be the most challenging, as its complex and ever-changing, ever-updated nature requires ongoing retraining of library staff.

Although the course was very intense and only covered the materials at an introductory level, course evaluations were generally very favorable and supervisors reported a high level of performance from the new staff. The course has been offered four times in the past 13 months to 89 reference staff. Incorporating the "Plan, Do, Check, Act" model of quality improvement, many adaptations and modifications have been incorporated into this model of quality improvement.

We have now packaged the core curriculum that was established for the group presentations so that individuals or small groups can do most of their learning in a self-directed format. The Library does not expect to be hiring enough LA's at any one time to make it economical to offer the two-week classroom model of training, so we are now moving to individualized learning modules.

New Staff Orientation

Having the opportunity to welcome over 150 new staff members and to help many existing staff prepare for promotions and new assignments in the organization is an enviable situation, but it also presented a challenge to provide adequate learning in a timely manner. Beyond the specific skills training offered by the "survival training" described above, we have revised and refreshed two in-service programs that had long been offered at Multnomah County Library.

All new staff are now invited to attend a four-hour welcome and orientation hosted by the Library's management team. This session outlines the mission of the Library, its history, and gives insight into current programs and initiatives. The orientation includes small group discussions with the executive team and representatives from the library's Quality Council.

Intellectual Freedom Training

The Intellectual Freedom course covers the basics of the importance of free and open access to ideas and the role of the public library. In recent years this has become the forum for training new staff to interact in a positive way with the community and the media on such topics as internet filtering, censorship, and the public library's concern for the safety of children. Trainers from all areas of library service, from youth services to materials selectors to associate directors, take part in directing this training. This course is required for all new staff and all employees are encouraged to take this class at least once every three years.

Technology Training

When MCL first implemented the Microsoft Office Suite (1996 to 1997), a full-time staff member was assigned to technology training.

Multnomah County contracted with an outside vendor to provide a series of classes on Word, Access, Excel, PowerPoint, and the NT environment. We also purchased online tutorials and made them available for individualized training.

These classes are still available to all staff, but they are generally all-day sessions that are difficult to schedule and sometimes too general to be helpful. We are now looking for shorter classes and desktop tutorials that can be customized for library purposes.

In the meantime, an important part of our technology training approach is the TechnoMentors. This group was developed when staff computers were first upgraded with email capabilities. The need for training was urgent and widespread. A staff member from each branch and section was selected to learn the software and became responsible for teaching others in their work group. The roles and responsibilities of TechnoMentors continue to evolve, but they are key to the continuing learning that occurs as new staff join a work group and as technology tools are deployed.

System Initiatives

Beyond survival training, orientation, and technology training, Multnomah County Library has several system initiatives that include staff learning objectives, and we have begun to develop training programs to address these issues.

The first example is called "Everyone Serves Youth" and was launched in March of this year. This comprehensive curriculum provides staff with the information and skills necessary to serve all young library users at an excellent level of service.

The curriculum consists of six half-day workshops. The introductory workshop has two versions, one for reference staff and one for all other library staff. This course examines the Library's services to youth from pre-birth through high school age, exploring stages of youth behavior and giving staff the opportunity to explore successful approaches to helping kids in library situations. This introductory course is now required for all new staff and strongly recommended for continuing staff.

Other courses cover reference services, reader advisory topics, and a course on working with the very young child. These courses are optional but highly recommended. As each course is scheduled twice a year, staff are able to include these sessions as learning objectives in their individual learning plans.

The process developed to put this curriculum together was an important learning experience for the organization. The Learning Systems Manager and the Youth Services Coordinator met to outline the breadth and scope of the curriculum. A youth services librarian was selected to be the project manager. Then teams of youth services librarians and library assistants were created to develop and deliver the individual courses. This was a significant allocation of time and energy. The teams had relatively short deadlines and for many staff this was a new way of working together. The teams were asked to evaluate their process as well as its product. These evaluations indicate that while working in teams can be challenging and even difficult, the results are worth it. Evaluations by the attendees indicate that the new approach resulted in excellent learning opportunities.

A second example of a system initiative is the "Branch Staff Readiness" program. As we plan for each branch renovation, we also plan a staff readiness program. Beginning with the development of an individual learning plan, staff members of a branch about to be renovated identify what they would like to learn before the branch reopens. This process is still under development, but some examples of learning activities include branch reference staff working at Central Library; circulation and page staff taking computer classes and working in branches that already have the new electronic capabilities in place; and branch leaders taking on special system-wide projects to develop project management skills.

About one month before the scheduled reopening, the staff comes together for a one-day workshop on team building and communication.

During this day together, the staff writes the branch mission, establishes ground rules for working together, and does several team exercises to increase communication.

About 10 days before the branch reopens, the staff begins an intensive period of training combined with the physical work of getting a branch ready for the public. This training gives staff the opportunity to gain some comfort with the electronic resources that will be available in the branch, as well as providing some practice time using library computer applications. Throughout this time, the staff is using team building skills and establishing working relationships that will help them deliver outstanding public service.

So far, 78 staff have participated in these training programs. Each branch staff member has made very useful suggestions for continuously improving the quality and quantity of this training. The best improvement so far is the addition of a brunch—prepared by the staff of the most recently renovated branch for the weary staff of the about-to-be reopened branch!

A third system initiative is to be responsive to learning opportunities as they arise. The budget for conference and travel has been significantly increased and targeted to fund team attendance at workshops or conferences on strategic topics. As part of this conference travel, each team is charged to return to the library and apply the new learning. As a result of this initiative, three staff members from different areas of the library attended a national conference on adaptive technology in Bloomington, Minnesota; four circulation staff members attended the circulation conference at the University of Wisconsin; and three people attended the Internet Librarian '98 Conference in Monterey, California. They brought back many exciting ideas that are now being incorporated into the operations of the library.

Staff Day

Multnomah County Library sponsored its seventh all-day staff in-service day this year. This event features a variety of classes and workshops and the chance for all staff to be together. A staff team representing a variety of job classifications and locations plans and produces the day's events. This year's theme, Back to the Basics, emphasized books and reading. The event was highlighted by the annual State of the Library address by library director Ginnie Cooper, and included 44 break-out sessions, which included sessions on book making, author presentations, a slide show on canoeing, and a session on "Everything You Didn't Want to Know About Menopause."

Results

Our measures for success are primarily anecdotal but we are working on data gathering methodologies. Every training session includes written evaluation and feedback mechanisms and this information is an important part of our improvement process.

We have also been tracking the public's response. The patron feedback mechanism in our library is known as "Ginnie Coupons." We encourage the public to send comments or suggestions on coupons that are available at all public service points. Coupons that include an address receive a written response from Library Director Ginnie Cooper. We have tracked the number and type of concerns while we have been incorporating this large number of new staff and were happy to find no significant increase in the number of complaints. And we were pleased by the number of compliments about great public service that we received from the public.

There are also downsides to any new program, and here are a few we experienced. This approach takes considerable time and energy. It is not a quick fix. It is difficult and challenging to be continually adapting and retraining. It is difficult to keep everyone informed. It is very hard to incorporate this much staff development into work schedules, and hard to incorporate new learning into day-to-day work. Dilbert cartoons often appear on staff bulletin boards, and it sometimes feels like we are caught in jargon and the management theme of the day.

Next Steps

The activities outlined here are only representative of the learning that is going on at Multnomah County Library. Every day, teams and committees meet and work to solve issues and complete projects. Staff help each other learn new skills by coaching and in over-the-shoulder training. Often these "just in time" learning opportunities are the most helpful way to assimilate new skills. We continue to work on developing team skills and implementing performance planning for all staff.

We also have several additional system initiatives that need curriculum development including reference, circulation, question handling for everyone and leadership development. We need to continue to fine tune and improve on programs in place and we need to continue talking about what works and what doesn't.

The learning organization literature emphasizes the amount of time, energy and resources it really takes to make change permanent. We are finding this to be true. But, we believe the challenge of providing excellent public service in an evolving information environment requires us to create a workplace that dedicates the required resources to staff development and training and learning.

Many people helped in the preparation of this article. Much of the theoretical thinking about the learning systems approach is being done by Deputy Director Ruth Metz. The Learning Systems staff has included Jane Mackinnon, Marilyn Shayegi, Lise Brackbill, Serena Gomez, Eva Miller, and Patricia Welch. Sharon Klemp and Jan Thenell assisted in compiling and editing.

Recommended Reading

Massis, Bruce E. "How to create and implement a technology training program." *American Libraries* Oct. 2001: 49–51.

Up to Our Ears in Lawyers: Legal Issues Posed by the Net

Have any technologies caused us as much ill-considered legislation as the Internet? Librarians have been forced into court to protect the threatened First Amendment and privacy rights of our users. Because the unregulated, anything-goes Internet brings a whole lot of stuff into our buildings that parents and community leaders and politicians don't want there, librarians have been afflicted with the Communications Decency Act, the Children's Internet Protection Act, the Child Online Protection Act, and other laws requiring libraries to install filters.

Publishers who think e-books and databases threaten their profits have lobbied for, and gotten, tighter copyright protections. The Copyright Term Extension Act has yanked works out of the public domain and back into copyright protection. The Digital Millennium Copyright Act limits our fair use and first sale rights in digital products. The Uniform Computer Information Transactions Act (UCITA), if ratified, would shift the balance of power toward vendors and away from buyers. The PATRIOT Act, of course, trumps existing state privacy laws that protect patron use records, and requires librarians to turn over such records as requested by the FBI.

What can librarians do to deal with these problems?

1. Gather information. The Internet Filter Assessment Project, for instance, did a careful analysis of the effectiveness of various filter programs, and ALA's Washington Office and the Government Documents Round Table Legislative Committee analyze and keep us informed about pending legislation that will cause an impact on our work.
2. Offer input before the laws get passed on how they would impact free expression and access to public

information. (See Julia F. Wallace's testimony in Chapter Nine on the proposal to shift responsibility for government printing away from the Government Printing Office.)

3. Try to understand what the law requires and abide by it, even while protesting it.
4. Write letters as individual citizens protesting or supporting or suggesting modifications to proposed legislation. The ALA Washington Office Web site offers copies of their own letters to Congress as well as talking points for your letters.
5. Argue the laws in court.
6. Craft policies that deal with problems while still honoring library values.
7. Teach children and parents safe use of the Net, create safe and delightful children's Web pages, encourage parental monitoring of children's Internet use. For ideas, see the Multnomah County Library's Family Guide to the Web, and the Free Expression Policy Project: Media Literacy, an Alternative to Censorship.
8. Be prepared. Make sure all staff understand your policies. Note that the Multnomah County training program discussed in Chapter Seven included intellectual freedom training for all staff.

Solution
Gather Information

Managing Internet Access:
Results of a National Survey

Leigh S. Estabrook and Edward Lakner

Sociology professors often ask their students to guess whether more people die in fires or by drowning each year. It is a trick question to teach them not to rely on their assumptions about the world, but to test them. Most people incorrectly answer by fire because fires are often covered in the media with pictures—and we have few pictures of drowning.

Similarly, media coverage of isolated abuses of Internet access in public libraries can distort public perceptions, leading people to assume that most public libraries offer children easy access to sexually explicit images online. The reality is that 99% of the public libraries in the U.S. control public Internet use in some way.

This fact emerged from a recent study conducted to understand how U.S. public libraries actually manage Internet access. The Library Research Center of the University of Illinois/Urbana-Champaign, under contract with ALA, mailed the survey to 1,297 public libraries across the U.S. that were randomly selected from the 7,049 reported in the 1997 Federal-State Cooperative System census as offering Internet access. Almost all the 1,015 libraries that responded, or 96.3%, say that they provide public access to the Internet. (The survey netted a 78.3% response rate; the numbers reported here are weighted so that the percentages of the libraries in the strata match the corresponding percentage for all libraries in the U.S.)

We found that America's public libraries are managing public Internet use in two ways. First, many provide guidance by developing policies and guidelines, as well as by holding classes for users and pre-selecting Internet sites of potential interest. Second, a substantial majority exert some kind of formal control, implementing one or more of the following measures: They filter access, require parents to give their permission for children to use the Internet, or place computers in locations the staff can monitor. Only 10 libraries out of 1,015 survey respondents report having no filtering, parental permission, or other Internet-management tools.

Outlawing the Offensive

Nearly all U.S. public libraries (94.7%) have a formal written policy or set of guidelines to regulate public use of the Internet. Of those that did not have a policy at the time they completed the questionnaire, almost half reported being in the process of formulating one. These policies reflect librarians' responsiveness to areas of public concern that have been the recent focus of talk shows and federal bills tying e-rate eligibility to the installation of filters. Almost 80% of public libraries' Internet acceptable-use policies address public use of online content that may be offensive to others and over 70% relate to public use of Internet content inappropriate for children. Further, almost 90% of the surveyed libraries report that they provide training to some or all of their staff in applying these guidelines, proving the importance of these policies to library practice.

Libraries also play a pivotal role in educating the public about how to use the Internet. Classes and workshops in Internet use are common in larger libraries, with 78.3% of those libraries serving over 100,000 providing training within the last 12 months. Even in libraries serving smaller populations, training is important: 62.5% serving populations of 25,000 to 100,000 and 39.2% serving less than 25,000 people have recently offered patrons Internet-use classes. Overall, almost half (46.2%) offer classes, half of which (51.1%) are intended for adults.

One of the central roles of public libraries is organizing their collections of materials to make them more usable to their patrons. This ranges from grouping easy readers together to providing public-access catalogs that can easily be searched. As the amount of material on the Internet has mushroomed, consequently making discrete items increasingly difficult to find, librarians are actively bringing those same aids to their patrons, most directly by pre-selecting Internet sites of potential interest.

Among the libraries serving more than 100,000 people, 69.6% provide Internet users with a set of sites pre-selected by the library staff. Smaller libraries are also making an effort to assist their users in this way, with 48.1% of those serving 25,000 to 100,000 and 25% of those serving fewer than 25,000 offering pre-selected sites. In most libraries these pre-selected sites are a guide, not a limit to Internet use; only

6.7% do not give children access beyond those sites. However, young adults in 2.3% and adults in 1.3% of the libraries have no access beyond those sites pre-selected by the library staff.

While librarians are clearly affected by public concerns over Internet content, they have retained control over policy development. According to the survey, the principal players in formulating Internet-use policies are the library director (cited by 92.5% of libraries), trustees (84.3%), and staff (73.1%). Fewer than 10% of the libraries included public officials (9.1%) and people in the community (8.3%) in policy formulation.

Consistent with traditional ways of handling user concerns, one-fifth of libraries (21.6%) that offer public access to the Internet have a formal written procedure for complaints about Internet content accessible in the library. Half the libraries (50.2%) serving over 100,000 persons report they have such a complaint procedure, compared to only 28.7% of those serving 25,000 to 100,000, and 17.3% of those serving less than 25,000.

Overall, formal complaints about content were reported by fewer than 20% of libraries. Librarians estimate that one-third of those complaints came from people who do not use the library, but heard about the Internet service. Complaints are notably more common in larger libraries (serving over 100,000 persons), more than half (57.5%) of which reported receiving complaints. Almost 90% of the complaints (87.5%) concerned sexually explicit material. Informal complaints, according to the librarians surveyed, are most likely to focus on problems with the computer, including equipment failure (24.9%), slow response time (25.9%), and too few computers (21.3%). Only 7.5% of the informal complaints related to Internet content.

Remote Controls

Beside guiding and educating users, libraries have implemented several methods to exert more direct control over public Internet use. However, the most commonly talked-about form of control—filtering—

is not the most widely used. Few libraries completely filter Internet access for the public. Most public libraries (83.2%) reported having no filters and fewer than 7% (6.8%) have filters on all their public access terminals. Those libraries with the greatest level of restrictions are, however, truly controlling: Of those that filter every public terminal, only 19.4% allow users to circumvent filtering.

Almost two-thirds (63.9%) of U.S. public libraries require parental permission for children's use of the Internet, with two-thirds (66.5%) of that group requiring patrons under 18 to have permission. Nine percent of public libraries lift the requirement for parental permission at age 13 or older.

The most widely used tool for oversight of Internet use is the location of public Internet terminals in the library, with 80.6% of the reporting libraries placing terminals in open spaces. A similar number (80.2%) say they have placed terminals near a staff desk. (Libraries could give multiple responses.)

The survey demonstrates that few public libraries are offering children easy access to pornography on the Internet. Instead, they chaperone youngsters' online sessions through a combination of tools that include filtering and parental permission and/or oversight restricting children in some ways. Moreover, the actual number of complaints about Internet content in public libraries is relatively small.

Terminal Issues

There are two particularly troubling issues raised in this survey, though, about how libraries are managing Internet access. First, why are so few libraries involving public officials and people in the community in formulating policies for Internet use? Perhaps librarians fear the public may have different views that would compromise professional standards. Perhaps they worry about the issue being seized by a small group in the community. Perhaps they worry about many Americans' ambivalent views of their First Amendment rights, as the "2000 State of the First Amendment" survey of 1,015 adults conducted in April by the online

Freedom Forum demonstrates: 67% felt that public remarks offensive to racial minorities should not be allowed and 51% said that art offensive to some community members should not be displayed publicly. [That survey is no longer available. The 2002 State of the First Amendment survey, posted at http://www.freedomforum.org/templates/document.asp?documentID=16840, reveals similar attitudes.] Whatever the cause, it is difficult to understand why more public libraries are not engaging their clientele in helping to draft Internet-use policies.

Second, the survey shows that at least 80% of public libraries locate terminals to maximize staff oversight. But what are the human and work costs of having librarians manage use by placement of terminals? And what are the costs to the librarians' relationship to the public if librarians are seen as the Internet "police"? The sexual harassment suit filed by staff in Minnesota (*American Libraries*, June/July 2000, p. 36–38) is but one of the problems that can result.

Librarians appear to be extraordinarily responsive to the concerns of citizens about public access to the Internet. It seems important also to look internally. Managing Internet access in public libraries challenges us beyond deciding who has access to what. We are equally challenged to consider the processes of decision-making in public, community-based institutions and to understand the new stress being placed on our staff and their relationships to users.

Participants in Policy Development (N = 926)
The public library director 92.5%
Library trustees 84.3%
Staff of the library 73.1%
Public officials 9.1%
People in the community 8.3%
Other 10.2%

Issues Addressed in Use Policies (N = 926)
Internet content offensive to others 78.8%
Internet content inappropriate for children 70.7%

Internet content about illegal conduct (e.g., gambling, obscenity) 64.6%

First amendment rights of library users 46.4%

Other 16.8%

America's Libraries Exert Local Control by

- Enforcing policies that forbid the display of offensive sites on library computers.

- Requiring parental permission before allowing children to surf on-site.

- Pointing browsers to a homegrown default page of pre-selected, age-appropriate Web sites.

- Deploying filters in some circumstances.

Reprinted from *American Libraries*, Sept. 2000. Copyright 2000, Leigh Estabrook and Edward Lakner. Used by permission.

Solution
Try to Change the Law

Fortunately, The Uniform Computer Information Transaction Act (UCITA) has so far only been ratified by two states, which leaves 48 chances to kill it. ALA is tracking its ratification status throughout the country and will update that information regularly on its UCITA Web page at htp://www.ala.org/washoff/ucita/library.html. AFFECT (Americans for Fair Electronic Commerce Transactions) is a coalition of consumer groups, technology professionals, and several librarians' organizations. Its Web page (http://affect.ucita.com/) contains talking points to present to state legislators.

Americans for Fair Electronic Commerce Transactions (AFFECT): Why We Oppose UCITA

If signed into law in any state, UCITA will undermine consumer and privacy protections. This proposed legislation would change the rules for purchase and use of computer software and information products for businesses, individuals and non-profits. And if successful, UCITA will cost software consumers billions. In essence, the UCITA legislation validates a "shrink-wrap" or "click-on" approach to electronic licensing, superseding consumer protections, copyright law, and privacy protections. UCITA would change software and informational purchases in the following ways:

The software purchased would no longer belong to the buyer.

UCITA allows consumers to become licensees who are bound to the terms of the contract provided in "shrink-wrap" products or "click-on" agreements.

UCITA allows restrictions on use to be revealed after purchase.

UCITA allows software publishers to change the terms of the contract after purchase.

UCITA allows software vendors to prohibit the transfer of software from one person to another or from one company to another, even in the course of a merger or acquisition.

UCITA allows terms that may severely limit the use of the product.

UCITA allows restrictions that prohibit users from criticizing or publicly commenting on software they purchased.

UCITA would permit invasions of privacy.

UCITA allows software publishers to legally track and collect confidential information about personal and business activities of licensees.

UCITA allows software and information products to contain "back door" entrances, potentially making users' systems vulnerable to infiltration by unauthorized hackers.

Software companies could knowingly ship defective products.

UCITA allows software publishers to deny both large and small businesses many of the current warranty protections they have under present law.

UCITA allows software publishers to sell their products "as is" and to disclaim liability for product shortcomings. Imagine buying a refrigerator or stove where the producer does not guarantee that the product will work correctly.

If the consumer wants to sue over a defective product, UCITA allows the software publisher to restrict legal action to a specific jurisdiction—a particular county, state or even a different country.

UCITA would allow software to be disabled without notification.

UCITA allows software publishers to shut down mission critical software remotely without court approval and without incurring liability for the foreseeable harm caused.

UCITA allows software publishers to modify the terms of contracts after the sale simply by sending an e-mail—regardless of whether the consumer receives the notification or not.

UCITA allows software publishers to remove their product, simply because usage fees arrive late.

UCITA puts consumers at the mercy of software publishers to "blackmail" users for more fees by their unhindered ability to disable or remove their product for unspecified "license violations."

UCITA would threaten existing privileges granted under federal copyright laws.

UCITA would permit an end-run around federal copyright law in mass-market licensing agreements that are used by virtually all consumers and that are the mainstay of most library and business operations.

UCITA threatens fair use privileges that allow for the provision of fundamental library services like inter-library loan, archiving and preservation.

UCITA threatens "first sale" privileges that permit donation, transfer or resale of a product.

Yogi Berra famously said, "The game ain't over 'til it's over." But sometimes it ain't over even when it IS over. Bad laws can be revised, amended, or overturned in court. The moral is, keep those letters flowing to your legislators.

DMCA Revision to Get New Push

Andrew Albanese

In a sign that the library community's pleas are not falling on deaf ears, Congressman Rick Boucher (D-VA) has editorialized for the need to rewrite the controversial Digital Millennium Copyright Act (DMCA). Writing for the popular computer web site C-NET, Boucher said that initial warnings by the library and university communities that the DMCA would threaten access to information are proving true.

Since its proposal and subsequent passage in October 1998, the DMCA has been strenuously opposed by the library community, which called it overly broad and argued that in a digital future the DMCA would gut currently existing fair use provisions. Boucher offered a series of unsuccessful amendments to preserve fair use when the act was being debated and has since criticized it frequently.

In his editorial, Boucher took aim at the anti-encryption provision of the DMCA, section 1201, which makes it a crime to circumvent encryption controls, even for materials legally purchased. "In the three years since the law was enacted, we have not seen an increase in digital content. Instead, we have seen a rash of lawsuits; the imprisonment by U.S. authorities of a Russian computer programmer who had come to the United States to give a technical talk; and, more recently, the release of compact discs into the market that cannot be played in computers or even some CD players." This could lead to a time when materials "on library shelves" will be available only on a pay-per-view basis.

ALA to Support Boucher

American Library Association officials say they are poised to support Boucher actively in his legislative efforts. ALA legislative counsel Miriam Nisbet said Boucher, who has been working with library advocates, was originally planning to introduce a broad, sweeping bill to reaffirm fair use.

Now, however, Boucher is expected to bring forth legislation that more specifically addresses section 1201, the anti-circumvention provision of the DMCA, making it clear that libraries and universities that need to go around technical controls to make fair use of copyrighted works could do so without fear of criminal prosecution.

New Discussion List

In a sign of growing concern over copyright, librarians at the University of Maryland's Center for Intellectual Property and Copyright in the Digital Age (CIP) have established a new electronic discussion list. In three days, the list gained over 1,500 subscribers <http://www.umuc.edu/distance/odell/cip/cip.html>.

"We hope this list will be the kind of forum where anything from the nuts and bolts questions to the philosophical will be addressed," said Olga Francois, the list moderator, noting that librarians—some 60 percent of the initial subscribers—can trade messages with non-librarians. Francois, senior reference librarian at the center, says the list will handle questions on issues ranging from online library services, plagiarism detection, faculty courseware ownership in the online classroom, and digital content to legislative issues such as copyright term extension and scholarly publishing initiatives.

Solution
Understand What the Laws Require of You

Filters and the Public Library: a Legal and Policy Analysis

Mary Minow

My analysis on options that libraries consider:

1. Filters on all terminals used by children under 18 (or under 13)

   Analysis: The library, as a government agency, is the restricting agency, not the parent. Probable First Amendment violation, unless filters closely match unprotected speech (not technically feasible). ALA Bill of Rights violation.

2. Filters on all terminals used by children under 18, unless the child has parental permission to use the full Internet

   Analysis: The library, as a government agency, is restricting use. Many, if not most, parents will not take affirmative action to lift the restrictions, even if they believe in open access. Parents are busy, and the burden of "opting in" will leave many children without access, by government design. Possible First Amendment violation (the closer the library is to imposing restrictions, the more probable the violation). ALA Bill of Rights violation.

3. Filters on terminals in the children's room, but no library-imposed restrictions. Parents have the option of requesting that their child's card is coded for filtered terminals only. Thus library enforcement is required, though only at the time of issuing cards. Librarians are not expected to monitor use.

Analysis: The library, as a government agency, is not directly responsible for restricting use. Many, if not most, parents will not take affirmative action to impose restrictions, because they are busy, and it is a burden to "opt out" of the default. Although older children will easily circumnavigate the restriction—by using a friend's card, for example—parents who wish to protect their younger children from accidentally calling up cyberporn will have a tool, albeit imperfect. Librarians, however, will be put in the untenable position of assisting different children differently (e.g., a child can't find information on the Republic of Georgia on the filtered terminal, or on the library's shelves). Does the librarian risk searching the unfiltered Internet, to circumvent these limitations? What if a site that a parent doesn't approve of shows up?

Probably not a First Amendment violation, as the parents are responsible for the restrictions. Informing the parents on what is being restricted would be advisable. ALA Bill of Rights violation (restricting material based on age).

4. Filters on one or more terminals in the children's room, but no library-imposed restrictions, nor enforcement. Parents may direct their children to use only these terminals, but the issue is purely between parent and child, with no library intervention.

Analysis: The library, as a government agency, is not restricting use. Children who wish to use an unfiltered terminal are not denied access by the library. No First Amendment violation. Arguably, no ALA Bill of Rights violation, since patrons are not restricted use of library materials on the basis of age. However, ALA has issued a strong resolution against the use of filtering software in libraries.

5. Pro-choice position: filters on terminals that can be turned on or off by the patron. The default setting is off. At least one search engine, Magellan, which is available as a free site on the Internet, gives the user a chance to search only "green light sites." Use this (or another with the same principle) as the default search engine, at least in the children's room.

Analysis: The library, as a government agency, is not restricting use. Users who choose to search only "green light sites," are depending on Magellan's definitions. No First Amendment violation. Arguably, no ALA Bill of Rights violation, since patrons are not restricted use of library materials on the basis of age. However, ALA has issued a strong resolution against the use of filtering software in libraries

6. Open Access Without Filters

Analysis: Children run the risk of inadvertently being exposed to obscenity, harmful matters, indecent, and other offensive material. For example, searches on the words "toys," "Barbie," and other terms or names can result in the display of inappropriate Web-based graphics. The most sexually explicit title that the Library owns is probably *Playboy*, and it does not shelve centerfolds in the middle of picture books.

As noted, the frequency of children "stumbling," which could downgrade First Amendment protection to a broadcast standard, is in dispute. No First Amendment violation. No ALA Bill of Rights violation.

I believe that different solutions are appropriate for different communities. In Cupertino, I personally recommend the pro-choice position. This option does not impose a burden on any user, but does give parents tools to use with small children. Ideally, a range of filtering choices will be available at the user level, including some which use PICS. In a community in which a library finds children inadvertently stumbling upon obscenity, harmful matters, and even indecent speech, I recommend library-chosen filters installed on terminals that young children are most likely to use. Even though all filters are over-inclusive in their screening, as long as children are not restricted from open terminals that are reasonably available elsewhere, I do not believe that free speech freedoms are compromised.

Other options include turning computer screens away from foot traffic and installing privacy screens. This has been done at Santa Clara County library, for the most part. Other libraries, grappling with the same issue, have come to the opposite determination that such placement encourages Cyberporn viewing. Still others are experimenting with a "tap on the shoulder" policy. Should a library offer its users privacy, or should their searches be displayed to passersby? I believe that these options raise significant privacy issues which merit further study. Nevertheless, my general recommendation is to follow library tradition in safeguarding patrons' privacy as much as possible. Further, privacy measures can reduce the chances of inadvertent exposure to both children and adults of offensive screens.

Finally, I recommend proactive approaches, such as working with the public, training parents on Internet use, working with the media, and continuing to study emerging technology. Libraries should identify their needs, and communicate them to a software and hardware developers, many of which are based in the Santa Clara Valley.

Excerpted from *First Monday,* Dec. 1997. Copyright 1997, Mary Minow. Used by permission.

Solution
Policies That Deal with Problems AND Honor Library Values

Laying Down the Law: Crafting Acceptable Use Policy

Rob Reilly

How Did We Get Where We Are?

When computers were first introduced to the classroom, these were the major concerns that teachers and administrators had: How would a whole class share a single computer? What software was available and how could it be acquired? Who is going to help me when I get in trouble? Computers were not much more than a very effective drill-and-practice mechanism—they were not consequential enough to spawn material for the 6 o'clock news. But then, in the mid-'90s, computers became more powerful, more capable of running software programs that touched all aspects of the curriculum, and Tim Berners-Lee fathered the World Wide Web, which in turn brought about Web browsers. Schools began to install computer networks, which connected students to that gold mine of information known as the World Wide Web. Much to their credit, administrators and computer-savvy teachers were quick to realize that student use of the computers and computer networks needed to have a written use policy so that students and teachers understood the "ground rules"—limits needed to be defined, and appropriate use needed to be understood and codified. Let me repeat this, as these two points are critical in crafting a use policy—limits need to be defined, and appropriate use needs to be understood.

These use-policy documents came to be known as "Acceptable Use Policy," or AUP. However in the early stages of development AUPs proved to be ineffective, as those who created them did not quite understand how computer networks or the World Wide Web would, or could for that matter, make teachers more effective or support them in their daily tasks. But then no one really understood the "potential" of the computer for education, and back then I'm not sure anyone really understood what constitutes appropriate use of computers. Thus AUPs did not clearly define inappropriate conduct but tended to focus exclusively on a mechanical/logistical concerns (e.g., change your password every 6 months, back up your files), or to be vague. When push came to shove, this lack of clarity caused the AUP mandates to be legally or even pragmatically unenforceable (e.g., do not send unwanted or harassing e-mail, only use the system in an appropriate manner).

What's an AUP to Do?

Historically, Acceptable Use Policy regulates user-to-computer behavior and defines other logistical and mechanical needs. In recent years there has been a radical change and a demographic shift in both the nature of the network and its uses. The World Wide Web, e-mail, and various curricular-centered mailing lists are becoming valuable educational resources that can revolutionize education as we know it. Those who craft policy must realize that the network is not just a mechanical entity but it is a forum where proper use in an educational setting must be defined (e.g., how is the Web going to be used in the social science curriculum, what constitutes proper conduct/use for students and for the professional staff). Both of these concepts are important. But lost in the laser-speed development of the technology is the notion that we must understand and constantly talk about the educational reasons that technology is in school. We need to set policy so that the "things" out on the Web that are supportive of a school's educational goals are identified and utilized to their maximum. We should understand what appropriate behavior is and what it is not. And we should have a theoretical understanding of the mechanics of the computer networks and the Internet.

On one hand, AUP rules for behavior are already understood by teachers and administrators—it's "understanding" the rules while using a computer or a computer network that may complicate the issue. To a large degree, the issues that an AUP addresses are not all that different from what happens in the school bathrooms, on the playground, and when walking in line when the teacher is not looking. Granted, there are some areas where an AUP is needed to define conduct or outline proper use, but generally people who have been in the educational system for more than a few years know what a computer AUP consists of; they just don't know that they know. It's really no different for a child to call another a jerk via e-mail than it is to write that same message on a piece of paper and give it to the "jerk." It just seems that when behaviors we see everyday occur on a computer we are not as sure of things!

On the other hand, AUPs are meant to convey the idea that the computer systems and the computer network are intended to be an integral part of the school's educational mission. In short, the computer resources are to be used for school work. When not used for school work, then chances are the student is using these tools inappropriately. When Web sites that are not in direct support of a student's school work are being accessed then the students may need to be directed elsewhere. This is a simple concept, but often absent in AUPs. I think this is due to the fact that those who craft an AUP are far more concerned with stopping misuse and defining punishment to such a degree that they neglect to define proper use.

Some Examples, Some Questionable Ideas, Some Good Practices

There are a number of sites that have their AUPs available online. Many of these sites have policy documents that can be adapted to the needs of various schools or school districts. The mandates of a number of the AUPs listed here will likely be evolved or changed by the courts or legislatures, but for now these are management documents. AUPs should define the following:

- Define what proper behavior is, in the same manner it's defined in the student handbook.

- Include a statement that the computer resources are for educational uses, and comment on the fact that anything else is likely inappropriate use.

- Offer some reasons for policy statements that may not be understood by the students and/or the faculty.

When reading the AUPs listed below, try to imagine what the rule would be in your school if student behavior that violated the rules occurred in a situation that did not involve a computer. For example, if a student sends a blatantly harassing message to another student that would lead to an AUP-mandated loss of computer access for a few months, would a student sending the same message to another student via paper during math class not be allowed to do any math for a few months? Beware of an academic punishment for a behavioral incident!

Helena, Montana, School District's AUP

<http://www.helena.k12.mt.us/policy/aup/StudentAUPfinal2001 -2001Rev.htm>

This district has a good policy with many good points and some bad points. But the bad points are defensible in their situation. For example, Internet use is defined as a "privilege" and "not a right." Courts have held that the difference between a "right" and a "privilege" is a hollow distinction and rarely exists. But the "it's a privilege" position can work until Internet/Web resources becomes an integral part of the school curriculum, then taking the Internet or computer access away from a student under the guise of "it's a privilege" becomes more severely problematic.

Grinnell, Kansas, Unified School District AUP

<http://skyways.lib.ks.us/kansas/schools/grinnell/accusepo.html>
Grinnell has a nice AUP. This one-pager is a good document. It's written so that the students understand and acknowledge the do's and don'ts for computer use. (But it also refers to computer use as a "privilege" and "not a right.") This document may be important for you, especially if you are unfamiliar with the Internet, the Web, Usenet, etc. It also advises the students that their e-mail is NOT private; this may obviate an outcry of "invasion of privacy" if you need to read a student's e-mail for good reason.

Salt Lake City, Utah, School System AUP

<http://www.slc.k12.ut.us/aup.html>
A nice AUP, but once again we see the "privilege versus right" debate. The Parent/Guardian statement that must be signed may be problematic for parents. Parents may be reluctant sign it. It also outlaws the use of MUDs (multi-user domains—simulations where multiple people can interact). The problem is that we have a MUD here at MIT that is quite educational (24th century space science simulation), and there are a number of educational MUDs/MUSEs out there. The point is that the AUP outlaws specific activities where it should use an "educationally appropriate" term to define itself.

Ada, Ohio, Public Schools AUP

<http://ada.k12.oh.us/acc_use.htm>
This is a fairly solid AUP; it's well worth a WWW trip.

Bowling Green, Ohio, Public Schools AUP

<http://www.b-g.k12.ky.us/Tech/AUP/AUP.htm>
A very good AUP, however, it assumes a fairly high degree of technology literacy. In places the policy is clear but I doubt that the average computer user would know what many of the policy statements mean in practice.

Paw Paw, Michigan, Public Schools AUP

<http://www.pawpaw.k12.mi.us/miscinfo/pppsaup.pdf>

A very interesting one-page AUP. It essentially outlaws quite a bit for no apparent reason other than the person receiving it might be offended. It does not prohibit behavior unless someone is offended (e.g., it's OK to call someone a "jerk" if the person receiving the e-mail does not take offense). This is not a great AUP, but it's worth seeing to appreciate why!

Shelby County, Kentucky, AUP

[no longer extant]

It's a bit too vague, but that's good in most cases as it allow for discretion. It does endow the right to search all user accounts onto network administrators and the technology director. In a number of places this AUP creates rights and allows things to happen that are legally questionable. For example, it appears to be questionable whether or not the principal/superintendent can delegate the authority to conduct a warrantless search of a student's computer space (employee workspaces are a different animal). The AUP also states that "all communications and information accessible via the network should be assumed to be private property." Stating this shoots the administrators in the foot when AUP contends that files can be searched—they want to have the user's directories and their contents NOT be "private property." It also nicely ties the AUP back to the student handbook where appropriate.

Lexington, Massachusetts, AUP

<http://sturtevant.com/lextech/aup.htm>

It's a decent one-page document. It has the force of a field trip permission slip—it just informs the consent of the parents and users. But...this is not a bad idea at all!!

Windham, Maine, Public Schools AUP

<http://www.windham.k12.me.us/wsdept/aup.asp>

It has good points and bad points, but it may get the job done when edited to suit your needs.

Those were acceptable use policies for school libraries, which operate under different legal requirements than public libraries, which are considered public forums. Now let's see a publicly posted acceptable use policy for a public library:

Guide to Multnomah County Library's Policies Regarding Internet Use

Access to Internet Resources

1.1 Multnomah County Library is committed to providing free and open access to informational, educational, recreational and cultural resources for library users of all ages and backgrounds. Throughout its history, the Multnomah County Library has made information available in a variety of formats, from print materials to audiovisual materials. The library's computer system provides the opportunity to integrate electronic resources from information networks around the world with the library's other resources.

1.2 The Internet, as an information resource, enables the library to provide information beyond the confines of its own collection. It allows access to ideas, information and commentary from around the globe. Currently, however, it is an unregulated medium. As such, while it offers access to a wealth of material that is personally, professionally, and culturally enriching to individuals of all ages, it also enables access to some material that may be offensive, disturbing and/or illegal, inaccurate or incomplete. Users are encouraged to be good information consumers by evaluating the validity of information accessed via the Internet.

1.3   In introducing the Internet as an information resource, the library's goal is to enhance its existing collection in size and depth and as a public access agency, give opportunity to anyone who wishes to participate in navigating the Internet, both in the library and at home through dial-up service.

1.4   Library staff will identify specific starting points for searches on the library's home page that are appropriate to the library's mission and service roles. The library cannot control or monitor other material that may be accessible from Internet sources because the Internet is a vast and unregulated medium with access points that can and do change often, rapidly and unpredictably. Parents and children are encouraged to read "Child Safety on the Information Highway," available free from any library location or on the World Wide Web.

In-Library Access

2.1   The library upholds and affirms the right of each individual to have access to constitutionally protected material. The library also affirms the right and responsibility of parents to determine and monitor their own children's use of library materials and resources.

2.2   Library staff is available to provide assistance and to help identify appropriate sites. The KidsPage, Outernet, Homework Center and Electronic Resources have been provided to assist users in finding age- and topic-appropriate sites. Parents and children are encouraged to read the pamphlet, "Child Safety on the Information Highway," available free from any library location. The user, however, is the selector in using the Internet and makes individual choices and decisions.

In order to make Internet resources available to as many users as possible and to ensure that this resource is used in a manner consistent with library policies, the following rules shall apply. Specific terms of use may vary by location.

Conditions and Terms of Use in the Library

3.1   Depending upon the demand placed on Internet resources at any particular library agency, users may have to sign up for a limited number of time slots per day. If this is required, users must sign up in person. Reservations will not be taken over the phone. Latecomers forfeit their time if more than 10 minutes late.

3.2   Misuse of the computer will result in the loss of computer privileges, potential loss of library privileges and possible prosecution. Such misuse includes, but is not limited to, using the computer for illegal activities; hacking into the library computer system or any other computer system; damaging or attempting to damage computer equipment or software; interfering with systems operations, integrity or security; gaining unauthorized access to another person's files; sending harassing messages to other computer users; altering or attempting to alter the library computer's settings; and violating copyright laws and software licensing agreements.

3.3   The library's computers are set up for optimal usage by a single individual. In some cases, such as a parent/guardian with children, it may be important for two or more people to work together at a computer. Otherwise, because of limited space, a maximum of two persons may sit/work together at any one computer.

3.4   All users are asked to respect the privacy of other users and not attempt to censor or comment upon what others are viewing.

Reprinted with permission of Multnomah County Library.

Solution
Be Prepared

What to Do Before, During, and After a "Knock at the Door": Understanding the U.S.A. PATRIOT Act

Lynne E. Bradley and Claudette W. Tennant

With passage of the U.S.A. PATRIOT Act on October 26, 2001, many questions have been raised about the act and how it relates to current state privacy/confidentiality laws, as well as criminal and foreign intelligence investigations. In some libraries, law enforcement authorities have sought access to patron and student records, including electronic mail and other electronic communications.

The act includes a series of changes to the U.S. Code in sections on criminal and foreign intelligence investigations (FISA). Under some circumstances, federal rules may supersede state confidentiality laws. Seek clear advice from your college or university attorneys. Librarians should cooperate with the authorities within the guidelines provided by state and federal laws, as well as the PATRIOT Act.

ALA has been working with colleagues in library and higher education associations (the American Association of Law Libraries AALL, the Association of Research Libraries ARL, the American Association of Universities AAU, and others) to develop preliminary guidelines to help academic libraries do what is legal and appropriate.

Before

- Consult local legal counsel. You will need legal experts familiar with your unique situations and local and state laws to help make sure that your policies and procedures are appropriate and legal.

- Review your policies. The PATRIOT Act does not require institutions to make changes in policies or computer systems. However, with a possible increase in requests from law enforcement and the pervasiveness of technology in the daily transactions of libraries, you will want to review and address your policies on retention of and access to all types of information.

- Train staff. Anyone on your staff could be approached by law enforcement, so every staff member should understand your policies. Some institutions designate one staff person to manage the details of such requests. Knowledgeable staff will ensure that your library is complying with all appropriate laws and protect against any institutional or personal liability.

During

- Follow your policies. Sound policies can provide order and justification during what can be a chaotic time and ensure that the best possible thinking and judgment go into your responses.

- Consult legal counsel. Most inquiries made by law enforcement are lawful and in good order; however, you should call your legal counsel when presented with a request. Legal counsel will help you respond properly and legally, while protecting you and your staff from possible liability due to an unlawful request.

- Document your costs. Your institution may be able to recoup some expenses if asked by law enforcement to perform certain types of assistance in data collection. It is unclear what the guidelines will be for reimbursement. Document all costs incurred.

After

- Consult legal counsel. Again, consult legal counsel to assure that you meet any legal requirements to conceal the inquiries of law enforcement or conversely to fulfill any affirmative legal requirements to disclose what records may have been released.

- Follow up. Keep counsel informed; implement your policies; pursue any appropriate reimbursements. Determine whether you will have to maintain any subsequent information or records.

The ALA Washington Office will be tracking the impact of this legislation, so when allowed by law and the advice of counsel, inform the Washington Office of your experiences.

Lynne Bradley wants us to know that this article was published before the FBI guidelines on investigations were released; since then people have often confused the PATRIOT Act with those guidelines. She recommends that you visit the ALA Washington Office Web page for updated information (http://www.ala.org/washoff/).

Recommended Reading

Carlson, Scott, and Andrea L. Foster. "Colleges Fear Anti-Terrorism Law Could Turn Them Into Big Brother: Provisions about networks and library records raise privacy and academic-freedom issues." *Chronicle of Higher Education* 1 Mar. 2002. http://chronicle.com/free/v48/i25/25a03101.htm

Electronic Frontier Foundation. EFF White Paper: Three Years under the DMCA. http://www.eff.org/IP/DMCA/20020503_dmca_consequences. html *The Electronic Frontier Foundation reviews numerous DMCA court cases that have had a chilling effect on research and open discussion.*

Free Expression Policy Project: Media Literacy, an Alternative to Censorship. http://www.fepproject.org/policyreports/medialiteracyfull.html *This argument for the teaching of media literacy also provides a detailed history of the media literacy movement.*

Fuller, Susan. "Ethics and the Internet." In *Managing the Internet Controversy.* Ed. Mark L. Smith. New York: Neal-Schuman, 2001. 159–177. *An account of a two-year process of involving the public in the creation of the Internet use policy for the Santa Clara County Libraries.*

Minow, Mary. "Library Records Post-Patriot Act (Federal Law)." *LLRX* 16 Sept. 2002. http://www.llrx.com/features/libraryrecords.htm

Pike, George H. "The Delicate Dance of Database Licenses, Copyright, and Fair Use." *Computers in Libraries* May 2002. http://www.infotoday.com/cilmag/may02/pike.htm

Richey, Cynthia K. "Molding Effective Internet Policies." *Computers in Libraries* June 2002. http://www.infotoday.com/cilmag/jun02/richey.htm

Schneider, Karen G. "Learning from the Internet Filter Assessment Project." 13 Sept. 1997. http://www.bluehighways.com/tifap/learn.htm

Schneider, Karen G. "The Patriot act: Last refuge of a scoundrel." *American Libraries* Mar. 2002: 86.

Chapter 9

Disappearing Data

Even as we are moving toward rescuing fragile print documents by preserving them digitally, we are discovering that digital data can be equally fragile—threatened by "link rot," technical disasters, the removal of government documents, the removal of articles from databases as the result of the Tasini decision, the degradation of electronic data over time, and obsolete data formats. While nobody as yet seems to have come up with a really good solution to the Tasini problem, librarians are confronting the other problems in a variety of ways.

Solution
Link-Checking

When we post links on our Web sites, we are obligated to make sure not only that the links remain valid but also that the Web sites continue to contain the data we're recommending—there have been some regrettable instances of "porn-napping," when those who created respected sites did not renew the domain registration and the domain name was then purchased by porn dealers.

In two postings on Web4Lib, Karen G. Schneider explained a model link-checking process used at Librarians Index to the Internet:

On the Link-Checking Policy of the Librarians' Index to the Internet

Karen G. Schneider, as posted on Web4Lib

Every week we run a report to show broken/moved links. In this past quarter, our Validation Report averaged 4% broken links—down from 5%—and that's doubly good, because we now do a trick with some URLs to extend their shelf life that ends up with them showing up as 302s when actually they're just fine. (It's triply good if you consider that not only our overall size, but also our rate of growth, have steadily grown over the past several years.) From talking to peers in the Web portal community, 4% reported broken links is highly respectable. I wish it were 0%, but then, most libraries only dream of the kind of production and data quality we sustain with the budget we have. (And of course, we ask indexers to inspect their batch of sites at least once a month, because any number of sites move or break and never show up on this report.)

A bit more: we have an active weeding/updating program, with both paid staff and volunteers participating in evaluating records, and run a weekly report of 404s, 302s, etc. We also have excellent documentation on how to use the report . . . and we have checks and balances where, for example, indexers cannot contribute content if they rise above a certain percentage of reported errors in the Validation Report; we don't want people to slap records in and walk away (and in fact we have weeders periodically review the sites from indexers who are no longer with us). Our training emphasizes life cycle management, including an entire section in our course for indexers reserved for maintaining and replacing records. (And speaking of data quality, we also teach copyright, and we have an excellent Style Manual, if this nationally known writer does say so herself.)

We also have a very new feature in which anyone can comment on an lii.org record. This has been wonderful in terms of providing one more venue for learning about broken, moved, abandoned or changed sites.

I would encourage a data-driven comparison of content quality between lii.org and any comparable portal, and I would be highly receptive to any "lessons learned" from such a study. We not only welcome, but encourage and plead [with] you to use the comment feature when you find a broken or moved link associated with an lii.org record. However, the data and the comments we receive about lii.org (barring this one on Web4Lib) very strongly suggest that this is a resource its staff, indexers, and funding agency can be very proud of.

Incidentally, the former boss at lii.org [Carole Leita]—who is a great library leader and who I would not dream of disappointing by dorking up this wonderful resource—crunched some numbers while I was blathering.

Last Friday, lii.org had 69 404s ("broken links") out of 10,786, for a percentage of .6% (six-tenths of one percent). Again, the real magic, which has been true of lii.org since birth, is that the quality continues to rise even as lii.org grows. That is because lii.org is a planned resource, with real management and oversight, not a pile of links on a page. It has had daily oversight for a decade.

Might I add, Carole is the senior indexer of all, with almost 1/3 of all sites in lii.org, and every week she puts in significant work (now volunteer!) grooming her excellent opus.

You don't even want to know what happens before a record goes INTO lii.org—our editors are merciless. A site gets scanned, viewed in both browsers, evaluated, and looked at upside and down. They compare the record with the site, and groom as needed. They rewrite MY stuff, too. ;)

I've considered putting up our quarterly reports and statistics so the world can see the magic. But now back to that "magic." Magic, btw, takes a lot of work.

Karen G. Schneider: kgs@lii.org, http://lii.org

Coordinator, Librarians' Index to the Internet

Solution
Have a Technological Disaster Plan

Coping with Disasters

Roy Tennant

Now that we've all witnessed a disaster that beggars the imagination, preventing disaster seems not only an appropriate topic but an imperative one. As Mike Handy, acting director of information technology services for the Library of Congress, said after September 11, "Until recently, our planning efforts have assumed the most significant threats to be from accidental disruptions such as natural calamity, fire, power failure, etc. Obviously, now our assumptions include previously unimaginable possibilities."

Although clearly the most unthinkable disaster would involve the loss of life or injury to library staff, that type of disaster planning is outside the scope of this column. Rather, I will consider what can be done to protect your digital library services and collections from the many disasters—whether they be outrageous or minor—that may befall those who do not prepare. Through planning and preparation, we can help prevent disasters from happening or minimize the damage once they do.

Prevention

"An ounce of prevention is worth a pound of cure" remains a valuable aphorism for disaster prevention. Everything that you can reasonably do to avoid or lessen the impact of disasters by planning ahead of time will be well worth your time, effort, and resources.

For digital systems, the classic prevention technique is an effective protection system. Effective computer protection systems are constructed in layers. The first layer is the disk itself—or, more accurately, the way in which data are stored on the disk.

The most secure way to store data on hard disks is by using RAID technology. RAID, an acronym for Redundant Array of Inexpensive (or Independent) Disks, specifies various methods of storing data that are optimized for different requirements. For example, if you want to provide a reasonable level of performance while achieving a moderate level of protection, you may choose a less-protective level of RAID (for example, RAID level 1, which is simply mirroring, or creating another complete copy of the data). If, on the other hand, protection is more important than response time, then a more protective level of RAID may be selected. For example, level 5 distributes both the data and information required to recover it across several physical disks, which can protect you from the failure of multiple drives.

Layers of Protection

The second layer of protection includes such strategies as uninterruptable power supplies (which can prevent disk drive damage in power failures), fire extinguisher systems, alarm systems, and other methods for securing the computer disks or the room where they are kept.

The third layer entails making copies of the data—backing it up. The typical computer backup system copies the data that you wish to retain to another disk, tape, or other digital medium. This backup can be incremental (only changed files are backed up) or complete. For better protection, the second copy should be stored at a location distant from the first (and I mean really distant—the farther the better, considering the impact of disasters such as earthquakes and hurricanes).

A common technique for locating data close to where it is needed can also serve as a default backup system. Called "mirroring," this technique was developed primarily in response to slow or costly Internet connections. For example, those in Australia must pay a per-byte charge for overseas Internet traffic. Therefore, it's helpful for them to copy, or mirror, popular sites locally. Not only can this serve as a default backup, but it can also be essential in emergencies where users can be shunted from the main site to the mirror location.

What might be considered the logical endpoint of this technique is represented by a preservation scheme advanced by Stanford University. Called Lots of Copies Keep Stuff Safe (LOCKSS), the strategy employs a large pool of interconnected and physically distant computers that constantly share copies of each computer's data. If any single computer crashes, the data it contained could be recovered from other computers still online.

The system is designed to use standard-issue PCs, even those that would be too underpowered to run standard office applications (a typical LOCKSS installation would only require something like a PC with a 100Mhz Pentium chip with 32MB of RAM and one or two large disks).

Whether LOCKSS is used or not, since the price of hard disk storage is so cheap (you can find disk drives for as low as $3/GB now, and prices continue to drop), there is no logical reason for not creating multiple redundant copies of critical data. This can (and should) be as simple as setting up a script to copy all of your data to additional hard drives each night. If those drives are physically distant—which the Internet enables easily—it is even better.

Emergency Response & Recovery

Good preparation includes knowing what you will do in the middle of an emergency. One of the quickest and easiest ways to solve an emergency situation is to route users to a mirror (see above). If, for example, www.xxx.org goes down, that domain name can quickly be assigned to the host computer that has a mirror. Once this change propagates to the Internet routing system (which can take from a few hours to a few days), users will be none the wiser that they are going to a different physical location, since the domain name remains unchanged.

If you're not lucky enough to have a mirror, you will need to do something else. What you do will depend on how essential your operation is to those who matter. If your data are important but not essential, then hang tight until the emergency passes and you can move on to the "recovery" stage. If your systems must be constantly responsive, then, one hopes, you will have determined ahead of time how you will cope. Again, planning is everything.

Once the emergency has passed, you should know what steps must be taken to get everything back up and functioning. Specifically, you should know in advance how to install new hardware and software, retrieve data from a backup system, and get everything back online. Here you will discover just how well (or poorly) you have prepared. Those who have planned well will find this process to be quick and smooth, while those who haven't will find it time-consuming and difficult.

Run with the Big Boys

If you have data you can't afford to lose, you can't afford to be without a disaster plan. The plan should include aspects dealing with prevention, emergencies, and recovery. Luckily, there is little to prevent small libraries from having a disaster plan similar to that of the Library of Congress, which uses many of the techniques outlined here.

If you don't know where to begin, start with the Federal Emergency Management Administration's Emergency Management Guide for Business & Industry, which will guide you through the process of making a plan that will get you through just about anything—except perhaps the unimaginable.

Link List

Disaster Recovery Journal's Glossary
<http://www.drj.com/glossary/drjglossary.html>

Emergency Management Guide for Business & Industry
<http://www.fema.gov/library/bizindex.shtm>

Keeping Memory Alive: Practices for Preserving Content at the National Digital Library Program of the Library of Congress
<http://www.rlg.org/preserv/diginews/diginews4-3.html>

LOCKSS <http://lockss.stanford.edu>

Public Library Association Tech Note: Disaster Planning for Computers and Networks <http://www.pla.org/publications/technotes/technotes_disasterplanning.html>

Solution
Advise Legislators on the Impact Proposed Laws Will Have

Since September 11, 2001, government agencies and librarians at depository libraries have become aware that some of the data they have made publicly available could be used to harm us. Given the conflict between librarians' professional obligation to preserve data and the request of a government agency that they destroy the data, what does the law require of librarians? The Association of Research Libraries requested an opinion on that from attorney Thomas M. Susman. His memo on "The Removal or Destruction of Federal Depository Library Documents" (available on ARL's Web site) explains why resisting government directives to return or destroy documents would be a legally risky strategy.

Also at issue is the preservation of digital government documents. Government agencies have never had to be concerned about the permanence of their documents, because once they were distributed in print form to depository libraries, librarians took care of cataloging and preserving them. Now that government documents are increasingly born digital, it is far easier for agencies to erase, alter, and replace documents, unaware of the importance to the historical record of even superseded documents. That's why Julia F. Wallace, on behalf of the American Library Association and several other librarians' organizations offered testimony against the transfer of printing functions away from the GPO.

Statement of Julia F. Wallace before the Joint Committee on Printing, on "Federal Government Printing and Public Access to Government Documents," July 10, 2002

Good morning. I am Julia F. Wallace, Head of the Government Publications Library at the University of Minnesota. We are the regional depository library for Minnesota and South Dakota, and I have been in my current position since 1989. I served as Head of the Government Documents Department at the Minneapolis Public Library, a large selective depository library, from 1983 to 1989. Additionally, I was a member of the Depository Library Council to the Public Printer from 1998 to 2000; served as Chair of the Government Documents Round Table of the American Library Association in 1992–1993; and am a frequent speaker on depository library issues at regional and national conferences. I am very pleased to appear this morning on behalf of the American Library Association (ALA), the American Association of Law Libraries (AALL), the Association of Research Libraries (ARL), and the Medical Library Association (MLA).

The issue before the Joint Committee on Printing today, the May Memorandum from the Office of Management and Budget (OMB) to executive departments and agencies on the "Procurement of Printing and Duplicating through the Government Printing Office," has an enormous impact on the Federal Depository Library Program and the public's access to tangible government publications. We commend you, Chairman Dayton and Vice Chairman Ney, for holding this important hearing on the OMB Memorandum. The library community has a very strong interest in

Federal information policy. Collectively, our four associations represent over 90,000 librarians, as well as the more than 1,300 libraries in every state and congressional district across the Nation that participate in the Federal Depository Library Program (FDLP). Librarians are the crucial access points for the public when they need information from their Government. We are very concerned that, if implemented, the directive to executive agencies to move away from procuring publications through the Government Printing Office (GPO) will further erode the FDLP and exacerbate the longstanding problem of fugitive documents, resulting in a loss of access by the American public to their government information.

Before going any further with my formal statement, which I ask that you please include in the record of today's hearing, I would like to thank you, Chairman Dayton, for visiting the regional depository collections at the Government Publications Library, University of Minnesota, last Friday. I very much enjoyed hosting your brief tour of the collections and introducing you to several librarians from our local selective depository libraries. Since we had representatives of a small public library in a growing suburban area, a large urban public library, a law library, and a private academic library, you were able to hear the many uses which are made of government information in these varied settings. I think you also sensed the commitment these librarians, and all staff members in depository libraries, have to the important goal of providing government information to all people. You heard about community members who are not comfortable with any information on computers, and about academic scholars who love finding data online but want to be able to compare it with historical information available only on paper.

You learned about the additional burdens the electronic transition is placing on libraries, and how they are meeting those challenges. And you also heard about our serious concerns about the long-term access to information that is produced only in digital form. In addition, we talked about the fact that 237 Minnesota printing firms are on GPO's master bid list, including seven small or disadvantaged businesses, and that in FY 2001, Minnesota printers received $954,442.32 in printing contracts from GPO. Minnesotans, like members of the public throughout the country, have many reasons to take interest in and be concerned about the important matters before this Committee.

I would like to make three key points this morning regarding the OMB Memorandum:

First, Federal agencies benefit by the transparent link that GPO currently provides between procuring agency publications and disseminating government publications to the public;

Second, the American people benefit when agency publications are disseminated through GPO to local Federal depository libraries in each congressional district across the country, where the public then has equal, efficient and ready access to that information;

And third, it is clear that the OMB directive will lead to more fugitive publications and less public access to government information. This comes at a time when Congress, the Executive Branch and the courts instead should be working together to improve public access and to meet the challenges of the electronic environment, particularly regarding the permanent public access to and preservation of electronic government information.

First, Federal agencies benefit by the transparent link that GPO currently provides between procuring agency publications and disseminating government publications to the public.

The OMB Memorandum at issue today will make it more difficult for agencies to meet their Title 44 obligations to inform the American public through the FDLP. Regardless of how they might procure or produce their government publications, agencies have an affirmative obligation to disseminate and provide broad public access to the information they create. From the earliest days of our democracy, Congress wisely recognized the importance of the public's right and need to have access to the information created by the Federal Government. To hold Government accountable for its actions, to educate and inform the citizenry, and to provide the public with information it has paid for with its tax dollars—it is for all these reasons that Congress and this Committee, in particular, have insisted that agencies fulfill their obligations under 44 USC Chapter 19 and disseminate their publications to Federal depository libraries and the public.

GPO provides agencies with an efficient and transparent mechanism to meet their Title 44 obligations and keep the public informed. The origins of the FDLP and its partnership with Congress date back to the Act of 1813, when Congress authorized legislation to provide one copy of the House and Senate Journals and other Congressional documents to certain universities, historical societies and state libraries. For more than 100 years, since the Printing Act of 1895, the link between producing, disseminating and no-fee public access to government publications, including those from Federal agencies, through the FDLP has worked effectively. When agencies comply with the

Section 501 provisions of Title 44, the GPO procures and manages the printing contract for the agency's publication. GPO then adds to the printing order the additional number of copies required for depository libraries, and distributes those copies to the libraries, with no effort or cost on the part of the agency. As part of this process, GPO also catalogs and classifies each publication and announces its availability in its online Catalog of government publications.

This efficient link—from GPO, to depository libraries, and to the public who needs and uses agency publications on a daily basis—is transparent (indeed, sometimes even unknown) to the issuing agency. This link has proven to be cost-effective for Government agencies and responsive to the needs of users. Breaking this link, as the OMB Memorandum proposes, would require a massive duplication of effort on the part of agencies and huge costs for the Federal Government. And should agencies fail to meet this additional burden, it will result in a dramatic erosion of the public's access to government information.

Moreover, the OMB Memorandum at issue here today states that "departments and agencies shall ensure that all government publications are made available to the depository library program through the Superintendent of Documents." OMB is basing this mandate on the assumption that today departments and agencies are complying fully with the 44 USC Chapter 19 requirements that government publications be part of the FDLP. Unfortunately, this is simply not so. In fact, when Title 44 was amended in 1976 to include law libraries and executive departments and agencies as part of the FDLP, many Federal libraries sought depository status in order to receive copies of their own agency's publications. For example, the National

Oceanic and Atmospheric Administration (NOAA) library became a FDLP library in 1993 in order to ensure that copies of NOAA publications would be available to their own scientists and to the public.

The FDLP serves as a cost saving for Federal agency libraries by allowing them to select publications from other agencies as well to add to their collections for use by their agency's personnel, and, in many cases, the public. The departmental policy of the Department of Interior (DOI), for example, requires two copies of DOI publications to be deposited to their library in Washington, DC, but the library also selects publications from other executive departments through the FDLP to supplement their collection. Publications from NOAA, for example, assist DOI's Fish and Wildlife Service library users in their research and in policy development. Other departments and agencies either are not able to or are unwilling to provide even their own libraries with copies of their publications, and so Federal libraries rely on a comprehensive FDLP to provide services, including cataloging and other finding tools, and permanent public access to government publications.

Second, the American people benefit when agency publications are disseminated through GPO to local Federal depository libraries in each congressional district across the country, where the public then has equal, efficient and ready access to that information.

The OMB Memorandum will make it more difficult for the public to access government information. Our Nation's libraries play a uniquely important role in helping the public access and use government information. Your constituents—whether they are rich or poor, young or old, live in a large city or in a remote rural area—all of them have equitable no-fee access to Federal government information through the collections and services provided by their local depository libraries. Indeed anyone, anywhere, can access the collections of depository libraries. Librarians working with and for the American public know first-hand, on a daily basis, the importance and impact that government information has on the health and lives of all Americans, on the economic well being of our Nation and on the preservation of our democracy. The more than 1,300 Federal depository libraries across the country, including public, academic, law, special, Federal agency, research and medical libraries, provide access to the tremendous amount of critically important Federal government information on all subjects and in many formats, and assist the American public in finding and sorting through this vital national resource. As knowledge experts in today's information society, librarians:

- Provide government information through our collections, and organize and develop these collections by making use of the cataloging and indexing services provided by GPO and other services, so that people can easily find the government information they need;

- Represent important channels of access for the public to government information, especially helping to close the digital divide for those in poor or rural areas without access to the latest technology by providing computers with Internet access and related services;

- Are educators and intermediaries who provide the necessary tools and expertise to assist the public in understanding and using the government information they find;

- Contribute $3 for every $1 in cost to the Government and spend millions of dollars annually for staff, space and equipment, and to buy commercial indexes, software, and access to networks to make government publications more accessible to the taxpayer;

- Provide feedback and expertise to Government agencies about how members of the public (who often are not the primary audience for agency publications) use government publications and assist agencies in developing information products, infrastructures, and policies for information in all formats;

- Partner with the Government in addressing the need for continuous, permanent public access to government information.

But librarians can't do any of these things if an agency's publications are not distributed to libraries and the public. The skills, expertise, and assistance that librarians can offer the public—services built on the historic partnership between libraries and the Federal Government to work together to help the public find and use the government information they need—these all go to waste if the Government doesn't hold up its end of the bargain and disseminate agency publications in the first place.

And third, it is clear that the OMB directive will lead to more fugitive government publications and less public access to government information. This comes at a time when Congress, the Executive Branch and the courts, instead should be working together to improve public access and to meet the challenges of the electronic environment, particularly regarding the permanent public access to and preservation of electronic government information.

There is no question that the OMB Memorandum will result in more fugitive government publications. Despite the requirements for agency dissemination in Title 44, it has been estimated that fifty percent of the government publications that Executive Branch agencies print today are "fugitive." This means that the printing or procurement is done outside of GPO or that agencies produce the publication on in-house printers. Most importantly, it also means that these publications are not known by GPO, are not cataloged by GPO and are not included in the FDLP, with the result that your constituents may be denied access to this information. Future generations also are denied the opportunity to benefit from, or even be aware of, this information that the Federal Government created at taxpayers' expense and that, by law, should be readily accessible to the public. Implementation of the OMB Memorandum will worsen this situation dramatically, not only because it will make it even more difficult to enforce the requirements of Title 44, but also because agencies will need to assume the additional costs of printing and distribution which are now borne by the GPO.

Locating a fugitive document to satisfy a user's important needs for information created by a Government agency is like trying to find a tiny needle in an endless row of haystacks. It is a very time-consuming and often fruitless search when you don't know which agency or department might have produced the information or data; when you don't know when the information was produced, or in what format; when the information has not been cataloged by GPO because the agency failed to meet its statutory requirements under Title 44; or when you don't know what the title is, or whether the information even exists. Unless GPO has cataloged the publication, it is going to be very difficult and frustrating to find. Particularly challenging and rarely successful is the task of searching for an electronic-only title that is hidden deeply within an agency web site—even when you know its title.

The fact of the matter is that when agencies use GPO, as required by law, to procure or print their publications, the public then has access to that information through the FDLP. When agencies do not use GPO, the public suffers because that information usually is lost and inaccessible. A 1998 review of the National Institutes of Health—an agency that has statutory authority to procure and print its publications—determined that only 22 percent of the NIH titles within the scope of the FDLP were actually provided to GPO for inclusion in the FDLP. This means that only about one out of every five publications issued by the NIH has been cataloged by GPO and provided to the public through depository libraries as mandated by law. The fact is that when agencies procure outside of GPO or print in-house, there is neither an economic incentive nor an enforcement mechanism in place today to ensure that they provide depository copies to the Superintendent of Documents. The effect of the OMB Memorandum will be to further exacerbate a problem that already is indefensible—it will result in more fugitive documents and less access to government information for the American public. Rather than looking for ways to help Federal agencies circumvent the law, OMB instead could and should be investing its time and resources in guiding agencies' commitment to dissemination and public access; to facilitating agencies' abilities to participate in the FDLP and make their publications accessible to the public; and to enforcing compliance where needed to ensure agencies' participation in the FDLP.

Finally, addressing the issues created by the OMB Memorandum will not, in itself, solve all the problems of public access to government information. During the past decade, Federal agencies, Congress and the courts have moved increasingly to rely on the Internet as the preferred system of public information access and dissemination. It is estimated that Federal entities today provide public access to more than 30 million Web pages. This number will continue to grow exponentially. GPO itself, as mandated by Congress, continues its transition to a more electronic FDLP. While it is distributing fewer documents in paper, it is including many more electronic publications in the program by providing cataloging and links to publications through the Catalog of Government Publications. GPO also ensures permanent public access for documents in the program by retaining documents permanently on GPO servers or entering into partnerships with agencies and other organizations.

As all parts of the Government embrace electronic dissemination, the consensus among librarians is that overall, Government-wide progress in information management has been slow, uncoordinated and without a clear vision for the future. This is despite the explosive growth of a more electronic environment and the concurrent financial investments in technology. Unfortunately, the move to an e-Government has not been accompanied by the development of a comprehensive policy framework focusing on the life-cycle of electronic government information. Such a framework is necessary to ensure that the public will have seamless, continuous and permanent access to important electronic information. Without sound and reasonable information policies supported by adequate funding for the life-cycle of government information, e-Government can not succeed. It is critically important to recognize the responsibility of the Federal Government to ensure the permanent public access to and preservation of government information in all formats. Documents distributed in paper or microfiche through the

FDLP are preserved permanently in the regional depository libraries that serve all states, thereby providing multiple points of permanent public access. Thus far, no similar system is in place for electronic government publications. Without a strong, coordinated national program to systematically capture, preserve, and maintain ongoing access to government information, important information is lost every day as files come and go from agency Web sites and computer servers. The information becomes inaccessible and thus useless to the American public whose tax dollars have supported its creation. We believe that this system of permanent public access can be accomplished through a comprehensively coordinated program that includes Federal agencies, the Superintendent of Documents, the National Archives and Records Administration, the Library of Congress and other national libraries, depository libraries, and other library partners.

Thank you very much for inviting me to participate in this very important hearing on the impact of the OMB Memorandum on public access to government information.

Used by permission of Julia F. Wallace.

Solution
Standards for Preservation of Digital Information

Time Is Not on Our Side: The Challenge of Preserving Digital Materials

Roy Tennant

Digital libraries are sitting on a time bomb. Yes, libraries are already familiar with deteriorating materials, but digital libraries face an even graver threat. While digital library materials do not decay like old paper, they nonetheless may become unusable. And digital librarians have learned that solutions must be different as well.

The Nature of the Problem

"Preservation," Yale's Paul Conway writes in the report "Preservation in the Digital World," "is the acquisition, organization, and distribution of resources to prevent further deterioration or renew the usability of selected groups of materials." The currently accepted preservation formats are acid-free paper, microfilm, and photographic reproduction. None of these are digital. In fact, there is no accepted format for preserving digital information. Rather, Conway and others discuss preservation strategies rather than formats. Preservation in the digital world, it turns out, has much more to do with long-term institutional commitment than with short-term fixes.

Why? Because preserving digital information is not simply a matter of determining which format will resist physical deterioration the longest—although that is still one aspect of the problem. The more serious threat is technological obsolescence. Remember 8-track tapes? Technology marches on and leaves previous, outmoded technologies in the dust.

The key publication that outlines the dilemmas of digital preservation and the need for a strategy to deal with the problems is "Preserving Digital Information: Final Report and Recommendations," from the Research Libraries Group (RLG).

This seminal report identifies the need for a migration strategy, so that as each technology reaches the end of its life, any information stored in that system or format can be brought forward into a new format or system. Migration therefore differs from the concept of refreshment, in which data from one deteriorating hard disk, CD-ROM, or tape are copied to another.

As outlined in the task force report, migration strategies can take several forms. One strategy is to change the storage medium, the most extreme solution being to print the item on acid-free paper, thus losing its digital nature altogether. An alternative: change format, i.e., move documents in proprietary word processing formats such as WordPerfect to ASCII or SGML-encoded text.

Central Repositories Needed

Standards for document formats, data storage, and information interchange are needed to help libraries and archives build effective data migration strategies. Given the specialized nature of this kind of work, as well as the costs to migrate information from one format to another, we may need to cooperate in funding central repositories to take on these tasks.

We already have models of similar kinds of cooperative efforts in organizations like the Center for Research Libraries (CRL), which collects rare items on behalf of a coalition of research libraries, and efforts such as JSTOR, which archives scholarly journals. A central digital archive could be supported by dues or fees from participating libraries and be responsible for migrating the information it holds to prevent its loss through media decay or technological obsolescence.

The More Complex the Material...

So far I've allowed you to assume that we are talking mainly about relatively straightforward materials—digital books, journals, and word processing files. Such mainly textual materials can typically be migrated from one technology to another without a great deal of information loss. For example, many of us can move files from one word processing program to another without much loss of content or context.

But what about much more complex materials that were born digital, such as multimedia presentations? What happens when the hardware and software environment required to run such an item is no longer available? What are the best preservation options for such complex items? We are just beginning to consider how these problems can be solved.

As may be apparent at this point, a viable digital preservation strategy requires institutional commitment and a structure of policies and procedures. "A Strategic Policy Framework for Creating and Preserving Digital Collections," produced for higher education institutions in the U.K., is a useful discussion of some of these issues.

This framework identifies three main stages in the life of a digital resource (creation, management/preservation, and use) and appropriate roles and functions of different stakeholders (funding agencies, libraries and archives, etc.) in preserving the resource. For an example of a specific digital preservation policy statement, see the National Library of Australia's "Statement of Principles for the Preservation of and Long-Term Access to Australian Digital Objects."

Doing the Job Once

An essential aspect of any preservation program is quality, or the importance of doing the job once and doing it right. This is particularly urgent for digital librarians, since standards for digital preservation are still being formulated. For example, what if you wish to digitize a deteriorating print item? Several years ago you would have probably scanned the item at 300 dots per inch (dpi). Since technology has both improved and dropped in price since then, now you would likely scan it at twice that resolution.

If there is this much difference in how an archival master is produced over just a few years, what does this bode for the long-term? What compromises in quality are we making now that we may regret later? It is just such issues that keep digital preservationists awake at night.

While they are unable to get any sleep, one thing digital preservationists can ponder is how things have changed. With print materials, preservation is an endgame. Typically, you don't have to think much about preservation until the book begins to crumble, or the binding starts coming apart. With digital material, everyone wants a commitment up front that you will keep this material around for the foreseeable future.

Within minutes of announcing the opening of the Berkeley Digital Library SunSITE February 1, 1996, I had a return message from a colleague wondering what commitment we had to preserving the material we were making available. What is it about digital information that turns the preservation process on its head?

Perhaps we need to cultivate an open market for digital information: when a library or archive no longer wants to maintain a particular collection, it announces the availability widely. If no person or organization steps forward to rescue it from extinction, then it probably is not worth saving anyway. After all, although individual libraries should check to see if they have the only copy of a print item before throwing it away, there is no formal mechanism for doing so, nor any requirement to do so.

Digital Preservation Resources

Besides the publications mentioned above, a number of resources can help you explore these issues further. "Preserving Access to Digital Information" (PADI), hosted by the National Library of Australia, points to a number of bibliographies, discussion lists, journals, web sites, and more; the "What's New" section is a good way to keep current. The "Conservation Online" (CoOL) web site is also an important resource, although it covers the preservation of non-digital material as well.

Organizations active in this issue include the Commission on Preservation and Access (CPA) and the Digital Library Federation (DLF), both of which are under the umbrella of the Council on Library Information and Resources (CLIR). Useful publications include the bimonthly "RLG DigiNews," the quarterly "Preservation and Access International Newsletter" [ceased publication in 2000] and the occasional "Conserve O Gram" from, yes, the National Park Service.

Link List

Center for Research Libraries <http://wwwcrl.uchicago.edu/>

Conservation Online <http://www.palimpsest.stanford.edu/>

Council on Library Information and Resources (CLIR)
<http://www.clir.org/>

Digital Library Federation <http://www.clir.org/
diglib/dlfhomepage.htm>

JSTOR <http://www.jstor.org/>

Preservation in the Digital World
<http://www.clir.org/pubs/reports/conway2/index.html>

Preserving Access to Digital Information (PADI)
<http://www.nla.gov.au/padi/>

Preserving Digital Information: Final Report and
Recommendations <http://www.rlg.org/ArchTF/>

RGL DigiNews <http://www.rlg.org/preserv/diginews/>

Statement of Principles for the Preservation of and Long-Term
Access to Australian Digital Objects
<http://www.nla.gov.au/preserve/digital/princ.html>

A Strategic Policy Framework for Creating and Preserving
Digital Collections <http://ahds.ac.uk/manage/framework.
htm>

Recommended Reading

"9/11: Businesses Rebuild. Reports from the Front Line of Disaster Recovery." *ZDNet: Tech Update* 10 Sept. 2002. http://techupdate.zdnet.com/techupdate/filters/specialreport/0,14622,6023411,00.html

Jobe, Margaret M. "Government information at a crossroads." *Library Journal* 15 May 2001: 62–6.

Kellogg, A. P. "An Order to Destroy a CD-ROM Raises Concerns Among University Librarians." *Chronicle of Higher Education* 14 Feb. 2002. http://chronicle.com/free/2002/02/2002021401t.htm

McKie, Robin and Vanessa Thorpe. "Digital Domesday Book Lasts 15 Years, Not 1000." *Guardian Unlimited Observer* 3 Mar. 2002. http://www.observer.co.uk/uk_news/story/0,6903,661093,00.html

Susman, Thomas. "Memorandum: The Removal or Destruction of Federal Depository Library Documents." 13 Mar. 2002. http://www.arl.org/info/frn/gov/Susman.html

Teper, Thomas H. "Where next? Long-term considerations for digital initiatives." *Kentucky Libraries* Spring 2001: 12–18.

United States. Cong. Senate. 107th Congress, 1st Session. Hearings before the Senate Committee on Governmental Affairs on S. 803, The E-Government Act of 2001, July 11, 2001. Statement of Sharon A. Hogan. http://www.senate.gov/~gov_affairs/071101_hogan.htm

Warner, Dorothy. "Why Do We Need To Keep This in Print? It's on the Web . . . A Review of Electronic Archiving Issues." *Progressive Librarian* Spring 2002. http://libr.org/PL/19-20_Warner.html

Chapter 10

How to Avoid Getting Blind-Sided

Solution
Scanning Present Indicators to Foresee Future Needs and Dangers

John Guscott, creator of *Library Futures Quarterly*, is running a continuing series he calls the Library Foresight System. Much more is to come, but this is his introduction to the system and his sketch of how to develop an early warning system.

Introduction to the Library Foresight System

John Guscott

Studying the future keeps a library in touch with its community and enduring in an ever-changing world. But how does one examine the future? Obviously, this is a difficult thing, since the future is not a fixed reality, and what seems to be a "sure thing" one day has vanished the next. Because the future is always in flux, smart decision makers don't rely on predictions or marketing hype about any one fixed future, but instead open their minds to a spectrum of futures, any of which may be pursued for realization. These optional futures fall under three basic categories:

- Possible: those futures that have a chance of occurring, whether they are imminent or only distantly possible, likely or unlikely, optimistic or pessimistic, conventional or unconventional.

- Probable: those futures that are likely to occur within a specified time frame. This form of future is usually the result of trend extrapolation, which describes what things would be like if present conditions remained fairly constant.

- Preferable/Undesirable: those futures that are either positive and desired or negative and undesired.

No one can accurately predict what will happen in the future, but we all have some control of what shape the future will take. The future of your library is more of a choice than a destiny. To help you manage your choices, *Library Futures Quarterly* has developed the Library Foresight System, a step-by-step approach to future building for libraries. This simple process leads you through the necessary stages to achieve a well-planned, vibrant future for your library.

The Library Foresight System Philosophy

The Library Foresight System is based on the following beliefs about the future:

- The future is shaped primarily by the decisions we make today.

- There is no one unavoidable future, but a range of alternatives from which to choose.

- The future is a product of interdependent and interrelated systems. A happening or trend in one field may affect the future of other fields.

Step 1: Create and Deploy Your Library's "Early Warning System"

For you to keep your library relevant and fresh in the 21st century, you need an early warning system to track and evaluate emerging trends and consider what they might mean for your library. Watching the library and media fields alone won't be enough to prepare your library for the future, although they are extremely important. Outside influences that change the way libraries are run are greater than ever. To get the big picture, other areas you might want to include on your watch list include business and economy, culture and society, politics and law, technology and other areas of innovation, and your own unique local environment.

Step 2: Screen the Hits from the Misses

Not everything your early warning system turns up will be usable for your situation—you'll have to carefully sift through the results to identify usable information for your planning. At this step, you will begin to rank the collected information according to the probability of occurring as well as its relative importance for the library and community. Be aware of certain possible futures that, even if they are a distant possibility, would have great impact on your library should they occur. Start developing a range of futures and divide them into what is possible, probable and preferable/undesirable.

Step 3: Choose Your Futures

From the range of futures you have identified, choose which of the desired futures your library will focus its attention and energy on. Choose futures that have high probability, high impact and are viable for your library. Examine which futures will fulfill a market need, and which build a new market altogether. Which ones will take full use of your library's competitive advantage, capabilities and unique values? By focusing on a future that is aligned with the core values of your library, you can confidently commit resources to creating that future. Determine which futures will build your library's legacy and will add value to the community it serves.

Step 4: Build the Scenarios

In order to breathe life into a selected future, you need to create brief, plausible stories that vividly describe a typical day, situation or event in that future. You become a storyteller and depict an imaginary time when your library is already in the desired future. For creativity purposes, the scenario begins with the end in mind, and isn't concerned with how the future came to be. It is also useful to create a few other "what if" scenarios that describe "what would happen if X occurred." You will want to write a few worst-case scenarios, or develop contingency scenarios should the desired future not occur.

Step 5: Create the Vision and the Plans

Having imagined the future through scenarios, you must choose the best scenarios and create a strategy that will make them happen. Specify the optimum scenarios for your library and focus on the means to achieve them. Many factors will be examined at this step, including consequences of actions, costs, market dynamics, life expectancy of services and return on investments. You will also have to consider factors such as marketing, features, styling and quality of the new products and services. Finally, use whatever method your library employs to get work done (e.g., action plans, to-do lists, etc.) and plug the vision into that system. Identify key personnel and other assets you'll need to realize the future.

Step 6: Promote the Vision

Inform and inspire the library staff, trustees and patrons with your vision of the future. Ensure that everyone involved in building the vision shares a unity of purpose and works toward making it a reality. Position your future vision as a fulfillment of the library's mission. Use marketing techniques to spread the vision and achieve a sense of excitement in the community.

Step 7: Evaluate Your Library's Progress

To learn from the successes and mistakes encountered during your
library's progress, you'll have to continually evaluate your library's
situation. The Library Foresight System is a process with no end, as
you are always scanning and remaining open to adaptations and the
fluctuating nature of the future. This step is like checking a map to
make sure you are headed in the right direction, and if not, you can
always make the necessary adjustments to get back on the right track.

Library Foresight System Step 1:
Building Your Library's Early Warning System

The first stage of the Library Foresight System is to build an early
warning system to detect the issues that are likely to affect the future
of your library. Although similar to conducting an environmental
scan, establishing an early warning system is quite different in the
way the collected information is viewed. Environmental scans provide a snapshot of the current state of affairs. Your early warning system will also capture the present, but it doesn't stop there. Through
the continued discovery of new material, your system will compel
you to continually reveal the various catalysts of change and forecast
how they might play out over time. This may be done through extrapolation, or through finding ongoing trends, emerging issues and new
ideas. Through a series of questions, interviews, and exercises, you
will start to deeply understand the community you serve and the
forces that drive it into the future. Setting up your library's early warning system is not entirely a scientific exercise. While it does require a
fair amount of analytical thinking, your intuition and creative mind
will inform you. The process requires you to tap into your powers of
insight and instinct and to reach into your gut-feelings. Since intuition can be a subjective thing, I recommend you work together
with only one or two other people on collecting the information for
your early warning system. I wouldn't necessarily recommend a
committee or task force for this job, since these approaches tend to

be time-consuming and the members often lack accountability. Also, too much subjectivity from a large group can cloud the real findings and offer only vague interpretations, especially when clarity, precision and unity are needed.

Where do you go to gather the data for your early warning system? Reading *Library Futures Quarterly*, particularly the Radar Scope section, will alert you to trends that affect libraries across the world. For local issues, you must identify the forces of change in your community and start to monitor them closely. Begin by talking to people who live in the community and use your library to identify the possible forces of change. The library staff is particularly invaluable, especially your circulation staff. In today's libraries, the circulation staff has the most contact with the general public, and have a sense of what people are interested in and how they behave. After talking to your staff, find a few trusted informants in the community who can give you additional information.

Finding the Forces of Change in Your Community

Constituents—This category includes all the people who live in your service area, whether they use your library or not. Before you begin to assess your constituents, it may be helpful to divide your service area into sections based on demographics and psychographics. People of a like mind tend to live close together in fairly homogenous—or at least harmonic—neighborhoods. No matter how small your service area, you can divide your city into a few separate "wards." For example, the community in which I work is only 6 square miles, but I can easily divide the map up into 10 distinct areas based on income level, housing type and ethnic or religious background. To help you divide your community, rely on both your unscientific assessments based on your experiences and intuition and hard demographic data. Libraries will soon receive Census 2000 data, which can assist your analysis. To get a glimpse deeper into the lives and values of your community, it is worthwhile to get a cluster segmentation report [see last issue of *Library Futures Quarterly*].

Take a close look at the populations in each of the areas, studying both the people who use your library and the people who don't. What issues are most important to them? What are their typical behaviors or habits? What are their values? What are their life situations like? Examine their political and social beliefs: where do the different segments of your community stand in terms of economic beliefs? Where do they stand on personal freedoms? A key area is their attitudes toward government institutions and organizations. How do they see public education and public space (e.g., as an area of pride or a wasteful use of taxpayer money)? What are their stances on family values? Who are the dominant community authority groups? Is your community generally matriarchal or patriarchal?

How has each area changed in composition of population over the last few years? Are any of the areas changing now? What elements are occurring that is causing this change? What are the housing patterns like? Many community newspapers publish listings of who bought and sold houses recently. Is the area's housing stock value increasing or decreasing? Are there a large number of government or bank repossessions? Based on your observations, will the areas be roughly the same in five years, or are they drifting to include new populations? How is your library providing service to the people in each of these areas? How can you attract people from each area to the library? If the composition of the area changes significantly, what strategies will you need to take to attract the new population?

Next, look at your community's schools. Is the school population growing or decreasing? Are the results because of changes in the birthrate or household types (singles vs. families)? Since many students will remain in the community in which they grew up, even after college, this can give you a sense of who will be living in the community in the near future. What is the makeup of your student body like?

What are the dominant subcultures in the schools? Are students using your library or do they choose other information sources?

Finally, look at your library's key customers. For what reasons do they use the library? Who are your most frequent patrons? Are they students, street people, business people, etc.? Who are your library's "lead users," the sophisticated customers who use your most up-to-date services (or recommend new services)? Who used to use the library, and why do they no longer come in as frequently, if at all? Do you notice any trends or issues that alert you to fundamental change in your constituents? Which will bear watching over a two-year period? A five-year period?

Social Identity—Every community has a social dynamic that makes it unique. Does your community have a "mystique"—something that makes it distinctive? How do people in your community see themselves? Are the social dynamics in your community negative, positive or neutral? Do people wish the community can get rid of some elements and increase others? What's your community's reputation with neighboring cities?

Have any of the answers to the above questions changed over the past few years? Where are they trending now? What steps does your library have to take in order to maximize the good elements?

Competitors & Enemies—Despite their elevated status as public institutions, libraries are in truth surrounded by competition. Libraries are constantly competing for market share against other information services (e.g., Internet), other forms of media distribution (bookstores, theaters, television companies, etc.) and even other libraries (public, school and otherwise).

Find out who your competitors are. This is a difficult task for librarians, since we often see ourselves as quasi-monopolies and were never trained to act as if we were doing business in the private sector, battling for market share through innovation or aggressive service models. What are your competitor's motives? What are they doing now? What are they doing better than you? Are they doing anything inferior? Do you know their future plans? Who are their leaders? Are there any alliances among your competitors? Is anyone ganging up on another, mutual competitor? Which of your competitors are national, and which are local? Are your competitors passive or aggressive? What are their weaknesses? Are there any blind spots to exploit? How do your constituents view your competitors? Do they see them as another option to fill their needs, or as a replacement for your services? When answering the above questions, imagine scenarios in which the trends are all drifting against you. How could you combat such a situation?

Also scan for your library's enemies. With a competitor, there is often friendly rivalry or even occasional cooperation but an enemy is rarely friendly. Is there any person or group actively combating the library? It could be a former employee or someone you didn't hire, an anti-public sector activist, a gadfly with an ax to grind, a champion of a political, moral or social cause or an overzealous reporter looking for a story. I'm not advising you to keep an enemies list, but know who they are, know their modus operandi and alert the appropriate people to possible scenarios. In the future, your library's enemies are likely to enter into the picture, and it's best to have a plan in place.

Economics—Keeping track of the national economy includes following the dynamics of financial markets, monitoring prices, suppliers who may be affected by environment, among other areas. *Library Futures Quarterly* will help you monitor the national economy, and in a future issue an article will be devoted to tracking the macroeconomic environment.

For your EWS, you will want to survey your local economy. Who are the largest employers in your service area? In what sectors do the bulk of your constituents work? Are they cyclical industries, government, etc.? Are the dominant companies in your service area resistant to recession? How does your community weather bad times, and how do they enjoy themselves when times are prosperous? What events would need to occur to brighten your community's economic future? What would cause it to dim? What is the attitude to taxes and public service costs in your community? In general, everyone believes that his or her taxes are too high, but all members of a community have an internal "tax priority" list. What are your community's priorities? Where does the library rank? What is viewed as indispensable? What can you do to move your library from the "nice to have" category to "indispensable"? What circumstances would have to occur to move your library out of the favored status? Monitor those circumstances regularly, and find ways to better position your library in the case of economic hardship.

Technology—Technologies affect libraries in two ways: as an opportunity for development or as threat to service, even existence. Often, a technology can take both roles. Which technologies are on the upswing and which are waning? Which ones have an impact on your services? Are technologies being developed that threaten the existence or functions of your library? How can you turn these technologies into an opportunity? Monitor early adopters and see how they are using the technology to further their own agendas.

Although libraries are not traditionally technology labs, they could be. Sometimes libraries find the most innovative uses of technologies, perhaps even better than the private sector. How could you develop technologies or technology solutions yourself? To fully be aware of technology's implications, library leaders need to read "hacker" publications. I'm not referring to computer criminals, but the creative individuals who find innovative uses for technologies and are often catalysts for change. These technophiles tend to be voracious readers and you probably know of some who use your library. These individuals are living one or two years ahead in the future already, and could provide valuable insight into the implications and realistic assessments of technologies.

Politics—National political philosophies usually set the tone for the whole country. Examine both elected and appointed officials, especially those in the overlooked "fourth branch" of government, which consist of the bureaucracies that carry out policy. What are the priorities of government? What are their attitudes toward education and libraries? [*Library Futures Quarterly* will devote an article to watching national government in a future issue.]

Who runs your local government? Does a "political machine" run it? Do people from the private sector dominate (popular in newer cities in the South & West)? Are there lifelong politicos moving up the *cursus honorum*? How are appointments made? If your library is part of the city government, who are the closest competitors for your funds? If you are a governed by a school board, who are your allies and detractors? How are the trends drifting? What steps do you have to take to protect your library for the future?

Law & Crime—On a national level, pay attention to litigation in the following areas: intellectual property, human resources, sexual harassment, copyright, obscenity, trademark, hate crimes and censorship. All these areas are likely to affect libraries in the future.

On a local level, a community's system of justice sets the pace of who will move in, who feels safe and who will leave. Pay attention to how crime is dealt with in your community—is there a public outcry when a crime crisis occurs? Does the act galvanize the neighborhoods or is it viewed as "business as usual"? How do long-time residents feel about the current state of law and crime? Do they feel safe or ready to move? If they are moving out, who is replacing them? Attitudes to crime show where a community's tolerance level is to unwelcome behavior. The more apathetic the community is toward crime, the more criminals will feel welcome. This can become problematic for your library, as it may become a target or gathering place for troublesome individuals or groups. Talk to police to get a sense of where problems are now or will likely occurring.

What is your community's feeling about non-violent vices (i.e., soft drugs, drinking, pornography)? Are there strict laws banning bars or "adult" entertainment? Are there activist groups seeking to minimize these elements? Generally speaking, the more tolerant a community is about these matters, the less citizen activism you will have in library matters.

Guiding the Future:

Having identified the forces of change, ask yourself (or your small EWS group) these questions:

- Are there any surprises that may occur that will alter the nature, course or impact of an identified force of change?

- Which of the identified forces does the library control?

- What forces can the library not control?

- How can I as the library leader alert, warn or advise other community leaders to opportunities and threats discovered in the early warning system process for the greater good of the community?

- What ways can I position the library to the greatest advantage for the future?

Keep in mind that even if you have absolute certainty about a force, there are still the possibilities for alternative futures. Factor in the impact and implications of these alternatives. The early warning system is a continuous process, not a final report, and must be continued on a regular basis.

Solution
Dream Big

The Defect in Realism

Marylaine Block

I'd like to suggest one possible reason why we let Amazon beat us at our own game of constructing catalogs: we may be too realistic for our own good.

We know that libraries exist either by the marginal grace of tax-payers, or by that of institutions which see them solely as a cost, rather than a generator of revenue. We understand that given the excessive rate of inflation in books and journal prices, and the techno-economic imperative that forces us to continually add to and upgrade our equipment, our funders view libraries as a black hole capable of sucking up all available revenue.

I suspect what that means for many of us is that we focus our energies on what seems doable—keeping what we've got, with maybe a few extras tacked on. If you're busy fighting for an extra $20,000 just to maintain, not expand, the periodicals budget, if you're working with an administration that would rather spend $150,000 over six years to buy compact shelving than shell out $60,000 in one year to buy it all at once, it's hard to think about, let alone try to sell, blue-sky ideas that may run into the millions.

Amazon could afford to spend millions of dollars on servers and software because they expected to make money doing it, and they got the start-up money up-front from other people who believed they would succeed. We know perfectly well that taxpayers and our administrations wouldn't fork over that kind of money, don't we?

Actually, I'm not sure we do, because I don't know if we ever asked them. Certainly we've gotten up the nerve to ask for bright, shiny, expensive, new buildings, and the equipment for them, because the benefits are obvious and highly visible, and there will be ribbons to cut and photo-ops when it's time for the grand opening. But who of us would go to our administrations and say, "Give me a few million dollars and I'll produce the ultimate user-friendly catalog that tells people everything they could possibly want to know about any book or video or recording in our library"?

Even if we could think of the idea in the first place, would we propose it? It would require so much explaining, to people who don't understand much about libraries, who might not think libraries are all that important, who might still resent our decision to dispose of the card catalog. It would require extraordinary persuasive skill to sell the idea, first to a few influential potential allies, and then to a wider public. It would require the library director to have enormous credibility, and to be well known for the ability to deliver promised services on budget and on time. And it would require the ability to build a scalable budget for the project, because sure as shooting, if the idea makes headway at all, it will be on a smaller budget than what you're asking for.

Daunting, isn't it? It's a lot easier to ask for what you're already getting, but more of it; people may not understand even these expenditures very well, but at least budget items like periodicals and equipment and databases have the benefit of tradition behind them.

The problem is, when we scale our dreams to fit our realistic budgets, we might end up with cut-rate dreams, and a world where people like Jeff Bezos zip right past us and create a future that makes libraries irrelevant. As Joe Janes of the University of Washington says: "The AskJeeves of the world did not steal our users. We gave them away and it's time to get them back."

The political problems for individual library directors are great enough that it seems to me serious blue-skying has to be done at the consortium level—it's always easier to convince our own funders to contribute just a portion of funding to a project some reputable larger organization is responsible for. Consortiums can also draw on a wider range of funding resources—state funding and grants, as well as member contributions. And larger organizations have greater clout with vendors.

How do we stop playing the incrementalism game and learn how to dream big? One way is to pay attention to emerging technologies and ask how our own services might be improved by using them.

Another way is to remember that the traditional ways of doing things are often habits based on the limitations of past technologies; we don't necessarily have to keep on doing them that way. Remember, the reason we used so few SEE references was because each entry required typing and filing another card. Guess what? It doesn't any more.

We should re-examine every single service we perform, and the way we perform it, from the point of view of our users: could we make it more accessible, or more convenient? Could fuzzy logic finally solve the age-old problem of users who can't find what they want because they can't spell it? Does our online catalog include only our own library's holdings, when it might include those of nearby libraries as well? Does it allow you to find out what's inside a book by listing tables of contents, or displaying book reviews or pictures of the book jacket?

Do our web pages let users ask questions? Do they let our users talk back, contributing reading recommendations or suggestions and comments? Can our users fill out any of our forms online and e-mail them to us?

This is a game we could—and maybe should—keep on playing forever, or at least until we are replaced by a new generation of librarians who have never ever seen a card catalog or a *Readers' Guide*— librarians who have no understanding of, or commitment to, the way we used to do things.

Question everything. Dream big, and worry about details later. If the dream is beautiful enough, it will attract money and partners.

Recommended Reading

American Demographics. This monthly magazine of market research is a treasure house of information about changing American interests, preferences, and expectations.

Futurist. A magazine about possible, or even probable, futures.

Library Futures Quarterly. John Guscott's publication includes articles such as his "Library Foresight System," but it also provides summaries of articles that touch on the future of libraries and of our library users.

About the Editor

From 1977 to 1999, Marylaine Block was Associate Director for Public Services at St. Ambrose University's library. In 1995, she acquired a reputation as an internet "guru" by creating Best Information on the Net (http://library.sau.edu/bestinfo/), one of the first librarian's indexes to the Web. As American correspondent for a British online publication, she began writing an Internet column called *My Word's Worth* (http://www.qconline.com/myword/archive.html). As a result, Fox News Online invited her to write a weekly column called *Observing US*, which ran from April 1998 through November 2000.

In 1999, she became a full-time writer, speaker, and publisher of two e-zines for librarians, ExLibris (http://marylaine.com/exlibris) and a site review service, Neat New Stuff I Found This Week on the Web (http://marylaine.com/neatnew.html). She has written numerous articles for library publications like *American Libraries*, *Library Journal*, and *Searcher*, and general interest publications like *Writer* and *Yahoo! Internet Life*. She also edited *The Quintessential Searcher: The Wit and Wisdom of Barbara Quint*, published by Information Today, Inc. in 2001.

Marylaine is a frequent speaker at librarians' conferences, where she has addressed topics like library marketing, mapping the information landscape, and how libraries can better serve men's interests. Links to all of her presentations and writings are available at http://marylaine.com/.

Contributors

Andrew R. Albanese is associate editor, *LJ Academic Newswire.*

Janet L. Balas is library information systems specialist at Monroeville (Pennsylvania) Public Library. She can be reached by e-mail at jbalas@telerama.lm.org or balasj@clpgh.org.

Steven J. Bell is director of Gutman Library at Philadelphia University, e-mail: bells@philau.edu.

Lawrence Biemiller is a senior writer for *The Chronicle of Higher Education.*

Chris Bradfield has been with the Vigo County Public Library for more than 10 years. She is currently serving as the associate branch manager for the library's East Branch. She is simultaneously pursuing her M.L.S. at Indiana University–Indianapolis. Her e-mail address is cbradfield@ vigo.lib.in.us.

Lynne E. Bradley is Office of Government Relations director of ALA's Washington office. Her e-mail address is lbradley@alawash.org.

Kelly Broughton is reference coordinator at the Jerome Library at Bowling Green State University in Bowling Green, Ohio. She holds an M.A. in library and information science from Rosary College in River Forest, Illinois. Her e-mail address is kmoore@bgnet.bgsu.edu.

James B. Casey, Ph.D., is director of the Oak Lawn (Illinois) Public Library.

Ron Chepesiuk, an *American Libraries* contributing editor, is a professor and head of special collections at Winthrop University in Rock Hill, South Carolina. He has also written or edited 10 books, most recently *South Carolina in the Civil War* (McFarland, 2000).

Leigh S. Estabrook, dean of the University of Illinois/Urbana–Champaign library school, surveyed the Internet access policies of more than 1,000 U.S. public libraries last spring along with Ed Lakner. Their full report is available at http://www.lis.uiuc.edu/gslis/research/internet.pdf/.

Darlene Fichter (fichter@lights.com) is data library coordinator, half-time, University of Saskatchewan Libraries, president and owner of Northern Lights Internet Solutions, and a frequent contributor to *Online* and other publications.

Fred J. Gitner is assistant head, New Americans Program, Queens Borough Public Library, Jamaica, New York.

Rachel Singer Gordon is head of computer services at the Franklin Park Public Library in Franklin Park, Illinois. She is the co-author of *The Information Professional's Guide to Career Development Online* (Information Today, Inc., 2001), author of *The Accidental Systems Librarian* (Information Today, Inc., 2003), and the Webmaster of the library careers site Lisjobs.com (http://www.lisjobs.com/). Her e-mail address is rachel@lisjobs.com.

Michele Gorman is the Wired for Youth librarian, Carver Branch, Austin Public Library, Texas.

John Guscott is the manager of electronic services at Lakewood Public Library (Ohio), and the creator and editor of *Library Futures Quarterly*.

Steven Heser is the north campus librarian and Web developer at Milwaukee Area Technical College. He holds an M.L.I.S. from the University of Wisconsin–Milwaukee and an M.A. from Marquette University in Milwaukee. His e-mail address is hesers@matc.edu.

Péter Jacsó is associate professor of library and information science at the University of Hawaii's Department of Information and Computer Sciences. He is also a columnist for *Information Today* and a popular conference speaker. His e-mail address is jacso@hawaii.edu.

Sarah Kaip, formerly reference librarian and the SOLIC coordinator at the Jackson County Medford Library, now has her own writing and editing business. She can be reached at sarahkaip@yahoo.com.

Janet Kinney is the community services director and learning systems manager, Multnomah County Library.

Cheryl H. Kirkpatrick is information technology librarian at the South Carolina State Library; her e-mail address is cheryl@leo.scsl. state.sc.us.

Ed Lakner, of the University of Illinois/Urbana–Champaign's Library Research Center, surveyed the Internet access policies of more than 1,000 U.S. public libraries last spring along with Leigh S. Estabrook. Their full report is available at http://www.lis.uiuc.edu/gslis/research/internet.pdf/.

Joyce M. Latham is an instructor at the graduate school of Library and Information Science, University of Illinois at Urbana–Champaign. She may be reached at latham1@uiuc.edu.

Jenny Levine is Internet development specialist at the Suburban Library System, Bur Ridge, Illinois. Known for her original Web sites, the Librarians' Reference Site du Jour and Jenny's Cybrary, she is now even better known for her blog, The Shifted Librarian. Contact her at Jenny@TheShiftedLibrarian.com.

Molly Susan Mathias, who was reference librarian and instructional specialist at Milwaukee Area Technical College when she wrote this article, is now teaching an Internet research class at the University of Wisconsin Milwaukee. She holds an M.L.I.S. and an M.A. from the University of Wisconsin–Milwaukee. Her e-mail address is mathias@sois.uwm.edu.

Shannon Maughan is audio news editor and children's audio/video review editor for *Publishers Weekly* and an executive editor for the Web site http://www.kidsreads.com.

Mary Minow is an attorney, consultant, and a former librarian and library trustee. She has taught library law at the San Jose State School of Library Science.

Catherine Buck Morgan is automation librarian at the South Carolina State Library. Her e-mail address is catherine@ leo.scsl.state.sc.us.

Elaina Norlin is undergraduate services librarian at the University of Arizona in Tucson.

Nancy Pearl, executive director for the Washington Center for the Book at the Seattle Public Library, created the One City One Book concept. She is editor of "The Reader's Shelf" column for *Library Journal*, and is also author of the book *Now Read This: A Guide to Mainstream Fiction, 1978–1998*.

Jeanne Holba Puacz is a systems and reference librarian at the Vigo County (Indiana) Public Library. Additionally, she is the library Webmaster and is responsible for the majority of the public computer training. She received her M.L.S. from the University of Illinois at Urbana–Champaign. Her e-mail address is jpuacz@ vigo.lib.in.us.

Rob Reilly, Ed.D., is the computer education teacher in the Lanesborough (Massachusetts) Elementary School. He is also a visiting scientist at the MIT Media Laboratory in Cambridge, Massachusetts. His e-mail address is reilly@media.mit.edu.

Karen G. Schneider is the new coordinator of lii.org, the Librarians' Index to the Internet. She wrote the "Internet Librarian" column for *American Libraries* from 1995 to 2002, and wrote *A Practical Guide to Internet Filters* (Neal Schuman, 1997), and *The Internet Access Cookbook* (Neal Schuman, 1996).

Eric Sisler (esisler@westminster.lib.co.us) is library computer technician, Westminster Public Library, Colorado.

Mary Stillwell, formerly with the Gates Foundation, is now library training coordinator, Library Division, Office of the Secretary of the State of Washington.

Peter Suber, professor of philosophy, Earlham College, is the creator and publisher of the *Free Online Scholarship Newsletter.*

Claudette Tennant is Internet policy specialist, ALA Office of Information Technology Policy. Her e-mail address is ctennant@alawash.org.

Roy Tennant (roy.tennant@ucop.edu) is manager, e-scholarship Web and services design, California Digital Library. He is founder and manager of the electronic discussion lists Web4Lib and Current Cites.

Ken Varnum (kvarnum@ford.com) is head of Web development at Ford Motor Company's Library Systems & Information Research department.

Julia F. Wallace has been head of the government publications library at the University of Minnesota since 1989. In 1996 she received the American Library Association's Government Document Round Table award for lifetime contributions to the field of documents librarianship.

Jeffrey R. Young is senior editor for student issues for *The Chronicle of Higher Education.*

URLs

Chapter One
Regaining Control over Selection

Librarians Index to the Internet, http://lii.org/

Colorado Virtual Library for Kids, http://aclin.org/index_cvl.html
*A great example of how selection can be educational—in the
section for teachers, sites are chosen for, and searchable by,
grade level, subject, and Colorado state educational standards
and benchmarks.*

Digital Library Federation, http://www.hti.umich.edu/cgi/b/bib/
bib-idx?c=dlfcoll *Where you can search through several hundred
digital library projects.*

JSTOR: The Scholarly Journal Archive, http://www.jstor.org/

Making of America, http://moa.umdl.umich.edu/ *A joint project of
the University of Michigan and Cornell to digitize a large number
of 19th century books and journals.*

Scholarly Electronic Publishing Weblog, http://info.lib.uh.edu/
sepb/sepw.htm *In which Charles Bailey acquaints you daily with
news in the world of scholarly publishing on the Web.*

Selection Policy, Best Information on the Net http://library.sau.edu/
bestinfo/selpolicy.htm *The selection policy I wrote for the Web site
I created for O'Keefe Library, St. Ambrose University.*

Chapter Two
Rescuing the Book

Blackwell's Tables of Contents Enrichment Service,
http://www.blackwell.com/level2/TOC.asp

Ferguson Library Catalog, http://www.futuris.net/ferg/

Ingram Library Services, http://www.ingramlibrary.com/

OCLC Announces Enhancements to WorldCat, http://www.oclc.org/oclc/press/20010918.shtm/

Table-of-Contents Enhancement of the Catalog, http://www.library.cornell.edu/cts/martyrep.htm

UC-Berkeley Library Proposal, http://sunsite.berkeley.edu/PEP/

Center for the Book at the Library of Congress http://www.loc.gov/loc/cfbook/ctr-bro.html

Vermont Center for the Book, http://www.vermontbook.org/

Colorado Center for the Book, http://www.aclin.org/~ccftb/

Washington Center for the Book at the Seattle Public Library, http://www.spl.org/wacentbook/centbook.html

If All of Seattle Read the Same Book, http://www.spl.org/wacentbook/seattleread/samebook.html

Guys Read: A Literacy Initiative for Boys, http://www.guysread.com/

Information Week: Breakaway, http://www.informationweek.com/breakaway/

BookCrossing.com, http://bookcrossing.com/

Chapter-a-Day, http://www.chapteraday.com/

StoryPlace: The Children's Digital Library, http://www.storyplace.org/

The Library Hotel, http://www.libraryhotel.com/

WPL: Waterboro Lib Blog, http://www.waterborolibrary.org/blog.htm

Morton Grove Public Library: MatchBook, http://www.webrary.org/rs/matchbookabout.html

Recommended Graphic Novels for Public Libraries, Selected and Annotated by Steve Raiteri, http://my.voyager.net/~sraiteri/graphicnovels.htm

Book Lists and Bibliographies, http://www.waterborolibrary.org/bklista.htm *A clearinghouse for the recommended reading lists that every library generates, courtesy of Waterboro Public Library (Maine).*

Books in Spanish and Portuguese, http://www.leercentral.net/ *A key resource for collection building. Choose from English, Spanish, or Portuguese versions, and search by author, title, or keyword.*

BuildLiteracy.org, http://www.buildliteracy.org/index.htm

E-Book Library at the Electronic Text Center, University of Virginia http://etext.lib.virginia.edu/ebooks/ebooklist.html *More than 1,600 titles for the MS READER and PALM Devices*

Future of the Book, http://www.futureofthebook.com/

ReadingGroupGuides.com, http://www.readinggroupguides.com/ *"The online community for reading groups." Includes author interviews, recommended books, and discussion questions.*

Waterboro Library Blog: "What Books Cities Are Reading Together." 13 Jan. 2003, http://www.waterborolibrary.org/blogs/blog381402.htm#onebook

"Yahoo: One Book Community Reading Programs." 2002, http://dir.yahoo.com/Arts/Humanities/Literature/Organizations/Reading_Groups/One_Book_Community_Reading_Programs/

Chapter Three
Training Our Users

X-Refer, http://w1.xrefer.com/

Bartleby, http://bartleby.com/

SearchGov, http://searchgov.com/

MedlinePlus, http://medlineplus.gov/

Academic Info's Biology and Biological Sciences Gateway, http://www.academicinfo.net/biology.html

Ask Jeeves, http://www.askjeeves.com/

Documents in the News, http://www.lib.umich.edu/govdocs/docnews.html

Find Articles.com, http://www.findarticles.com/Pl/index.jhtml

Google, http://www.google.com/

Internet Public Library, http://www.ipl.org/

Librarians' Index to the Internet, http://lii.org/

MagPortal, http://magportal.com/

MSN Search, http://search.msn.com

Multnomah County Library's Social Issues page, http://www.multnomah.lib.or.us/lib/homework/sochc.html

Online Books Page, http://digital.library.upenn.edu/books/

Polling Report, http://www.pollingreport.com/

Purdue University's Online Writing Lab, http://owl.english.purdue.edu/

Scout Report Archive, http://scout.wisc.edu/archives/

Statistical Resources on the Web, http://www.lib.umich.edu/govdocs/stats.html

Vivisimo, http://www.vivisimo.com/

PC Webopedia, http://www.pcwebopedia.com/

Virtual Acquisition Shelf and News Desk, http://resourceshelf.freepint.com/

Search Day, http://searchenginewatch.com/searchday

SurfWax, http://www.surfwax.com/

ThinkQuest, http://thinkquest.org/

Chapter Four
Adapting to the Changing Expectations of Our Users

The Shifted Librarian: The Web Site, http://theshiftedlibrarian.com/

The Shifted Librarian Presentation, http://www.sls.lib.il.us/infotech/presentations/infoshifting/infoshifting.ppt

Vigo County Public Library: Questions, http://www.vigo.lib.in.us/ref/ask.htm

Vigo County Public Library: Request to Add an Item, http://www.vigo.lib.in.us/suggest.htm

Doc Searls, http://doc.weblogs.com/

Slashdot, http://www.slashdot.org/

Pitas.com, http://pitas.com/

Blogger.com, http://blogger.com/

GrokSoup.com, http://www.groksoup.com/

Moreover's news headline service, http://www.livejournal.com/www.moreover.com/

LiveJournal.com, http://www.livejournal.com

Open Journal (OJ), http://grohol.com/downloads/oj/

Master WebLog, http://willmaster.com/master/weblog/index.shtml/

Squishdot, http://squishdot.org/

Open Directory, http://www.dmoz.org/

The AcqWeblog, http://acqweb.library.vanderbilt.edu/acqweb/ms_acqs.html

'brary' blog, http://chickeninthewoods.org/brary/index.php

Liblog: A Library Weblog, http://www.rcpl.info/services/liblog.html

Library News Daily, now Peter Scott's Library Blog, http://blog.xrefer.com/

Neat New Stuff I Found on the Net This Week, http://www.marylaine.com/neatnew.html

Newsresearch.weblogs.com—"A Resource Guide for News Researchers," http://newsresearch.weblogs.com/

Research Buzz, http://www.researchbuzz.com/news/index.shtml

RSS for Non-Techie Librarians, http://www.llrx.com/features/rssforlibrarians.htm

RSS Workshop, http://gils.utah.gov/rss.html

ELITE Project Web site from the University of Leicester, http://www.le.ac.uk/li/distance/eliteproject/elib/

Sloan, Bernie. Digital Reference Services Bibliography: a Supplement. October 14, 2002, http://alexia.lis.uiuc.edu/~b-sloan/digiref.html

DIGREF listserv, http://www.vrd.org/Dig_Ref/dig_ref.shtml

LiveReference e-group, http://groups.yahoo.com/group/livereference/

AvantGo, http://www.avantgo.com/

brarydog, http://www.brarydog.net/

StoryPlace, http://www.storyplace.org/

BizLink, http://www.bizlink.org/

HealthLinkPlus, http://www.healthlinkplus.org

Public Library of Charlotte and Mecklenburg County Family of Web Sites, http://www.plcmc.org/sharedPages/PLCMCwebSites.htm

E-Book Library at the Electronic Text Center, University of Virginia, http://etext.lib.virginia.edu/ebooks/ebooklist.html *More than 1,600 downloadable titles for the MS READER and PALM Devices.*

Introduction to RSS from www.WebReference.com/ http://webreference.com/authoring/languages/xml/rss/intro/

LiveRef: A Registry of Real-Time Digital Reference Services, http://www.public.iastate.edu/~CYBERSTACKS/LiveRef.htm

Portal Webliography, http://infomotions.com/portals/ *From Eric Lease Morgan, "The purpose of the webliography is to collect, organize, and disseminate pointers to information and examples of user-driven and customizable interfaces to sets of Internet resources—portals."*

Wilton Library: Innovative Internet Applications in Libraries, http://www.wiltonlibrary.org/innovate.html

Wireless Librarian, http://people.morrisville.edu/~drewwe/ wireless/ *Wireless librarian Bill Drew talks about his own library's experiences instituting a wireless LAN, and also includes links to articles, LibWireless discussion group, vendors, and other related resources.*

Chapter Five
Access Issues

Bobby Worldwide, http://bobby.cast.org/bobby/bobbyServlet/ *Have Bobby check your Web site for free to analyze what problems it will cause people with disabilities.*

CAST (Center for Applied Special Technology), http://www.cast.org/ *"A not-for-profit organization that uses technology to expand opportunities for all people, especially those with disabilities."*

EASI—Equal Access to Software & Information, http://easi.cc/ *A source for adaptive technology and training.*

Web Standards Project, http://www.webstandards.org/ *"... a grass-roots coalition fighting for standards that ensure simple, affordable access to Web technologies for all." Tutorials, reference charts, and templates help you learn to use the standards.*

Ai Squared, http://www.aisquared.com/

DBH Attachments, Inc., http://www.dbhattachments.com/

Duxbury Systems, Inc., http://www.duxburysystems.com/

Freedom Scientific, http://www.freedomsci.com/

Gus Communications, Inc., http://www.gusinc.com/

Troll Touch, http://www.trolltouch.com/

Zines, E-Zines, The Book of Zines, http://www.zinebook.com

HotMail (free e-mail), http://www.hotmail.com/

Yahoo! (free e-mail), http://www.yahoo.com/

Angelfire (Web-page hosting), http://angelfire.lycos.com/

Tripod (Web-page hosting), http://www.tripod.lycos.com/

Geocities (Web-page hosting), http://geocities.yahoo.com/

Fortune City (Web-page hosting), http://www.fortunecity.com/

Free Web Space, http://www.freewebspace.net/

Webmonkey for Kidshot, http://hotwired.lycos.com/webmonkey/kids/

WebKIDS, http://www.webkids.info/html.html

Web Genies, http://www.webgenies.co.uk/

CoolText.com, http://www.cooltext.com/

html Gear, http://www.htmlgear.lycos.com/

RocketDownload.com, http://www.rocketdownload.com/
default.asp

CNET's download.com, http://download.com.com/

The Internet Movie Machine, http://www.16color.com/

Celebrating America's Library & America's Libraries,
http://www.ala.org/celebrating/

Escondido Public Library, http://www.ci.escondido.ca.us/library/

Public Libraries as Partners in Youth Development http://www.ala.
org/plpyd//dwtoc.html

Digital Divide Network, http://www.digitaldividenetwork.org/
content/sections/index.cfm/

Libraries—Bill & Melinda Gates Foundation, http://gates
foundation.org/libraries/default.htm

REFORMA—National Association to Promote Library and
Information Services to Latinos and the Spanish-Speaking,
http://www.reforma.org/

Sitios hispanohablantes escogidos por bibliotecarios, http://
cityofnewhaven.com/library/spanish/bibredesp.htm *Links to
libraries' pages of links to Web resources in Spanish. Critical annotations of the links are in English.*

SOL (Spanish in our Libraries) and PLUS (Public Libraries Using
Spanish), http://www.sol-plus.net/plus/home.htm *An archived
e-zine full of good ideas and tools for serving Spanish-speaking
populations.*

Spanish Subject Headings, http://clnet.ucr.edu/library/bplg/
sujetos.htm *This subject-heading list, developed by the Oakland
and San Francisco public libraries, provides equivalents for
Library of Congress Subject Headings.*

Chapter Six
The Techno-Economic Imperative

Innovative Internet Applications in Libraries, http://www.wilton library.org/innovate.html

"Best Practices" 2001, http://ln-rb.ic.gc.ca/e/about/bestprac/

Waterfront Bookboat Complex, http://www.bookboat.com/

Media release, 3M Award for Innovation in Libraries, http://www.lianza.org.nz/award_3m.htm

SIRSI Corp.—Clients, http://www.sirsi.com/Sirsiclients/index.html#spotlight/

Eric's Linux Information, http://gromit.westminster.lib.co.us/linux/

Internet Library for Librarians—Library Projects, http://www. itcompany.com/inforetriever/project.htm

The Free Software Foundation, http://gnu.org/fsf/fsf.html

Google's Linux search engine, http://www.google.com/Linux/

Linux Online—general Linux Information, http://www.linux.org/

The Linux Documentation Project, http://www.tldp.org/

The Open Source homepage, http://www.opensource.org/

O'Reilly publishing, home of the "Animals" & "Nutshell" series, http://www.oreilly.com/

Free Online Scholarship Newsletter, http://www.earlham.edu/~peters/fos/

Peter Suber, FOS Lists, Journal Declarations of Independence, http://www.earlham.edu/~peters/fos/lists.htm#declarations/

The Public Library of Science, http://www.publiclibraryof science.org/

Budapest Open Access Initiative, http://www.soros.org/openaccess/

Nature Debates: e-Access, http://www.nature.com/nature/debates/e-access/

Budapest Open Access Initiative FAQ, http://www.earlham.edu/~peters/fos/boaifaq.htm

BioMed Central, http://www.biomedcentral.com/

Create Change, http://www.createchange.org/faculty/issues/quick.html

Caltech Collection of Open Digital Archives, http://library.caltech.edu/digital

Scholarship Repository, California Digital Library, http://escholarship.cdlib.org/

Dspace, http://web.mit.edu/dspace/

Eprints.org, http://www.eprints.org/

Open Archives Initiative, http://www.openarchives.org/

MERLOT (Multimedia Educational Resource for Learning and Online Teaching), http://www.merlot.org/Home.po/ *Provides peer-review of discipline-specific scholarly Web resources.*

Franklin Park Library, http://www.franklinparklibrary.org/

Phil Agre's "How To Help Someone Use a Computer," http://dlis.gseis.ucla.edu/people/pagre/how-to-help.html

Information Today, Inc.'s NewsBreaks, http://www.infotoday.com/newsbreaks/

InfoWorld's newsletters, http://www.iwsubscribe.com/newsletters/

FOS News Blog, http://www.earlham.edu/~peters/fos/fosblog.html

Gaining Independence: A Manual for Planning the Launch of a Nonprofit Electronic Publishing Venture, http://www.arl.org/sparc/GI/ *"SPARC intends this manual to help universities, libraries, societies, and others implement alternatives to commercially published scholarly and scientific information."*

oss4lib, http://oss4lib.org/ *Where you can find out about free software for library purposes and news about how other libraries are using open source.*

Chapter Seven
Continuous Retraining

Marylaine's Bookmarks, http://marylaine.com/home.html

Search Day, http://searchenginewatch.com/searchday/

Search Engine Watch, http://searchenginewatch.com/

Research Buzz, http://www.researchbuzz.com/

New Site Announcement Services, http://marylaine.com/
netnew.html

Chronicle of Higher Education, http://chronicle.com/

WebReference Update, http://www.webreference.com/new/

WebPromote Weekly, http://www.webpromote.com/

Internet Tour Bus, http://www.tourbus.com/

MindIt, http://www.netmind.com/

AlertBox: Jakob Neilsen's Column on Web Usability, http://www.
useit.com/alertbox/

New York Times technology page, http://www.nytimes.com/
pages/technology/index.html

Networking: The Node, http://thenode.org/networking/

Educational Technology & Society, http://ifets.ieee.org/periodical/

Steven Bell's Keeping Up Web Page, http://staff.philau.edu/
bells/keepup/

Why a Learning Organization?, http://world.std.com/%7Elo/
WhyLO.html

Sources for General Library News

Peter Scott's Libary Blog, http://blog.xrefer.com/

LIS News, http://www.lisnews.com/

Sources for Search Engine News and Tips

Research Buzz, http://researchbuzz.com/ *Tara Calishain offers
extended reviews of Web sites and search engines weekly. Available
by e-mail.*

Search Day, http://searchenginewatch.com/searchday/ *Invisible Web guru Chris Sherman offers tips on searching and new developments in search engines four days a week. Available by e-mail.*

Search Engine Watch, http://searchenginewatch.com/ *Search engine expert Danny Sullivan's Web site includes extended reviews of search engines, comparison tests, and more.*

Sources for New Web Sites of Note

Neat New Stuff I Found This Week, http://marylaine.com/neatnew.html

Scout Report, http://scout.wisc.edu/report/sr/current/ *The most venerable of the site review services, which has been thoroughly analyzing sites with substantial reference and academic value for seven years, accumulating more than 10,000 reviewed sites in its archive.*

Virtual Acquisition Shelf and Reference Desk, http://resourceshelf.freepint.com/ *From invisible Web guru Gary Price, daily tips on new Web sites, government reports, and professional reading. Available by e-mail.*

Sources for Technology of Interest to Librarians

The Shifted Librarian, http://www.theshiftedlibrarian.com/ *A blog from Jenny Levine (see Chapter Four).*

Steven Bell's Keeping Up Page, http://staff.philau.edu/bells/keepup/

Wired, http://wired.com/

Wireless Librarian, http://people.morrisville.edu/~drewwe/wireless/

ZDNet, http://www.zdnet.com/

Chapter Eight
Legal Issues

ALA Washington Office, http://www.ala.org/washoff/

The Multnomah County Library's Family Guide to the Web, http://www.multcolib.org/kids/famweb.html

Free Expression Policy Project: Media Literacy, an Alternative to Censorship, http://www.fepproject.org/policyreports/medialiteracyfull.html

Freedom Forum 2002 State of the First Amendment Survey, http://www.freedomforum.org/templates/document.asp?documentID=16840

ALA Washington Office UCITA Library, http://www.ala.org/washoff/ucita/library.html

AFFECT, http://affect.ucita.com/

Electronic Mailing List, Digital Copyright, http://www.umuc.edu/distance/odell/cip/listserv.html

Helena, Montana, School District's AUP, http://www.helena.k12.mt.us/policy/aup/StudentAUPfinal2001-2001Rev.htm

Grinnell, Kansas, Unified School District AUP, http://skyways.lib.ks.us/kansas/schools/grinnell/accusepo.html

Salt Lake City, Utah, School System AUP, http://www.slc.k12.ut.us/aup.html

Ada, Ohio, Public Schools AUP, http://ada.k12.oh.us/acc_use.htm

Bowling Green, Ohio, Public Schools AUP, http://www.b-g.k12.ky.us/Tech/AUP/AUP.htm

Paw Paw, Michigan, Public Schools AUP, http://www.pawpaw.k12.mi.us/miscinfo/pppsaup.pdf

Lexington, Massachusetts, AUP, http://sturtevant.com/lextech/aup.htm

Windham, Maine, Public Schools AUP, http://www.windham.k12.me.us/wsdept/aup.asp

Guide to Multnomah County Library's Policies Regarding Internet Use, http://www.multcolib.org/about/pol-internet.html

American Library Association. State Privacy Laws Regarding Library Records, http://www.ala.org/alaorg/oif/stateprivacylaws.html *State laws are downloadable in PDF or RTF.*

Freedom of Information Center at the University of Missouri, http://www.missouri.edu/~foiwww/ *This "reference and research library in the University of Missouri School of Journalism" answers questions about access to government documents and information.*

GODORT Legislation Committee, http://sunsite.berkeley.edu/ GODORT/legislation/ *Links to government actions that threaten libraries and the First Amendment, and GODORTs responses to them.*

LibraryLaw.com, http://www.librarylaw.com/ *Who better than Mary Minow, a lawyer and a librarian both, to explain the law we have to abide by?*

The UT System Crash Course in Copyright. 2001, http://www.utsystem.edu/OGC/IntellectualProperty/cprtindx.htm *Tutorial for faculty on what they can and can't do, on campus and in distance education: what is fair use, how to find out who owns what, what licensing resources are available, and more.*

Chapter Nine
Disappearing Data

LOCKSS, http://lockss.stanford.edu/

Emergency Management Guide for Business and Industry, http://www.fema.gov/library/bizindex.shtm

Disaster Recovery Journal's Glossary, http://www.drj.com/glossary/drjglossary.html

Keeping Memory Alive: Practices for Preserving Content at the National Digital Library Program of the Library of Congress, http://www.rlg.org/preserv/diginews/diginews4-3.html

Public Library Association Tech Note: Disaster Planning for Computers and Networks, http://www.pla.org/publications/technotes/technotes_disasterplanning.html

Center for Research Libraries, http://wwwcrl.uchicago.edu/

Conservation Online, http://www.palimpsest.stanford.edu/

Council on Library Information and Resources (CLIR), http://www.clir.org/

Digital Library Federation, http://www.clir.org/diglib/ dlfhomepage.htm

JSTOR, http://www.jstor.org/

Preservation in the Digital World, http://www.clir.org/pubs/reports/ conway2/index.html

Preserving Access to Digital Information (PADI), http://www.nla. gov.au/padi/

Preserving Digital Information: Final Report and Recommendations, http://www.rlg.org/ArchTF/

RLG DigiNews, http://www.rlg.org/preserv/diginews/

Statement of Principles for the Preservation of and Long-Term Access to Australian Digital Objects, http://www.nla.gov.au/ preserve/digital/princ.html

A Strategic Policy Framework for Creating and Preserving Digital Collections, http://ahds.ac.uk/manage/framework.htm

ALAWON: ALA Washington Office Electronic Newsline, http://www.ala.org/washoff/alawon/ *Current news about govern-ment actions of concern to librarians. Includes texts of laws, testi-mony, and talking points for you when you're writing your legislators.*

D-Lib Forum and D-Lib Magazine, http://www.dlib.org/ *"Facilitating and supporting the community developing the tech-nology of the global digital library." Basic resource for digital preservation issues and standards.*

A Framework of Guidance for Building Good Digital Collections (IMLS - Publications & Resources), http://www.imls.gov/scripts/ text.cgi?/pubs/forumframework.htm

Information Longevity, http://sunsite.berkeley.edu/Longevity/ *Links to articles, research, and organizations devoted to preserving digi-tal information and access to it.*

OMB Watch, http://www.ombwatch.org/ *OMBWatch is keeping a list of information removed from government Web sites and any other changes in public access to government information since the September 11, 2001 terrorist attacks.*

Chapter Ten
How to Avoid Getting Blind-Sided

Innovative Internet Applications in Libraries, http://www.wiltonlibrary.org/innovate.html

Library Futures Institute, http://www.wpi.edu/News/Conf/LFI/webliography.html

Library Futures Quarterly, http://libraryfutures.com/

LITA Top Tech Trends, http://www.lita.org/committe/toptech/mainpage.htm

OWLS Links for Librarians: Planning, http://www.owls.lib.wi.us/info/links/plans.htm

Works Cited

"AFFECT: Why We Oppose UCITA." AFFECT. August 2002, Americans for Fair Electronic Commerce Transactions, Washington DC. http://affect.ucita.com/why.html

Albanese, Andrew. "DMCA Revision to Get New Push." *Library Journal* 1 Mar. 2002.

Balas, Janet L. "Can You Build It? Yes You Can!" *Computers in Libraries* Feb. 2002. http://www.infotoday.com/cilmag/feb02/balas.htm

____. "Reading Is 'In.'" *Computers in Libraries* Sept. 2001: 64–66. *WilsonSelectPlus.* OCLC FirstSearch. O'Keefe Library, St. Ambrose University, Davenport. http://www.ref.oclc.org/

Bannan, Karen J. "RSS: Lo-fi Content Syndication." *EContent* Jan. 2002: 30–33. *WilsonSelectPlus.* OCLC FirstSearch. O'Keefe Library, St. Ambrose University, Davenport. http://www.ref.oclc.org/

Bell, Steven J. "To Keep Up, Go Beyond: Developing a Personal Professional Development Plan Using E-resources Outside the Bounds of Library Literature." *College & Research Libraries News* July–Aug. 2000: 581–584. *WilsonSelectPlus.* OCLC FirstSearch. O'Keefe Library, St. Ambrose University, Davenport. http://www.ref.oclc.org/

Biemiller, Lawrence. "California State U. Adopts New Model to Pay for Journals." *Chronicle of Higher Education* 16 July 1999: A26–A27. *Periodical Abstracts.* OCLC FirstSearch. O'Keefe Library, St. Ambrose University, Davenport. http://www.ref.oclc.org/

Block, Marylaine. "The Defect in Realism." *ExLibris* 2 Feb. 2001. http://marylaine.com/exlibris/xlib86.html

____. "In Praise of the Best Little Library System in the World." *ExLibris* 21 Jan. 2001. http://marylaine.com/exlibris/xlib40.html

____. "Making Bookstores Your Partners." *ExLibris* 25 Jan. 2002. http://marylaine.com/exlibris/xlib128.html

____. "Planning for Side Effects: The Case for Semi-Luddite Management." *ExLibris* 31 Aug. 2001. http://marylaine.com/exlibris/xlib112.html

____. "Reference as a Teachable Moment." *ExLibris* 5 July 2002. http://marylaine.com/exlibris/xlib146.html

____. "Stop the World, I Want to Catch Up." *ExLibris* 12 Apr. 2002. http://marylaine.com/exlibris/xlib137.html

____. "Teaching Kids Indirectly." *Library Journal NetConnect* July 2001. http://libraryjournal.reviewsnews.com/index.asp?layout= article&articleid=CA106237/

Bradley, Lynne E. and Claudette W. Tennant. "What to Do Before, During, and After a Knock at the Door?" Understanding the U.S.A. Patriot Act." *College & Research Libraries News* Feb. 2002: 129. *WilsonSelectPlus.* OCLC FirstSearch. O'Keefe Library, St. Ambrose University, Davenport. http://www.ref.oclc.org/

"brarydog.net Launches Web Portal for Students." *Information Today* Oct. 2000. http://infotoday.com/it/oct00/news10.htm

Broughton, Kelly. "Our Experiment in Online, Real-Time Reference." *Computers in Libraries* Apr. 2000. http://www.infotoday.com/cil mag/apr01/broughton.htm

Casey, James B. "The 1.6% Solution." *American Libraries* Apr. 2002: 85–86. *WilsonSelectPlus.* OCLC FirstSearch. O'Keefe Library, St. Ambrose University, Davenport. http://www.ref.oclc.org

Chepesiuk, Ronald. "JSTOR and Electronic Archiving." *American Libraries* Dec. 2000: 46–48. *WilsonSelectPlus.* OCLC FirstSearch. O'Keefe Library, St. Ambrose University, Davenport. http://www. ref.oclc.org/

Davis, Philip M. and Suzanne Cohen. "The Effect of the Web on Undergraduate Citation Behavior 1996–1999." *Journal of the*

American Society for Information Science and Technology 52.4 (2001): 309–314. Abstract. http://www.asis.org/Publications/JASIS/vol52n4.html

Estabrook, Leigh S. and Edward Lakner. "Managing Internet Access: Results of a National Survey." *American Libraries* Sept. 2000: 60–62. *WilsonSelectPlus*. OCLC FirstSearch. O'Keefe Library, St. Ambrose University, Davenport. http://www.ref.oclc.org/

Fichter, Darlene. "Blogging Your Life Away." *Online* May–June 2001: 68–71. *WilsonSelectPlus*. OCLC FirstSearch. O'Keefe Library, St. Ambrose University, Davenport. http://www.ref.oclc.org/

Gibson, Susan and Joanne Tranter. "Internet Information: The Whole Truth?" *Canadian Social Studies*, Summer 2000: 77–80. *WilsonSelectPlus*. OCLC FirstSearch. O'Keefe Library, St. Ambrose University, Davenport. http://www.ref.oclc.org/

Gitner, Fred J. "The New Americans Program: Twenty-One Years of Successful Partnerships Serving Diverse and Changing Communities." *Reference & User Services Quarterly* 38.2 (1998): 143–145. *WilsonSelectPlus*. OCLC FirstSearch. O'Keefe Library, St. Ambrose University, Davenport. http://www.ref.oclc.org/

Gordon, Rachel S. "A Course in Accidental Systems Librarianship." *Computers in Libraries* Nov.–Dec. 2001: 24–28. *WilsonSelectPlus*. OCLC FirstSearch. O'Keefe Library, St. Ambrose University, Davenport. http://www.ref.oclc.org/

Gorman, Michele. "Wiring Teens to the Library." *Library Journal NetConnect* 15 July 2002. http://libraryjournal.reviewsnews.com/index.asp?layout=article&articleid=CA232351/

Guscott, J. "The Library Foresight System." *Library Futures Quarterly* 1.1 (2000).

____. "The Library Foresight System: Step One." *Library Futures Quarterly* 1.2 (2001).

Hastings, Jeffrey. "Technology and the School Library: Great Expectations and Unintended Consequences." *LISNews* 9 Apr. 2002. http://www.lisnews.com/article.php3?sid=20020409095751/

Hildreth, Charles R. "Accounting for Users' Inflated Assessments of On-Line Catalogue Search Performance and Usefulness: An Experimental Study." *Information Research* 6.2 Jan. 2001. http://InformationR.net/ir/6-2/paper101.html

Jacsó, Péter. "Working with, Not Against, Web-Savvy Users." *Computers in Libraries* Jan. 2002: 50–51. *WilsonSelectPlus*. OCLC FirstSearch. O'Keefe Library, St. Ambrose University, Davenport. http://www.ref.oclc.org/

Kaip, Sarah. "It's Not Just for Term Papers: Solving Real-Life Problems in an Information Literacy Course." *College & Research Libraries News* May 2001: 496–498. *WilsonSelectPlus*. OCLC FirstSearch. O'Keefe Library, St. Ambrose University, Davenport. http://www.ref.oclc.org/

Kinney, Janet. "The Learning Systems Approach to Staff Development and Training at Multnomah County Library." *OLA Quarterly* Winter 2000: 9–13 *WilsonSelectPlus*. OCLC FirstSearch. O'Keefe Library, St. Ambrose University, Davenport. http://www.ref.oclc.org/

Kirkpatrick, Cheryl H. and Catherine Buck Morgan. "How We Renovated Our Library, Physically and Electronically, for Handicapped Patrons." *Computers in Libraries* Oct. 2001: 24–29 *Periodical Abstracts*. OCLC FirstSearch. O'Keefe Library, St. Ambrose University, Davenport. http://www.ref.oclc.org/

Latham, Joyce M. "To Link, or Not to Link." *Library Journal NetConnect*. 15 Apr. 2002. http://libraryjournal.reviewsnews.com/index.asp?layout=article&articleid=CA210718/

Levine, Jenny. "What Is a Shifted Librarian?" *The Shifted Librarian* Jan. 2002. http://www.theshiftedlibrarian.com/stories/2002/01/19/whatIsAShiftedLibrarian.html

"Library Policies: Acceptable Use of the Internet: Guide to Multnomah County Library's Policies Regarding Internet Use."

Multnomah County Library, Portland. 26 Oct. 2000. http://www.
multcolib.org/about/pol-internet.html

"lii.org Selection Criteria." Librarians' Index to the Internet. 30 Aug.
2002. http://lii.org/search/file/pubcriteria/

Martin, Julia and David Coleman. "The Archive as an Ecosystem."
Journal of Electronic Publishing 7.3 (2002). http://www.press.
umich.edu/jep/07-03/martin.html

Mathias, Molly S. and Steven Heser. "Mobilize Your Instruction Program
with Wireless Technology." *Computers in Libraries* Mar. 2002: 24–30.
Periodical Abstracts. OCLC FirstSearch. O'Keefe Library, St. Ambrose
University, Davenport. http://www.ref.oclc.org/

Maughan, Shannon. "You Go, Guys!" *Publishers Weekly* 7 May 2001:
41–42. Periodical Abstracts. *OCLC FirstSearch.* O'Keefe Library, St.
Ambrose University, Davenport. http://www.ref.oclc.org/

Minow, Mary. "Filters and the Public Library: A Legal and Policy
Analysis." *First Monday* Dec. 1997. http://www.firstmonday.dk/
issues/issue2_12/minow/index.html

Morton Grove Public Library's Webrary: Readers Services: Match-
Book. 25 Feb. 2002. http://www.webrary.org/rs/matchbook
about.html

National Education Association. NEA Poll on the Reading Habits of
Adolescents, conducted by Peter D. Hart Research Associates from
February 9–15, 2001. Originally (but no longer) available at
http://www.nea.org/readingmatters/readpoll.html (A summary of
some of the results is available at American Library Association's
Teens and Reading page http://www.ala.org/pio/factsheets/
drivetoread.html.)

Norlin, Elaina. "University Goes Back to Basics to Reach Minority
Students." *American Libraries* Aug. 2001: 60–62. *WilsonSelectPlus.*
OCLC FirstSearch. O'Keefe Library, St. Ambrose University,
Davenport. http://www.ref.oclc.org/

OCLC White Paper on the Information Habits of College Students. OCLC Online Computer Library Center, Dublin OH. 24 June 2002. http://www2.oclc.org/oclc/pdf/printondemand/infohabits verbatim.pdf/

Pearl, Nancy. "Re: Article on 'If All of Seattle Read the Same Book.'" E-Mail to Marylaine Block. 22 July 2002.

Puacz, Jeanne H. "Catching (and Keeping) E-Patrons." *Computers in Libraries* Jan. 2002: 12–15. http://www.infotoday.com/cilmag/jan02/puacz.htm

Puacz, Jeanne H. and Chris Bradfield. "Surf's Up for Seniors! Introducing Older Patrons to the Web." *Computers in Libraries* Sept. 2000: 50–53. Periodical Abstracts. OCLC FirstSearch. O'Keefe Library, St. Ambrose University, Davenport. http://www.ref.oclc.org/

Reilly, Rob. "Laying Down the Law: Crafting Acceptable Use Policy." *Multimedia Schools* Oct. 2000: 78–80. *WilsonSelectPlus.* OCLC FirstSearch. O'Keefe Library, St. Ambrose University, Davenport. http://www.ref.oclc.org/

Schneider, K. G. "Creating a Yahoo! with Values." *Library Journal NetConnect* 15 July 2002. http://libraryjournal.reviewsnews.com/index.asp?layout=article&articleid=CA232358/

____. "Re: Second Web Directory?" Online posting. 24 Apr. 2002. Web4Lib. http://sunsite.berkeley.edu/Web4Lib/archive/0204/0218.html

____. "Re: Second Web Directory?" Online posting. 24 Apr. 2002. Web4Lib. http://sunsite.berkeley.edu/Web4Lib/archive/0204/0220.html

Sisler, Eric. "Linux in Your Library?" *Library Journal NetConnect* Fall 2001. http://libraryjournal.reviewsnews.com/index.asp?layout=article&articleid=CA177575/

Stillwell, Mary. "Partnerships That Support Public Access Computing." *Journal of Youth Services in Libraries* 15 (2001): 29–32. *WilsonSelectPlus.* OCLC FirstSearch. O'Keefe Library, St. Ambrose University, Davenport. http://www.ref.oclc.org/

Suber, Peter. "Where Does the Free Online Scholarship Movement Stand Today?" Feb. 2002. http://www.earlham.edu/~peters/writing/cortex.htm

Tennant, Roy. "Digital Libraries—The Convenience Catastrophe." *Library Journal*, Dec. 2001. http://libraryjournal.reviewsnews.com/index.asp?layout=articleArchive&articleId=CA185367

____. "Digital Libraries—Coping with Disasters." *Library Journal*, 15 Nov. 2001. http://libraryjournal.reviewsnews.com/index.asp?layout=articleArchive&articleId=CA180529

——. "Time Is Not on Our Side: The Challenge of Preserving Digital Materials." *Library Journal*, 15 March 1999. http://libraryjournal.reviewsnews.com/index.asp?layout=articleArchive&articleId=CA156503

"Turning into Digital Goldfish," *BBC News*, Sci/Tech, 22 Feb. 2002. http://news.bbc.co.uk/1/hi/sci/tech/1834682.stm/

United States. Cong. Joint Committee on Printing. Hearings on Federal Government Printing and Public Access to Government Documents. Statement of Julia F. Wallace. 107th Cong., 2nd sess. 10 July 2002. http://jcp.senate.gov/jcp_testimony_wallace.htm

Varnum, Kenneth. "Information @ Your Fingertips: Porting Library Services to the PDA." *Online* Sept.–Oct. 2000: 14–17. *WilsonSelectPlus*. OCLC FirstSearch. O'Keefe Library, St. Ambrose University, Davenport. http://www.ref.oclc.org/

Weeks, Linton. "An Industry Insider's Gloomy Book Report: Michael Cader Foresees Continued Drop in Sales." *Washington Post* 14 May 2002: C1.

Young, Jeffrey R. "'Superarchives' Could Hold All Scholarly Output: Online Collections by Institutions May Challenge the Role of Journal Publishers." *Chronicle of Higher Education*, 5 July 2002: A29. http://chronicle.com/free/v48/i43/43a02901.htm

Young, Nancy J. and Marilyn Von Seggern. "General Information Seeking in Changing Times: A Focus Group Study." *Reference & User Services Quarterly*, 41.2. 2001: 159–169. *WilsonSelectPlus*. OCLC FirstSearch. O'Keefe Library, St. Ambrose University, Davenport. http://www.ref.oclc.org/

Index

More Great Books from Information Today, Inc.

The Accidental Webmaster

By Julie Still

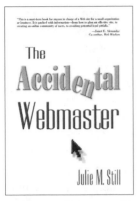

Here is a lifeline for the individual who has not been trained as a Webmaster, but who—whether by choice or under duress—has become one nonetheless. While most Webmastering books focus on programming and related technical issues, *The Accidental Webmaster* helps readers deal with the full range of challenges they face on the job. Author, librarian, and accidental Webmaster Julie Still offers advice on getting started, setting policies, working with ISPs, designing home pages, selecting content, drawing site traffic, gaining user feedback, fundraising, avoiding copyright problems, and much more.

2003/softbound/ISBN 1-57387-164-8 $29.50

Business Statistics on the Web

Find Them Fast—At Little or No Cost

By Paula Berinstein

Statistics are a critical component of business and marketing plans, press releases, surveys, economic analyses, presentations, proposals, and more—yet good statistics are notoriously hard to find. This practical book by statistics guru Paula Berinstein shows readers how to use the Internet to find statistics about companies, markets, and industries, how to organize and present statistics, and how to evaluate them for reliability. Organized by topic, both general and specific, and by country/region, this helpful reference features easy-to-use tips and techniques for finding and using statistics when the pressure is on. In addition, dozens of extended and short case studies demonstrate the ins and outs of searching for specific numbers and maneuvering around obstacles to find the data you need.

2003/336pp/softbound/ISBN: 0-910965-65-X $29.95

The Librarian's Internet Survival Guide

Strategies for the High-Tech Reference Desk

By Irene E. McDermott
Edited by Barbara Quint

In this authoritative and tremendously useful guide, Irene McDermott helps her fellow reference librarians succeed in the bold new world of the Web. *The Survival Guide* provides easy access to the information librarians need when the pressure is on: trouble-shooting tips and advice, Web resources for answering reference questions, and strategies for managing information and keeping current. In addition to helping librarians make the most of Web tools and resources, McDermott covers a full range of important issues including Internet training, privacy, child safety, helping patrons with special needs, building library Web pages, and much more.

2002/296 pp/softbound/ISBN 1-57387-129-X $29.50

The OPL Sourcebook

A Guide for Solo and Small Libraries

By Judith A. Siess

Judith A. Siess, editor of the monthly newsletter, "The One-Person Library," has created the definitive handbook and directory for small and one-person libraries (OPLs). Taking an international approach to reflect the growing number of OPLs worldwide, this new book covers organizational culture, customer service, time management and planning, budgeting, accounting, technology, collection development, education, downsizing, outsourcing, and many other key management issues. Includes a comprehensive directory.

2001/260 pp/hardbound/ISBN 1-57387-111-7 $39.50

The Information Professional's Guide to Career Development Online

By Rachel Singer Gordon and Sarah L. Nesbeitt

This book is designed to meet the needs of librarians interested in using online tools to advance their careers. It offers practical advice on topics ranging from current awareness services and personal Web pages to distance education, electronic resumes, and online job searches. New librarians will learn how to use the Internet to research education opportunities, and experienced info pros will learn ways to network through online conferences and discussion lists. Supported by a Web page.

2002/softbound/ISBN 1-57387-124-9 $29.50

The Quintessential Searcher
The Wit and Wisdom of Barbara Quint

Edited by Marylaine Block

Searcher magazine editor Barbara Quint (bq) is not only one of the world's most famous online searchers, but the most creative and controversial writer, editor, and speaker to emerge from the information industry in the last two decades. bq is a guru of librarians and database professionals the world over, and, as her readers, publishers, and "quarry" know, when it comes to barbed wit she is in a class by herself. Whether she's chastising database providers about unacceptable fees, interfaces, and updates; recounting the ills visited on the world by computer makers; or inspiring her readers to achieve greatness; her voice is consistently original and compelling. In this book, for the first time anywhere, hundreds of bq's most memorable, insightful, and politically incorrect quotations have been gathered for the enjoyment of her many fans.

2001/232 pp/softbound/ISBN 1-57387-114-1 $19.95

The Evolving Virtual Library II

Edited by Laverna M. Saunders

The Evolving Virtual Libray II documents how libraries of all types are changing with the integration of the Internet and the Web, electronic resources, and computer networks. It provides a summary of trends, developments in networking, case studies of creating digital content delivery systems for remote users, applications in K-12 and public libraries, and a vision of things to come.

1999/194 pp/hardbound/ISBN 1-57387-070-6 $39.50

The Web Library
Building a World Class Personal Library
with Free Web Resources

By Nicholas G. Tomaiuolo
Edited by Barbara Quint

With this remarkable, eye-opening book and its companion Web site, Nicholas G. (Nick) Tomaiuolo shows how anyone can create a comprehensive personal library using no-cost Web resources. If you were to calculate the expense of purchasing the hundreds of print and fee-based electronic publications that are available for free with "the Web library," you'd quickly recognize the potential of this book to save you thousands, if not millions, of dollars (fortunately, Nick does the calculating for you!). This is an easy-to-use guide, with chapters corresponding to departments in a physical library. *The Web Library* provides a wealth of URLs and examples of free material you can start using right away, but, best of all, it offers techniques for finding and collecting new content as the Web evolves. Start building your personal Web library today!

2003/softbound/ISBN 0-910965-67-6 • $29.95

Web of Deception

Misinformation on the Internet

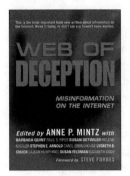

Edited by Anne P. Mintz
Foreword by Steve Forbes

"Experts here walk you through the risks and traps of the Web world and tell you how to avoid them or to fight back ... Anne Mintz and her collaborators have done us a genuine service." —Steve Forbes, from the Foreword

Intentionally misleading or erroneous information on the Web can wreak havoc on your health, privacy, investments, business decisions, online purchases, legal affairs, and more. Until now, the breadth and significance of this growing problem have yet to be fully explored. In *Web of Deception*, Anne P. Mintz brings together 10 information industry gurus to illuminate the issues and help you recognize and deal with the flood of deception and misinformation in a range of critical subject areas.

2002/278 pp/softbound/ISBN 0-910965-60-9 $24.95

Net Crimes & Misdemeanors

Outmaneuvering the Spammers, Swindlers, and Stalkers Who Are Targeting You Online

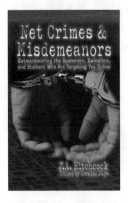

By J. A. Hitchcock
Edited by Loraine Page

Cyber crime expert J.A. Hitchcock helps individuals and business users of the Web protect themselves, their children, and their employees against online cheats and predators. Hitchcock details a broad range of abusive practices, shares victims' stories, and offers advice on how to handle junk e-mail, "flaming," privacy invasion, financial scams, cyberstalking, and indentity theft. She provides tips and techniques that can be put to immediate use and points to the laws, organizations, and Web resources that can aid victims and help them fight back. Supported by a Web site.

2002/384 pp/softbound/ISBN 0-910965-57-9 $24.95

Creating Web-Accessible Databases

Case Studies for Libraries, Museums, and Other Nonprofits

Edited by Julie M. Still

Libraries, museums, and other not-for-profit institutions are increasingly looking for (and finding) ways to offer patrons and the public Web access to their collections. This book from Julie Still and her expert contributors explores the unique challenges nonprofit archival institutions face in leveraging the Internet and presents a dozen case studies showcasing a variety of successful projects and approaches.

2001/200 pp/hardbound/ISBN 1-57387-104-4 $39.50

The Accidental Systems Librarian

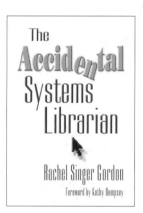

By Rachel Singer Gordon

Author Rachel Singer Gordon believes that anyone with a solid foundation in the practices and principles of librarianship and a willingness to confront changing technology can serve effectively in a library technology position—with or without formal computer training. Gordon's advice on using research, organizational, and bibliographic skills to solve various systems problems helps "accidental" systems librarians develop the skills they need to succeed.

2003/softbound/ISBN 1-57387-104-4 $29.50